Alternative Dispute Resolution

Alternative Dispute Resolution

An Essential Competency for Lawyers

Mark V. B. Partridge

OXFORD
UNIVERSITY PRESS

OXFORD
UNIVERSITY PRESS

Oxford University Press, Inc., publishes works that further Oxford University's objective of excellence in research, scholarship, and education.

Oxford New York
Auckland Cape Town Dar es Salaam Hong Kong Karachi Kuala Lumpur Madrid Melbourne Mexico City Nairobi New Delhi Shanghai Taipei Toronto

With offices in
Argentina Austria Brazil Chile Czech Republic France Greece Guatemala Hungary Italy Japan Poland Portugal Singapore South Korea Switzerland Thailand Turkey Ukraine Vietnam

Published by Oxford University Press, Inc.
198 Madison Avenue, New York, New York 10016

Library of Congress Cataloging-in-Publication Data
Partridge, Mark V. B.
Alternative dispute resolution : an essential competency for lawyers / Mark V. B. Partridge.
p. cm.
Includes bibliographical references and index.
ISBN 978-0-19-537205-2 ((pbk.) : alk. paper)
1. Dispute resolution (Law) 2. Mediation. 3. Compromise (Law)
4. Trial practice. 5. Law—Vocational guidance. I. Title.
K2390.P37 2009
347.73′9—dc22

2008055216

1 2 3 4 5 6 7 8 9

Printed in the United States of America on acid-free paper

Note to Readers

This publication is designed to provide accurate and authoritative information in regard to the subject matter covered. It is based upon sources believed to be accurate and reliable and is intended to be current as of the time it was written. It is sold with the understanding that the publisher is not engaged in rendering legal, accounting, or other professional services. If legal advice or other expert assistance is required, the services of a competent professional person should be sought. Also, to confirm that the information has not been affected or changed by recent developments, traditional legal research techniques should be used, including checking primary sources where appropriate.

(Based on the Declaration of Principles jointly adopted by a Committee of the American Bar Association and a Committee of Publishers and Associations.)

Contents

About the Author

Mark V. B. Partridge is a partner with Pattishall, McAuliffe, Newbury, Hilliard & Geraldson, LLP, a specialty firm with a global practice helping businesses defend their brands. With over twenty-five years of experience representing major companies, his practice focuses on ADR, litigation, and transactions involving trademarks, copyright, and the Internet.

A graduate of Harvard Law School, Partridge is also an adjunct professor at the John Marshall Law School in Chicago, where he has taught advanced courses in trademark law, litigation, and transactions since 1987.

In 1998, Partridge was selected by the World Intellectual Property Organization as an expert on the Internet Domain Name Process. In 1999, he was selected to serve as an initial member for the WIPO Arbitration and Mediation Center, Domain Name Dispute Resolution Service. As a WIPO Panelist, he has issued over 150 published decisions resolving Internet domain name disputes. Partridge has also served as an arbitrator or mediator with the Illinois Cook County Courts, United States District Court for the Northern District of Illinois, and the American Arbitration Association. As an advocate, he has used his ADR experience to achieve mediated settlements in a variety of areas, including software development, domain names, product brands, and video program licensing.

Partridge is the author of many legal and business articles and a previous book entitled *Guiding Rights: Trademarks, Copyright and the Internet* (2003). He has been a featured speaker at conferences throughout the United States and abroad on a range of legal and business topics, including the use of ADR to reduce litigation costs and achieve better results. For more information, visit www.Pattishall.com and www.MarkPartridge.com.

Introduction

As the expense and complexity of litigation continue to rise beyond reasonable expectations, as the importance of legal assets such as intellectual property becomes manifest as a major component of corporate value, as business relationships for all sizes of organizations become increasingly global, it becomes increasingly apparent that the traditional methods of resolving disputes by court adjudication are often inadequate. Attorneys of all types need to explore and understand alternative methods of dispute resolution (ADR) if they hope to give their clients effective advice and service.

My view of litigation is shaped by over twenty-five years of experience handling intellectual property litigation for small businesses and major corporations, including Nabisco, Nike, S.C. Johnson, Sunbeam, Disney, PepsiCo, Frito-Lay, and others. I've also served as an arbitrator for the Cook County Court in Illinois and for the American Arbitration Association, as a mediator for the Northern District of Illinois and for the International Trademark Association, and as a panelist deciding cybersquatting disputes for the World Intellectual Property Organization. These experiences have persuaded me that ADR has become a critical competency for attorneys whether they be litigators, transactional attorneys, or in-house counsel. This book explores that theme as it provides a guide for attorneys to obtain that competency.

ADR encompasses all of the tools and techniques of dispute resolution that reside in the gap between interparty negotiation and formal judicial adjudication. A common feature of the various ADR procedures is that they are facilitated processes for reaching resolution. The two principal options are mediation and arbitration.

Mediation and related methods are a form of facilitated negotiation. The neutral entity involved (i.e., the mediator) does not decide the dispute. Instead, the mediator leads the parties through a process that helps them reach a resolution. The process is nonbinding, so there is no resolution unless the parties agree to a final result.

In contrast, arbitration and related methods involve a neutral entity in the role of a judge. The parties must agree to the process, but the arbitrator determines the result, as is the case with a judge or jury. The result may be final, with no option for appeal, or binding unless appealed to a higher court or tribunal.

Variations on these two principal methods also exist, including facilitated settlement negotiations, neutral evaluation, advisory opinions, mini-trials, summary jury trials, and more.

This book is for general counsel, their in-house colleagues, and their outside litigators. It explores what lies in that gap between negotiation and adjudication. It considers whether there is a better alternative. It poses the question: why ADR?

One answer is that ADR provides alternatives to negotiation and adjudication—neither better nor worse, just different. The existence of alternatives increases the pool of options available to us as counsel to achieve the client's goals. If we ignore these alternatives, then we are neglecting part of our job.

Another answer is that both negotiation and adjudication are flawed and that better options must be found. The hope is that ADR provides those better alternatives. It does this by providing a facilitator to negotiation who becomes a catalyst for overcoming the paralysis posed by hardened positions and for inducing forward momentum to overcome the delay inherent in power posturing. It brings in a neutral party to negotiations to help each side achieve better results than would seem likely from bilateral negotiation alone.

The flaws in adjudication are widely recognized and become more acute each day: expense, delay, lack of confidentiality, burdensome discovery, endless appeals, all-or-nothing results, limited options for resolution, and generalist judges with no subject matter experience relevant to the dispute. ADR offers options that are faster and cheaper with the possibility of better results—results that preserve or build business relationships and uncover creative ways to achieve the interests of the parties.

However, none of these benefits will be realized if we fail to understand and master the options available. The traditional role of in-house counsel and outside litigator concentrated solely on negotiation and adjudication, but this focus was too limited and too narrow. It failed to serve client needs because it ignored alternatives that yielded better results. The goal of counsel is not to win a hardball negotiation or a victory before a jury, as these are small goals personal to the advocate. The true goal is a solution to a client's problem. A traditional victory may provide that solution, but often such victories prove merely Pyrrhic. Advocates who consider, use, and master only negotiation or adjudication serve the client poorly because they neglect possibilities that may provide a better route to the client's desired result. Advocates who understand, use, and master the full range of ADR options serve the client better because they achieve better results.

When should you consider ADR? Whenever there is a dispute. When should you use ADR? Whenever there is a possibility that ADR will help the client achieve its goals. ADR is a tool, one of many, in an advocate's toolkit, which may be used to help build the desired result: an effective, efficient, creative solution to the client's problem.

This is a new mind-set for litigators, who tend to master only a few tools in the advocate's toolkit, or perhaps only one. Increasingly those tools mastered are motion practice and discovery. It is natural to focus on what you know and seek to do it well. It is also natural to avoid those things you don't know. Thus, this focus leads to the dedication of more resources to motion practice and discovery. Yet does anyone claim that motion practice and discovery are good tools for achieving a client's goals? Are they in themselves *ever* desired goals? Does the CEO ever say to her general counsel, "Our shareholders want us to file more motions"? Does she say, "Our long-range goals require more time spent on discovery" or "Please have our executives spend more time in depositions"? Simply stating the question reveals the obvious answer—litigation with its accompanying tools is not the client's goal. At best, it is a necessary evil.

But litigation is not always desirable or even necessary, as alternatives exist that can be a more direct route to the client's goal and produce better results. These alternatives can reduce the impact of the flaws inherent in modern litigation.

However, it takes a new mind-set. Corporate counsel and litigators must understand, consider, use, and master the full range of tools available. A narrow, limited focus on negotiation or adjudication fails to serve well the needs and goals of clients. The effective advisor and advocate will recognize this.

It is a new way of looking at victory. Winning isn't the only way—and often it isn't the best way. A win at trial isn't a victory if it fails to solve the client's problem or if it replaces one problem with a bigger problem. The goal of an advisor or advocate should be finding fast and cheap solutions to the client's problem. This goal may sometimes be achieved through negotiation or adjudication, but not always or exclusively. This goal will be achieved more often over time if advisors and advocates understand, consider, use, and master a greater range of dispute resolution tools. The purpose of this book is to provide information and advice on the ADR options and how they may be used to achieve better client results.

CHAPTER 1

Need

1.01 Why ADR?

Why do you as in-house counsel or outside counsel advising companies in dispute resolution need to know and master the tools and methods of alternative dispute resolution (ADR)? Why is ADR an essential competency for lawyers? Four key trends dictate this conclusion: the growing cost of litigation, the declining incidence of resolution by trial, the attitudes and expectations of the client, and the opportunity for better results in an in creasingly complicated and global business world.

In the early part of this century, I was selected as an expert in a long-running copyright dispute. It was an unusual assignment. I wasn't asked to opine on the meaning of copyright law or the application of that law to a particular infringement problem. Instead, I was brought into a dispute by the plaintiff after a jury had awarded him over $1 million in damages for copyright infringement—and after he had received his bill from his trial counsel. It was an amazingly good result on its face, but therein lies the problem. The legal fees incurred to obtain that result exceeded $2 million—twice as much as the jury award. And that had resulted in a new lawsuit. (To see why, do the math.)

My task as an expert on copyright litigation was to provide an opinion about what constituted reasonable attorney's fees for a case of this typeI reviewed what had been done, analyzed all reported copyright infringement decisions involving attorney's fees, and considered industry information about the costs of copyright infringement litigation. All the time a thought lurked in my mind: *there has to be a better way*. I'm sure my client had similar thoughts.

The desire—and demand—of clients for a better way is echoed in the experience of others. As former in-house counsel to MCI and Elan Pharmaceuticals, Harrie Samaras had a prime vantage point for recognizing the need for ADR.[1] While at MCI as Director of Intellectual Property Litigation, Samaras became familiar with the use of ADR to resolve business disputes for her company. She gained additional experience with ADR in her role as head of intellectual property (IP) for the drug delivery business unit of Elan Corporation. Her views were also shaped by her experience as a clerk at the Federal Circuit Court of Appeals for the late Judge Helen W. Nies. Samaras has observed many situations where ADR could have been used to good advantage, but sadly was not.

Now in private practice focused on ADR, Samaras sees clear benefits from the process. "It can be a powerful business tool," she says, as an effective way "to sort through the emotional, technical and business issues attendant on many intellectual property disputes and to craft business resolutions that would not have been attainable from litigation."[2]

While at MCI, Samaras had experience using ADR to resolve regular disputes between MCI and a major competitor over advertising claims. The two companies created an expedited arbitration process yielding quick, low cost resolution of those disputes and providing the certainty they needed to carry on with business. Samaras also used arbitration for international disputes that would have been far more costly and time-consuming to pursue in foreign courts. In short, Samaras found ADR to be an important strategic tool in many situations to achieve business objectives in a timely manner.

Based on her experience, Samaras favors mediation as a low-cost alternative that can yield better and more certain business results than litigation or arbitration. It is a good starting point for dispute resolution. However, if mediation doesn't work, arbitration may be the next step due to its potential benefits over litigation in terms of flexibility, autonomy, efficiency, cost, expertise, and confidentiality. Both arbitration and mediation are a necessary part of the dispute resolution toolkit, along with negotiation and litigation. Samaras says companies need ADR:

> because they deal with disputes in all shapes and sizes on a regular basis and they can't treat them as a one-size fits all proposition. That is, all roads cannot lead to litigation because that process is too costly (monetary, internal resources) and time-consuming. Companies cannot suspend their businesses for years at a time while a case works its way through the court system. Also, ADR can help to maintain relationships in small business communities and create new

---

1. Harrie Samaras is a shareholder with Ratner & Prestia, P.C., a Pennsylvania law firm specializing in IP. She is cochair of the litigation/dispute resolution department. *See* http://www.ratnerprestia.com.
2. *An Interview with Harrie Samaras*, 23 IPL Newsletter, Spring 2005.

> business opportunities. Companies need to understand more about the various forms of ADR and how to avoid pitfalls in ADR. The key factors creating a need for ADR are the cost of litigation generally and in IP cases in particular [hourly rates in the IP field, extensive discovery in IP cases, need for multiple experts, length of time to get to trial, distraction to businesses (time of business, marketing and attorneys taken up for months, years to support litigation, there is a cloud over the business (accused product in a TM or patent case, for example)]. Also, e-discovery has upped the ante in litigation in terms of costs for compliance and costs for possible noncompliance. Corporate budgets for litigation are not limitless, and although they may have grown over time to deal with our litigious society, there are limits and decisions that have to be made regarding who gets a piece of the pie and how much of it. If [the companies] don't fully appreciate what the processes are, they won't choose ADR or understand the benefits. Both attorneys and business folks need to understand what the processes are and how they can use [them].[3]

As Samaras indicates, the need to master the methods of alternative dispute resolution (ADR) as an adjunct or substitute to the traditional litigation is increasingly evident in several critical trends.

[A] Expense of Litigation

The dramatic rise in the cost of legal services in recent years is well known. Veterans of litigation often sympathize with Voltaire's saying: "I was never ruined but twice—once when I lost a lawsuit, and once when I won one." The rise in cost is particularly steep in IP litigation to the point that many businesses balk at it and either don't enforce their rights or simply cave in to avoid litigation expense.

The press regularly reports on litigation costs. The starting salary for fresh graduates from the top law schools is pushing $200,000 per year. Overall billing rates rise to pay these climbing salaries. Clients plead for relief, yet those faced with critical commercial risks still turn to the highest paid firms. After all, who wants to explain to members of a board of directors that they're going to jail because someone decided to save money on legal fees?

A dispute decided at trial in 2008 provides heart-stopping evidence of the high cost of litigation. The well-publicized lawsuit between Mattel Inc. and MGA Entertainment (involving a battle between Barbie and Bratz dolls) resulted in an award of $100 million in Mattel's favor. The reported amount of legal fees was more than $93 million.[4]

---

3. Letter from Harrie Samaras to Mark V.B. Partridge (Mar. 30, 2008).
4. Debra Cassens Weiss, *Legal Fees a "Breathtaking" $93M-Plus in Bratz Battle*, ABA J. (Sept. 10, 2008), *at* http://abajournal.com/news/legal_fees_a_breathtaking_93m_plus_in_bratz_battle/.

Every two years, the American Intellectual Property Law Association conducts a survey regarding the costs of IP litigation. The survey questions both corporate and private practitioners about patent, trademark, copyright, and trade secret litigation. Participants are asked to respond "only if you have personal knowledge either as a service provider . . . or as a purchaser of such services . . . of the costs incurred within the relatively recent past."[5]

The growth in litigation expenses reported by the AIPLA surveys since 2001 has been dramatic, as shown by these trends over time from 2001 to 2007:[6]

Trademark (median, inclusive of all costs, $1 to $25 million at stake)—30 percent increase.	
2001	$502,000
2003	$602,000
2005	$700,000
2007	$650,000

Copyright (median, inclusive of all costs, $1 to $25 million at stake)—25 percent increase.	
2001	$400,000
2003	$499,000
2005	$440,000
2007	$500,000

Trade secret (median, inclusive of all costs, $1 to $25 million at stake)—43 percent increase at highest point.	
2001	$699,000
2003	$875,000
2005	$1,000,000
2007	$800,000

Patent (median, inclusive of all costs, $1 to $25 million at stake)—a 67 percent increase.	
2001	$1,499,000
2003	$2,000,000
2005	$2,000,000
2007	$2,500,000

---

5. American Intellectual Property Law Association, *AIPLA Report of the Economic Survey 2007*.
6. American Intellectual Property Law Association, *AIPLA Report of the Economic Survey 2001, 2003, 2005* and *2007*.

When the amount at stake is over $25,000,000, the mean inclusive cost for patent litigation escalates to $5,499,000 and goes as high as $10,000,000 in certain regions.

The growing cost of litigation in the IP field is no doubt mirrored by litigation costs in other areas of the law. Increasing litigation expenses certainly encourage clients to look for ways to resolve disputes at a lower cost. Federal Court of Appeals Judge Randall Rader recognizes that the search for alternatives is a necessary and positive consequence of an effective legal system in which private dispute resolution plays a major role. In a keynote address to the University of Washington School of Law, Judge Rader explained this view:

> But what I'm really saying is that the costs keep the courts in their proper place in the system. The courts are not a guarantor of all resolution of all disputes; rather, in the American system of Justice we prefer to encourage private settlement. In America, the courts are not here to solve all the problems. They're not here to repair all the holes in the stairways in every department store in America, they're not here to guarantee that everyone gets the right cost for anything, whether it be intellectual property or the rent they pay on their apartment. Rather, the court is a kind of a safety net. It is the final arbiter to whom you can turn when all private resolution mechanisms fail. The cost of the system ensures the courts stay within that limited role in the system.
>
> Now it's a little against my interest to say this because, you know it would be much better for me to tell you that I am important and that you must come to me to resolve all of your disputes. But I think that is not true. I think the system operates, and can only operate, when I am the exception to the rule for dispute resolution. Indeed I think if you ask my brother colleagues here, if we had to resolve all of the disputes that are filed with the courts, the courts would collapse under the workload. We could not manage to handle such a continuing growth curve. We have to rely on settlements—not just settlements, there are many forms of private resolution outside of the court system—but we are as reliant on that as the system is for its entire functions.[7]

From a client's point of view, the costs of litigation compel them to seek private resolution outside the court system. As costs rise, the force of that compulsion increases, as does the need for attorneys who are skilled in both private resolution methods and traditional litigation.

---

7. Randall Rader, *The Pace and Expense of Litigation in the United States Courts*, Keynote address at the 1999 Summit Conference on Intellectual Property, University of Washington, CASRIP Symposium Publication Series No. 5, (July 2000) *at* http://www.law.washington.edu/CASRIP/Symposium/Number5/pub5atcl1.pdf.

[B] The Vanishing Trial

Coincidentally with the rise of litigation costs, the opportunities for obtaining skills in traditional litigation decline as trials become an increasingly endangered species.

When we think of litigation, we're trained and conditioned to think of trials—Jimmy Stewart in *Anatomy of a Murder*, Charles Laughton in *Witness for the Prosecution*, or even Joe Pesci in *My Cousin Vinnie*. However, the reality for civil litigation is that very few cases reach trial.

The Administrative Office of the U.S. courts tracks filing and disposition statistics for the federal district courts. The 2007 *Annual Report of the Director on Judicial Business of the United States Courts* provides a wealth of facts, figures, and tables that tell a remarkable story about the vanishing trial in civil litigation. During the twelve-month period ending September 30, 2007, a total of 239,292 civil cases were terminated. Of that group, only 4.1 percent were terminated during or after trial. The numbers for commercial disputes involving IP are even more striking. During that one-year period, the disposition of IP cases during or after trial in total numbers and as a percent of total disposition of that case type were as follows:

- 50 copyright cases (1.0 percent)
- 61 trademark cases (1.7 percent)
- 94 patent cases (3.4 percent)

Several observations can be drawn from these statistics:

- Expense apparently increases as experience with trial practice declines.
- Persons tend to focus on the familiar. Thus, as lawyers become less familiar with trial and more familiar with discovery and other pretrial matters, it is understandable that more time and attention is given to pretrial practice and less to actual trial.
- We are far more likely as practicing attorneys to spend our time resolving disputes by means other than trial. Yet the focus at law school and in continuing legal education (CLE) is largely on trial practice, with little time given to other methods of dispute resolution. We should instead dedicate more attention and energy to mastering alternative methods for resolving disputes such as negotiation, mediation, and arbitration.

[C] Client Attitudes

As an apparent reaction to the increase expense of litigation, client attitudes are shifting in favor of alternative forms of dispute resolution. Business leaders and general counsel increasingly look to litigators to explore other options. A study of general counsel reported in the October 2004 issue of *Corporate Legal Times* indicated that 40 percent favored arbitration and 60 percent favored meditation over court litigation as a means to resolve commercial disputes. The message to litigating counsel is clear: your clients now expect you to at least consider ADR as one of the tools for resolving disputes. Outside counsel who fail to hear this message are likely to be replaced by those who do.

Michael Leathes confirms this perception. With over thirty years of corporate legal experience, including serving as legal counsel for The Gillette Company, general counsel for Pfizer International Inc., general counsel for International Distillers & Vintners (now part of Diageo) and head of IP at British American Tobacco, Leathes has been a champion of ADR in the commercial world, especially mediation, which he sees as a critical tool for helping his companies reduce expense and achieve better results.

As corporate counsel, Leathes has long advocated widely on the need for litigation counsel to master the strategies and tactics of ADR. It was an important factor in his selection of outside counsel. "I checked their Web sites," he said. "I looked for an expression of their attitude about ADR. If it was not highlighted convincingly, if it was not apparent from the site and promoted, I thought twice before hiring that firm to take on my work."

Client attitudes no doubt are driven by reported accounts of other corporations that have reinvented and improved their dispute resolutions practices and legal budgets through the use of ADR. Georgia-Pacific Corporation, for example, has reaped large benefits from emphasizing early case evaluation and ADR as part of its dispute resolution strategy. Phillip M. Armstrong, principal counsel for litigation at Georgia-Pacific, has described the company's approach:[8]

> For many years, the company followed the path of litigation common to most major companies. When a lawsuit was filed against the company it was assigned to a member of the legal department, often a junior attorney with little litigation experience. The in-house attorney would then hire outside counsel in the jurisdiction where the case was filed to answer, conduct discovery, and represent the company in the litigation until the case was resolved, usually through settlement months later. This typical method of dispute resolution was expensive and time consuming.
>
> This dispute resolution practice is guided in large measure by a win-at-all costs, never surrender philosophy held by top management and litigators. We did nothing wrong, why should we settle? We have to fight back, otherwise we

8. Phillip M. Armstrong, *Case Study: Georgia-Pacific's Aggressive Use of Early Case Evaluation and ADR*, 16 (6) ACCA Docket 42–48 (1998) at http://www.allbusiness.com/human-resources/careers-job-training/1014905-1.html.

> will be a target for lawsuits. If we fight hard, people will avoid bringing action. In the end, the belief is that an aggressive litigation defense policy will avoid lawsuits and reduce costs. To a degree, this may work. If you don't stand up for your rights you get pushed around. But not all cases fit this philosophy. And experience shows that when applied across the board, the aggressive defense philosophy is more expensive and time-consuming than it needs to be, wasting valuable company resources which could be profitably directed elsewhere.
>
> In 1993 the Georgia-Pacific legal department, led by general counsel James F. Kelly, sought and found a better way. Kelly analyzed the company's caseload and concluded that many cases could have been resolved earlier at a substantial savings to the company. One of Kelly's cost-cutting steps was to mandate early case evaluation with an emphasis on ADR for disputes filed against the company. Lawyers were trained in ADR. Instead of sending cases off to outside counsel as soon as they came in, Georgia-Pacific legal staff would review every case; consider early case evaluation, mediation, arbitration and other ADR options; and seek to resolve most within the first sixty to ninety days. The process is especially valuable for dealing with suits that involve a legitimate claim against the company or a business relationship that should be preserved. If a case is bogus or grossly inflated, Georgia-Pacific will stand firm.

By 1998 Kelly was pleased with the results:

> We are constantly reviewing our litigation strategy, but early case evaluation and ADR seem to be working. If you properly evaluate a case early in the process and can arrive at a settlement that is consistent with that evaluation, it's hard to argue with the results.

In 2005 Armstrong provided an assessment of the company's ADR program after ten years of implementation.[9] Georgia-Pacific estimated that the program saved the company several million dollars during its first ten years. Armstrong offers several tips for companies wanting to follow Georgia-Pacific's example:

- Maintain management support for the program. Educate new and existing managers on why ADR is good for the company.
- Train the legal staff in ADR processes and benefits. Remarkably, lawyers receive little ADR training in law school.
- Use mediation clauses in contracts.
- Litigate when necessary to protect the company from frivolous or unwarranted claims.
- Develop a positive settlement mentality. You can settle without being weak.

9. Phillip M. Armstrong, *Georgia-Pacific's ADR Program: A Critical Review after 10 Years*, Dispute Resolution J. (May–July 2005).

- Focus on early case evaluation and mediation as the most effective methods.

Armstrong hopes that Georgia-Pacific's success with its ADR program will encourage other companies to reevaluate their dispute resolution practices and embrace the benefits of ADR.

[D] Empirical Studies

In addition to anecdotal evidence and individual case studies, there have been several empirical studies in the dispute resolution field. Of particular interest are a 1998 study by Cornell University professors David B. Lipsky and Ronald L. Seeber entitled "The Appropriate Resolution of Corporate Disputes: A Report on the Growing Use of ADR by U.S. Corporations" (The Cornell Study), a 2003 study by the American Arbitration Association reported as "Dispute-Wise Business Management: Improving Economic and Non-Economic Outcomes in Managing Business Conflicts" (The AAA Study), and a 2004 study by the Maryland Mediation and Conflict Resolution Office (the MACRO Study).

In 1997, Cornell University surveyed more than 530 U.S. corporations in the Fortune 1000 regarding dispute resolutions practices. Ninety percent of the survey respondents reported that they considered mediation to be a cost savings method. The study also reported that corporations with effective ADR practices enjoyed significant litigation cost savings. For example, engineering and construction firm Kellogg Brown and Root, a subsidiary of Halliburton, reported an 80 percent reduction in outside litigation costs. Likewise, Motorola reported a 75 percent reduction in litigation costs over a period of six years, and NCR reported a 50 percent reduction in litigation costs and a drop in pending lawsuits from 263 in 1984 to 28 in 1993. Finally, the Toro Co., a lawn mower and small engine manufacturer, reported reduced per claim litigation costs from an average of $47,252 to $10,420 after it implemented a two-step national mediation program for disputes. Toro also reported a reduction in the average settlement and verdict amount from $68,368 to $20,248.

The AAA Study was based on phone interviews with 101 Fortune 1000 companies with mean revenues of about $9 billion, 103 mid-size public companies with mean revenue of about $380 million, and 50 privately held companies with mean revenue of about $690 million.[10] The AAA report on the study finds two key factors driving a steady growth in acceptance of ADR. Executives want to preserve valuable business relationships while also

10. *Dispute-Wise Business Management: Improving Economic and Non-Economic Outcomes in Managing Business Conflicts* (American Bar Association), 2006.

being determined to avoid costly litigation. Among the findings of the study was the recognition that companies that are effective users of ADR experience lower legal department expenses as compared to those that were the least effective users. The total budget for legal services was $10,292.000 for effective ADR users versus $12,221,000 for the least effective. Further, the price/earnings ratio of the effective ADR users was 28 percent higher than the mean for all publically held companies and 68 percent higher than the mean for companies that were not effective users of ADR.

The economic benefits of using ADR are striking at the corporate level. The most effective approach appears to involve a redefinition of "winning." Rather than viewing victory as the goal of each dispute, the companies who enjoy the greatest economic benefits seem to be those who approach individual disputes as being part of a portfolio of disputes. A portfolio view of winning looks for an overall reduction of risk, cost, and time spent on the full array of disputes. The goal is to win the overall war, not just the individual battle, and that war involves an overall improvement in terms of reduced risk, cost, and time commitment.

In companies that are effective ADR users, the legal department is likely to have a good understanding of broader business issues, to be involved in the general corporate planning process, and to work with a management team focused on preserving relationships rather than winning cases. In contrast, in companies that are the least effective users of ADR, the legal department is more likely to take an aggressive approach to disputes, to focus primarily on contract review, and to favor litigation over ADR.

Overall the AAA study found that only 15 percent of companies "often favor litigation over ADR." The top reasons given in the AAA study for favoring ADR were (1) saves money; (2) saves time; (3) provides a more satisfactory process; (4) allows parties to resolve disputes themselves; and (5) requires only limited discovery.[11] Seventy-seven percent of survey respondents believed the use of mediation reduced costs while 58 percent believed that arbitration reduced costs.[12]

These findings again support the point that corporate attitudes favor ADR as a dispute resolution option. Therefore, it behooves counsel to understand and master ADR as a dispute resolution tool.

The MACRO study involved information from three sources: (1) published literature about ADR, (2) two surveys distributed to Maryland employers, and (3) interviews with officials from business, government, and ADR institutions. The study revealed an interesting lack of knowledge about ADR.

The key findings of the MACRO study were that most Maryland businesses surveyed (and presumably other businesses nationwide) did not have

11. *Id.* at 19.
12. *Id.* at 23.

well-developed ADR practices in place in their company, suggesting much room for further development. The survey found, for example, that less than 30 percent of respondents extensively or frequently explored ADR as a means of resolving disputes. Only 35 percent provided ADR training and education for the legal staff. Less than 11 percent extensively or frequently used corporate ADR policy statements endorsing interest or institutional support for ADR. Instead of ADR, survey respondents most frequently turned to negotiation, settlement conferences, and litigation for the resolution of disputes. In conclusion, the authors state: "Our study clearly revealed that there generally is a low level of familiarity or sophistication about dispute resolution processes in Maryland businesses."[13]

The findings in Maryland seemed at odds with the more positive views of ADR voiced in the Cornell study and the AAA study. Based on the benefits revealed in those other studies, the MACRO report urged Maryland companies to invest more attention, training, and time in ADR programs, indicating "the benefits that businesses following these recommendations can expect" include among others, "saving money, saving time, preserving good business and employee relationships, avoiding bad press, improving public image, [and] increasing employee satisfaction and retention . . .."

The MACRO study also noted the need for better integration of ADR into law firm practice. Most practitioners have not been specifically trained in ADR techniques and processes. In addition, many attorneys continue to view litigation as having a more important role in resolving disputes than ADR. Acceptance of ADR by private practitioners was seen as essential to the type of systematic use of ADR that leads to the greatest benefits, such as those observed in the Cornell study.

[1] In-House Counsel Perspective

The business case for the effective use of ADR emerges from these studies. From the in- house perspective, the effective use of ADR may result in a significant reduction in legal expense. The AAA studies indicate there is about a 20 percent reduction compared to companies that are not effective ADR users. Is ADR the cause of this reduction, or can the reduction be attributed to other characteristics? The AAA study found that the effective users of ADR had legal departments who understood broader business issues and were integrated into the general corporate planning process. If the legal players are integrated into the business, it is likely to take less time and expense to resolve disputes and other legal issues, and it is likely that ADR will be more effective. Better integration of lawyers into the company's business and the effective

13. *The Use of Alternative Dispute Resolution (ADR) in Maryland Business: A Benchmarking Study*. Maryland Mediation and Conflict Resolution Office (2004).

use of ADR to resolve disputes become complementary tools to achieve the same goal.

From the in-house perspective, we also see that effective users of ADR have higher price-to-earnings ratios. Is ADR a factor in this increase? It is possible that a company's reputation with respect to litigation is a factor in market value. Reports of high stakes litigation can drive down share prices, and certainly high stakes losses may reduce share prices. Consider for example the effect on share value for RIM, the makers of Blackberry PDAs, when it was sued for patent infringement. Increased litigation suggests increased risk that probably leads to lower market valuations. In contrast, companies that avoid high stakes public litigation may seem to be more stable and, therefore, a better, less risky investment. ADR can contribute to this perspective by resolving disputes in a private setting. Whether ADR itself is a cause of reduced legal expense and improved market value, it does appear to be part of a suite of best practices that in-house counsel can use to improve the effectiveness of the services delivered to their company.

[2] Outside Counsel Perspective

From the perspective of outside counsel, compelling reasons to use ADR flow directly from the fact that effective ADR users will want counsel who are also effective users. If outside counsel can bring ADR practices to bear on the disputes they handle for their clients, they may be able to contribute to reducing corporate legal expense and increasing market value. Outside counsel may also be able to serve their clients better by using ADR to obtain better results—ones that are cheaper, faster, and more satisfactory to the company's business goals—than those obtained through litigation. As our clients recognize the benefits of using ADR, those attorneys who focus on litigation as the only dispute resolution tool will see a decline in demand for their services.

In short, the trends in favor of ADR are strong. Litigation has become too expensive. Disputes are not likely to be resolved by trial in any event. Client attitudes demand that we consider alternatives as a means of resolving all forms of commercial disputes, including IP ones. Thus, our need to embrace ADR is acute.

CHAPTER 2

Benefits

2.01 What Are the Benefits?

What is the goal we seek as lawyers involved in lawsuits? Is it winning? Or is it dispute resolution? Winning at all costs can simply result in replacing one problem (the dispute) with another—an expensive legal bill.

A study by the Department of Justice suggests that ADR is proving to be a better way to resolve disputes.[1] The DOJ study of civil cases found that 65 percent of cases settled when ADR was used compared with only 29 percent when ADR was not used. During the period of the study from 1995 to 1998, 511 DOJ cases (or 3.3 percent) used ADR. The DOJ attorneys estimated the use of ADR saved eighty-eight hours of staff time, six months of litigation time, and about $10,753 in litigation cost *per case*. A higher percentage of

1. *Dispute Resolution and the Vanishing Trial: Comparing Federal Government Litigation and ADR Outcomes*, Ohio State J. Dispute Resolution (forthcoming). *See* http;//www.adr.org/sp.asp?id=34835.

cases settled (71 percent) when ADR was voluntary as compared to the rate (50 percent) when ADR was mandatory.

Another intimation regarding the benefits of ADR is found in a study reported in the *Journal of Empirical Legal Studies* by Randall L. Kiser, analyst at DecisionSet; Martin A. Asher, an economist at the University of Pennsylvania; and Blakeley B. McShane, a graduate student at the Wharton School of the University of Pennsylvania.[2] In analyzing the results of 2,054 civil law suits between 2000 and 2005, the survey researchers found that most of the plaintiffs who passed up a settlement offer and went to trial received less money than if they had taken the settlement offer, at an average loss of about $43,000. Defendants were wrong less often in rejecting settlement offers, but when they were wrong, the average loss was much higher: $1.1 million. Plaintiffs most often made bad choices in cases in which contingency fee arrangements are common while defendants were more likely to make mistakes in cases where insurance coverage is generally available to cover the costs of defense and the amount of an adverse award, indicating their greater willingness to gamble when the risk of personal loss is low. The implication of this study for ADR is that a greater emphasis on a facilitated settlement, such as mediation, may lead to overall better results for litigants.

The commonly recognized benefits of ADR—either arbitration or mediation—include the potential for improvements over court adjudication in the following key areas:

[A] Privacy

Privacy refers to the ability to hold hearings in private, away from the glare of the media. Court litigation necessarily entails the likelihood the proceedings will be open to the public, including competitors, government agencies, and the media. The concern for privacy has grown in recent years as courts increasingly make all court documents available online. What once took a trip to the dusty files of the courthouse to uncover can now be found via one's own computer and sent around the world electronically with a few clicks of the mouse. This can hinder ongoing business dealings, lead to embarrassment, and cause positions to harden.

In contrast, ADR proceedings are normally private, with only the parties, witnesses, and counsel involved. Business matters can be kept out of media scrutiny.

---

2. Jonathan D. Glater, *Study Finds Settling is Better than Going to Trial*, New York Times, Aug. 8, 2008.

[B] Confidentiality

Confidentiality is an adjunct to privacy, but instead of focusing on the nature of the hearings *per se*, confidentiality focuses on protection of information disclosed during the litigation process. Although it is possible to obtain a protective order in court litigation, there seems to be a growing reluctance in the courts to maintain records on a confidential basis. In any event, even if a protective order is entered early, the information used at trial generally becomes public record.

In contrast, materials used in ADR proceedings can be maintained on a confidential basis, restricted from public disclosure or use for any purpose not related to the dispute.

[C] Discovery

Discovery in court litigation, especially in the U.S. federal courts, is wide ranging and burdensome, involving interrogatories, document production, requests for admissions, and depositions. Not only is discovery expensive in terms of attorney fees, but the entire process can be disruptive to the organization. This burden has been increased in recent years by the increased demand for electronic discovery, leading to revisions to the Federal Rules of Civil Procedure and court rulings imposing new burdens and obligations on litigants.

ADR methods of arbitration and mediation can reduce the burden by limiting the extent of discovery or avoiding the obligation altogether, depending on the rules of the ADR Institute and the desires of the parties.

[D] Expertise

Expertise refers to the specific knowledge a judge or other neutral entity brings to bear on the case. Subject matter and legal expertise relevant to the dispute can yield faster and better results. Yet in our judicial system, judges usually are generalists with no specialized training in a given field of law or industry experience in a particular field. Federal judges in particular bear a caseload that runs the gamut from criminal disputes to patent infringement—and everything in between. State court judges are sometimes classified into more defined categories (e.g., criminal, domestic, traffic, civil), but within the civil category state court judges are still likely to be generalists.

In ADR, the parties have the ability to select neutrals who are industry, technology, or legal experts in areas directly relevant to the dispute.

[E] Location

Location can be an important factor in the economics of litigation. In court, the selection of location is limited by the requirements of jurisdiction, venue, and convenience. Indeed, side litigation over these issues can occupy major resources and delay ultimate resolution of the dispute.

In ADR, the location can be chosen at the convenience of the parties without regard to jurisdictional issues. In some circumstances, such as domain name disputes handled under the Uniform Dispute Resolution Policy ("UDRP") of the Internet Corporation for Assigned Names and Numbers ("ICANN"), conflicts are handled via online submissions, eliminating the need to convene in a fixed location. For example, I was involved in one dispute in which a complaint by a trademark owner in the United Arab Emirates was decided against a domain name owner in India by a three-member panel comprised of one person in Australia, another in England, and me in the United States (Chicago). The proceeding was decided on written submissions exchanged via e-mail with no live hearing. This flexibility ADR offers regarding location can reduce costs.

[F] Timing

Timing is also a factor in the expense and inconvenience of litigation, both in terms of the scheduling of hearings and the length of time from filing to decision. ADR increases the control that parties have over scheduling and timing.

[G] Reduced Expense

Reduced expense is cited as a benefit of ADR, and clearly is a goal of ADR in most instances. Whether it is achieved depends on the type of ADR employed, the cooperation of the parties in efficiently pursuing a resolution, and the power of the panel to manage the proceeding in a manner that reduces many of the causes of added expense, including runaway motion practices and discovery.

There is a general consensus that successful mediation prior to trial will result in a significant cost savings. This savings will be enjoyed even if that case has advanced through discovery and motion practice as the time involved in a mediation will most probably be less than that required for trial.

However, views on the cost savings of arbitration tend to be more mixed. Many note a growing pressure by participants to push arbitration into the litigation mold by seeking more discovery, greater motion practice, and lengthier hearings. If a three-member panel is used for the case, their fees added to the cost of counsel may cause arbitration to be more expensive than traditional litigation. However, the extreme instances in which cost may not in fact be a benefit of ADR can be acknowledged without the benefit being surrendered completely. If used properly, the benefit on cost should go to ADR especially when it is used over time as part of a corporate program of dispute resolution.

Studies making cost comparisons paint a positive picture of this ADR benefit. In one study reported in the Dispute Resolution of the American Arbitration Association, a panel of experienced construction litigators and arbitrators estimated the claimant's cost of arbitrating or litigating a state court claim in a construction dispute.[3]

This is the hypothetical dispute involved:

> The owner of a commercial building has a claim against an architect arising out of a remodeling project. The claim is for design defects and inadequate workmanship in connection with the flooring, which the owner contends is unstable and suffers from vibration problems. The owner seeks $600,000 in damages for repair costs and loss of use. The dispute raises issues of professional malpractice, the standard of care, the scope of repair and loss of use.

The panel based its cost estimates on several assumptions. The dispute was primarily handled by a partner billing at $300 per hour. The arbitration involved discovery with four depositions along with four days of the arbitration hearing itself. In comparison, the experts concluded the court litigation would involve six depositions and six days of trial. Each track would involve typical preliminary hearings, discovery disputes, a dispositive motion to dismiss, an expert report and testimony, and briefing before and after the hearing. The experts also considered the potential cost to prepare and participate in mediation as lasting eighteen hours over the course of two days. The detailed cost estimates, which broke out the anticipated expense of each step in the dispute, found a cost savings from ADR in comparison to litigation as follows:

Mediation—Total Cost $10,140
Arbitration—Total Cost $94,500
Litigation—Total Cost $120,300

As with any hypothetical, the assumptions control the result and may be subject to challenge. Nevertheless, these figures provide a well-reasoned estimate of the likely savings in a typical commercial dispute.

---

3. Susan Zuckerman, *Comparing Cost in Construction Arbitration & Litigation*, DISPUTE RESOLUTION J. 42 (May–July 2007).

[H] Finality

ADR can offer the benefit of finality by eliminating appeals and ongoing judicial review. In the typical arbitration, the decision of the arbitrator is final and cannot be appealed. Mediation generally also involves a negotiated agreement that terminates further litigation.

[I] Relationships

Relationships are critical in the business world. However, the dynamics of litigation often lead to bitter antagonism between the parties. ADR offers parties the ability to work together to maintain the relationship. Mediation is especially useful for this goal when the process cultivates collaboration in problem solving. Mediation can also facilitate creative solutions to disputes in which both parties can sometimes enjoy an improved position that would not be possible as the result of a court decision.

[J] Results

Perhaps most importantly, ADR offers the prospect of better results. Consider this example: The first company (Acme) was a manufacturer of a patented design for plastic acoustic surround boxes. These plastic boxes are placed between wall joists behind wallboard and serve as housing for stereo speakers, reflecting the sound forward into the room for improved acoustic results. The second company, Beta, obtained similar boxes manufactured in China that it imported for sale in the United States over the objection of Acme. The result was a federal civil action for patent infringement in the District Court for Minnesota.

Beta was outraged to be sued for this conduct. "This idea's been around for years," Beta's president insisted. "When I worked construction, we'd buy cat litter boxes from the hardware store for the same purpose. What do you mean they have a patent?"

Clearly Beta had a basis for challenging the invalidity of the patent, but at what cost? Both sides recognized the time and expense of litigation were destined to become the real problem, so mediation was arranged with the magistrate judge assigned to the case. Although Beta initially refused to consider doing business with Acme ("Why would I want to work with someone who sues me over crap like this?"), with the help of the magistrate counsel was able to steer the discussion to a business solution that could not have been reached through litigation.

In the end, the president of Beta was able to report to his board that he had resolved the dispute without further legal cost or payment to Acme and had secured Acme as a supplier for its needs at a discount, saving the company substantial expense for the next five years. Similarly, the president of Acme was able to report that he had stopped the infringement of Acme's patent and secured a five-year order that would provide more in profit than Acme had estimated it could recover in damages even if it were successful.

This story illustrates the possibility of better results through ADR. If this matter had been litigated through trial, the likely result was either that the plaintiff would have paid thousands (maybe millions) of dollars in legal fees to obtain an injunction and a small recovery of damages, or that the defendant would have prevailed, therefore paying no damages but still incurring substantial legal expense.

[K] Image

Finally, effective use of ADR may help restore public confidence in lawyers and the legal process. Unsurprisingly, the legal profession has a poor image, with lawyers being rated below politicians and used car salesmen in public opinion polls. It has long been such, well before Shakespeare put the words "First, we kill all the lawyers" in the mouth of an anarchist. More recently, Joseph G. Bisceglia, president of the Illinois Bar Association, commented on the image problem of lawyers:

> Much of the popular perception of lawyers revolves around their role as advocates. . . . Unfortunately, this image of lawyers as advocates and warriors has also contributed to many of the negative portrayals of our professions. Pitting litigants against each other through their respective attorneys naturally creates resentment and antagonisms—and winners and losers. To make matters worse, the party that "wins" can be as unhappy as the loser at the end of the process . . .[4]

To improve the image of lawyers, Bisceglia, an experienced trial lawyer himself, urges greater use of ADR: "Embrace the growing use of alternative methods of dispute resolution at every opportunity. In the process, our image as lawyers—as problem solvers—is enhanced."

4. Joseph G. Bisceglia, *ADR and the Image of Lawyers*, 96 Ill. B. J. 8–9 (Jan. 2008).

CHAPTER

3

Avoidance

Despite the apparent benefits, ADR is not right for all disputes. The studies mentioned in Chapter 2 showing favorable attitudes toward ADR also show that about 40 percent of corporate respondents have an unfavorable opinion of arbitration, and 20 percent have an unfavorable opinion of mediation.

What are the reasons behind these unfavorable opinions? In some cases, negative views flow from bad past experiences. In other instances, the views are likely attributable to a person having an incomplete understanding of the available options and nature of the process.

Some resistance, however, goes beyond lack of understanding or bad past experience. Even those who acknowledge a desire to settle most disputes and the value of ADR as an aid to settlement find broader concerns in the effect of the promotion of ADR on the integrity of the judicial system. This concern was well stated in a letter to the editor of the *Illinois Bar Journal*:

> [I]nordinate pressure to settle denigrates and undermines confidence in the judicial system. Litigants are routinely told that the results of litigation are random and unpredictable, that the costs and risks of obtaining justice outweigh the vindication of rights, that standing on principles is anti-social, and that all concerned have better uses for their time and money. While uncertainty and risk are attendant to litigation, most objective observers believe that most courts most often reach an appropriate result. In the meantime, the argument that the justice system is essentially a lottery tends to be a self-fulfilling

prophecy because the system focuses on "getting rid of the case" rather than on "doing justice."[1]

Similarly, critics of ADR at the policy or systemic level voice concerns on a variety of grounds: (1) the privatization of dispute resolution is problematic because the elaboration of law through public trials and published decisions is necessary to protect and enhance individual rights, (2) treating disputes as private matters eliminates public accountability, (3) public dispute resolution has an important education function that is lost when matters are resolved privately, (4) the establishment of ADR processes often weakens the position of less powerful members of society, and (5) the private ADR process may increase the expression and impact of prejudice.[2]

Hostility toward arbitration has been seen at the legislative level as well. For example, Alabama enacted a state statute prohibiting the enforcement of pre-dispute arbitration agreements. The Alabama statute was challenged in a dispute between a pest control company and a homeowner over the enforcement of an arbitration clause in the parties' contract. When the matter reached the U.S. Supreme Court, twenty state attorneys general submitted an amicus brief urging the Court to uphold the state statute. Instead, the Court concluded that the Alabama statute was preempted by the Federal Arbitration Act (FAA).[3] Nevertheless, the controversy illustrates a certain level of antipathy toward ADR, at least as to coerced consumer obligations.

The systemic, policy, and legislative critiques deserve discussion elsewhere, and should be recognized by counsel learning the tools of ADR. However, they are largely beyond the scope of our concern here as we are focused on ADR as an essential competency for lawyers. In short, we are less concerned here with the possibility that ADR may be bad from a public policy point of view as we are looking at the use of ADR as a tool to serve our client's best interests.

3.01 Why Is ADR Avoided?

Given the recognized need for alternatives to litigation, why do clients and their counsel resist ADR? Joseph Bisceglia, trial attorney and Illinois Bar Association President, sees several reasons.[4] First, there is a widely held view that attorneys get the best result by showing strength. Clients want strength

---

1. Letter to the Editor from Jack Joseph, "ADR has become an industry," 96 Ill. B. J. (Mar. 2008).
2. Jean R. Sternlight, *Is Alternative Dispute Resolution Consistent with the Rule of Law? Lessons from Abroad*, 56 DePaul L. R. 569.
3. Allied-Bruce Terminix Cos., Inc. v. Dobson, 513 U.S. 265 (1995).
4. Joseph G. Bisceglia, *ADR and the Image of Lawyers*, 96 Ill. B. J. 8–9 (Jan. 2008).

and will find a better "warrior" if the attorney suggests otherwise. Second, when money is the issue, the defendant has little incentive to settle early. It can also be difficult to assess a reasonable settlement without discovery. Finally, client psychology can be a factor.

Sometimes the parties need a catharsis and time to heal the pain (economic, emotional, or otherwise) that lies at the heart of the dispute. Sometimes litigants are simply unrealistic, unreasonable, vindictive, or unwilling to compromise at any cost, particularly at an early stage. And sometimes people simply and honestly want to prove a point for the greater good.[5]

Thus, not all cases are well suited to ADR, and some disputes should be addressed in open court to further public policy and discourse. Nevertheless, most of the explanations for resistance to ADR in commercial disputes don't withstand scrutiny.

The specific reasons cited to avoid the use of ADR usually fall into the following categories.

[A] Loss of Control

Participants sometimes feel they lack control over the process. Attorneys trained in, experienced with, and accustomed to traditional litigation work inside a process that constantly changes—which is like trying to build a house while someone else is trying to tear it down—and feel comfortable operating within a familiar set of rules and practices. They know generally what will happen next, and they benefit from a vast pool of resources in the form of published decisions, treatises, and manuals.

In contrast, the various ADR options seem to place the participants in an arena where they have little control and little framework for taking control—as if they were on a boat adrift in a stormy sea, without sails, paddles, compass, or landmarks.

Control in ADR can be gained by obtaining greater knowledge and experience with the process. There are rules, practices, and methods for directing an ADR process to a good result.

[B] Unwanted Disclosure

A commonly expressed sentiment is that if a party becomes involved in ADR early, it will need to disclose information and strategy that could be used against it in litigation if the ADR process fails. Litigants want to hold their

5. *Id.*

cards close to their vest in the belief that doing so will give them a future advantage.

However, this attitude usually fails to withstand scrutiny. The formal litigation process is designed to avoid surprise by requiring disclosure through a variety of mechanisms, including mandatory initial disclosures, formal discovery (interrogatories, document production, requests for admission, depositions, etc.), elaborate pretrial orders, pretrial briefs, and motion practice. Information not disclosed during the pretrial process may be excluded from us at trial.

Not only is it likely that disclosure will take place before trial in any event, but also the statistics cited above about the incidence of trial indicates that it is highly likely the dispute will be resolved before then anyway. Therefore, there is little or no advantage to delaying disclosure. The more prudent and productive course is early disclosure to encourage early resolution. Granted, there may be circumstances in which nondisclosure of facts or strategy can yield advantages, but a blanket stand against disclosure during ADR is unwarranted.

[C] Weakness

Participants in a dispute naturally seek advantages and strive to avoid the appearance of weakness. Most lawyers and clients want to negotiate from a position of strength. It doesn't follow, however, that proposing the possibility of ADR or settlement demonstrates weakness. Handled properly, the introduction of alternatives to litigation should have no adverse effect on bargaining strength. Trial savvy Joseph G. Bisceglia says, "There is no inherent weakness in compromise; in fact, some would say it indicates greater wisdom and intelligence."[6]

It is a commonly held belief that proposing settlement or ADR displays weakness, but this belief is shortsighted and often foolish. Is the goal to win at trial at all costs? Or is the goal to solve a problem, to resolve the dispute? The latter *should* be the goal.

The litigation process includes natural junctures for exploring settlement without displaying weakness. The process also includes rules and practices that require the parties to consider settlement in a way that neither participant displays weakness. The rules direct the parties to consider settlement options at various pretrial conferences, and the court will also usually raise the issue at status conferences and the like.

Rather than showing weakness, if used correctly ADR can be a remarkable opportunity to show strength to your opponent. An effective presentation at

---

6. *Id.*

an ADR session can display that you are confident, well prepared, and ready and capable of going to trial, if necessary.

[D] Expense

Some parties are reluctant to participate in ADR because of the added expense. ADR often costs more in filing fees to initiate than traditional court proceedings. Hiring an ADR neutral can be an added cost. Mediators and arbitrators are generally paid by the hour for their roles in ADR, whereas there is no added cost for a judge's involvement in a state or federal court case. Even when there is no additional cost for participating in ADR by way of filing fees and cost for the neutral, extra legal expense may be incurred for the attorneys to prepare and appear at the ADR hearing.

These added costs, however, are small in comparison to the overall cost of litigating a case through trial. If the use of ADR leads to an early resolution short of trial, it will be money well spent and will result in an overall reduction of cost.

[E] Time

Parties may also avoid ADR due to the perceived time commitment. First, ADR can require added attorney time for preparation. This is primarily a cost issue that fades to insignificance if the matter is resolved early. In that event, the cost savings will far outweigh the added cost for attorney time devoted to ADR.

Second, arbitration can sometimes be a slow process if the arbitrator and parties do not press forward for a prompt resolution. Usually the added time in this regard can be reduced by effective case management. The added time involved is not endemic to the process itself. Arbitration rules, for example, normally allow the neutral to limit the discovery and length of hearing to reduce the time spent on the case. The award is usually due a few weeks after the conclusion of the hearing, which is often much faster than litigants experience in court litigation. The lack of an appeal also reduces the time involved.

Another time issue associated with ADR is the prospect that participating in the process will delay the litigation process. For example, in the Cook County, Illinois mandatory arbitration program, all newly filed civil cases involving less than $75,000 must first proceed through arbitration. Some may argue that this step delays a party's ability to bring the matter before the court. In reality, the program has dramatically shortened the overall time for the resolution of disputes in the Cook County system.

Likewise, proceedings in court may be suspended when the parties elect mediation. It is not uncommon to suspend discovery and other deadlines while the parties engage in mediation. Although mediation often involves a single mediation session, multiple sessions are possible, and the mediator may facilitate ongoing settlement negotiations over a period of time. If successful, of course, there will be no further need for court proceedings. Although there is the possibility of added delay, on the whole the cumulative time benefit from using ADR should outweigh the additional time resulting from ADR on occasion.

[F] Uncertainty

Similar to the concern about loss of control is the uncertainty of the process itself. Loss of control relates primarily to the feeling by counsel and the parties that they don't understand or control their role in the process. Uncertainty is related to the feeling that counsel and the parties do not understand the process itself or they are unsure about the range of results that may be achieved.

Bill Frank served as in-house counsel with S.C. Johnson & Son, Inc. for nearly twenty years and now has a growing ADR practice with a private firm bearing his name.[7] He has seen resistance to ADR from clients and peers. The main reason, he says, was fear of the unknown:

> In-house counsel didn't understand the benefits and process. Business clients weren't educated on the benefits. Because they were unfamiliar with the process they resisted ADR clauses in agreements and ad hoc ADR for the resolution of disputes. The devil you know is better than the devil you don't. Lack of knowledge can be a real impediment. Outside counsel also seemed threatened by the unfamiliar. When you're the hammer everything looks like a nail. Anything else can be seen as a threat to your livelihood.

As always, the darkness caused by uncertainty is alleviated by the bright light of knowledge, education, and experience. Given the importance of ADR as a dispute resolution tool, counsel should invest time and resources in learning more about the process. Counsel should also educate clients about the ADR options available for resolving commercial disputes.

[G] Loss of Fees

Certainly no readers of this book would avoid the use of ADR due to the belief that they would make less money as a consequence. Of course that is a

---

7. Interview with J. William Frank III, Of Counsel, McCracken & Frank LLP, www.mccrakenandfrank.com (Chicago, Illinois, Sept. 24, 2008).

cynical attitude that applies only to others, and perhaps should not even be mentioned as a serious consideration. Nevertheless, this attitude is raised in the literature as a reason some attorneys have been slow to adopt and implement ADR in their litigation practice. Not all reasons for avoidance are client focused or strategic. Harvard Law School professor Frank E.A. Sander has observed a "widespread perception by lawyers that [ADR] will be bad for their pocketbooks."[8]

To the extent this attitude does exist, it is certainly shortsighted and unethical. Lawyers have a duty to place the best interests of their clients above their personal interest in larger legal fees. Attorneys who do place the interests of their client first will no doubt be rewarded with more business and referrals from satisfied clients.

---

8. E. J. Pollock & M. Gayelin, *Law Firms Promise to Encourage Litigation Alternatives to Clients*, Wall St. J., Oct. 1991.

CHAPTER

4

Options

ADR affords parties a wide range of creative options for the resolution of disputes. Michael Leathes shares a story about his creative use of ADR while head of IP at British American Tobacco.[1] The UK-based tobaccocompany

1. *See Einstein's Lessons in Mediation*, MANAGING INTELLECTUAL PROPERTY 23 (July–Aug. 2006).

owned a collection of clothing trademarks licensed to PMEC, a small company selling upscale casual clothing. Eventually, BAT agreed to sell the marks to PMEC. The hitch was price. Both parties obtained independent reports with very different valuation results; therefore, they couldn't agree on a selling price for the transaction. Leathes describes the impasse:

> There was really only one buyer—PMEC. They had built a business using these brands and it would have been irresponsible of a company like BAT to threaten to sell the brand rights to a third party just to intimidate PMEC into paying more. So I didn't do it. On the other hand, the trademarks in question were certainly not worthless, and the company's shareholders had the right to expect that I would sell them for a fair value. I had an independent valuation in my hands, and I had shared it with Bob, but it was far above the valuation he had in his hands.[2]

The parties were reluctant to determine the selling price by binding arbitration, as BAT was concerned the result would be too low and PMEC that it would be too high. Mediation was considered but rejected out of concern that it might be a waste of time and money if the process failed to produce agreement.

The parties agreed on a creative blend of arbitration and mediation. First, they would present their case to a neutral in the role of arbitrator. He would decide on a fair selling price based on the valuation reports and other evidence. However, the decision would not be disclosed immediately to the parties but instead sealed in an envelope. In the afternoon, the neutral, now well versed in the facts, would turn into a mediator. If the mediation was successful, the mediated agreement would control. If the mediation did not produce agreement, the sealed arbitration decision would control.

This process not only had the benefit of guaranteeing a result by the end of the day, but also encouraged the parties to reach an amicable agreement rather than an imposed result. In fact, the mediation did result in agreement, bridging the gap in perceived value and putting nonmonetary issues into the mix to enable each side to get an acceptable result, something that would not have been obtained via a one-dimensional arbitration decision.

But what about that sealed decision? Curiosity might get the best of some, but here the wiser path was followed and the envelope was never opened. Leathes explains:

> We had shaken hands. Both of us were happy with the outcome. If we opened the envelope, that situation would most likely change. One of us would suddenly

---

2. *Id.* at 24.

> have become unhappy. It's not about turning a blind eye. Some things are just better not knowing.[3]

My partners, Robert Newbury and Joseph Welch, explored innovative ADR options for dispute resolution while working for AT&T in the 1990s. Harrie Samaras, who was introduced in Chapter 1, worked on the same situation from inside MCI. The problem arose from extensive and expensive litigation over many allegedly false advertising claims brought by AT&T and MCI against each other. Those claims eventually settled, but both parties were anxious to avoid further litigation of that magnitude. Thus, as part of the settlement, AT&T and MCI agreed to find an alternative method of resolving advertising disputes. Joe Welch described the approach taken by the parties:

> In 1991, a detailed Alternative Dispute Resolution Agreement was negotiated, agreed to, and implemented. The ADR Agreement provided essentially that all advertising disputes between AT&T and MCI involving long distance telephone service could only be resolved through the ADR. Rules were established for bringing complaints and procedures established for holding mini-trials. No discovery was allowed and the mini-trial could not last more than one day. From the filing of the complaint to reaching trial, the whole process took from two to three weeks. Decisions generally had to be issued within three business days of trial. The law to be followed was that of the Second Circuit. While there were liquidated damages provisions for failure to comply and some possibility of monetary award in exceptional circumstances, in actuality the relief in successful challenges always was injunctive.
>
> Both AT&T and MCI used the procedure often and found it helpful. The ADR Agreement was repeatedly amended and renewed over many years. Perhaps the most important amendment was the provision allowing the judge to determine the message of the challenged advertisement without a survey. That both speeded the proceedings and made them much less expensive.
>
> Through the years, somewhere between 600 and 800 cases were decided under the Agreement. Many were relatively minor advertising claims, but some were very important. For example, in 1993 when 800-numbers became portable, AT&T advertised it had the most reliable network and was able to defeat MCI's challenge of that claim. AT&T business executives believed that sustained claim was the major reason AT&T did not lose 800-number business. A notable result of so many actions was a rapid evolution in precedent and principles, so that in many instances the ADR actions were much more sophisticated than what one finds in federal court.
>
> As lawyers working under the ADR, we noted two important effects of the Agreement. One was that each company was much more willing to challenge advertising by the other, because the cost was not great and executive time was not taken up by discovery. The other was that both companies became more aggressive

3. *Id.* at 26.

in their advertising claims because the risks in losing a challenge (an injunction) were not as serious as losing in litigation (with possible monetary relief).

Through the years of the AT&T-MCI ADR Agreement, AT&T also entered into advertising ADR Agreements with several other competitors. These Agreements, however, were not effective because they did not make the ADR the only method of resolving disputes.

The stories of Michael Leathes and my partners, Robert Newbury and Joseph Welch, are examples of the creative use of ADR to address specific problems. They illustrate the benefits of understanding and exploring the various options to find an effective solution for the clients' needs. This chapter takes a look at a sampling of the various ADR options that have developed over the years with the goal of exposing counsel to the wide range of possibilities.

4.01 Options for ADR

Options for dispute resolution fall into two camps. First are those methods that assist the parties to reach a voluntary settlement, and the second are those in which participation can be coerced and a result enforced without the cooperation of all parties. Professor Stephen J. Ware suggests the first step in dispute resolution is to identify the "default processes" available for the dispute,[4] meaning those in which participation can be compelled. Litigation is the default process for most disputes unless there is an enforceable arbitration agreement covering the parties and the dispute. If a default process is available, the parties may turn to negotiation and processes in aid of negotiation to resolve the dispute under "the shadow of the law." In other words, the parties seek to work out a deal that is more favorable than proceeding to litigation or adjudication.

When evaluating the options, it is helpful to avoid comparing apples and oranges. The nondefault processes can be compared to one another. Similarly, litigation and arbitration can be compared on an equal footing. But as Professor Ware notes:

> Far trickier is to try to compare a default process with a non-default process. Those who compare mediation to arbitration, for example, must be especially careful. Such comparisons often go awry due to a failure to appreciate the basic differences between a process that casts the shadow of the law and a process that occurs in that shadow.[5]

The general options for ADR tend to fit within the following categories.

---

4. Stephen J. Ware, Principles of Alternative Dispute Resolution 10 (2007).
5. *Id.* at 11.

[A] Negotiation

Negotiation takes place directly between the parties. Usually it does not involve the use of a neutral party as a facilitator. Sometimes, however, the parties may turn to counsel who is not directly involved in the litigation to lead the negotiation discussions. In commercial disputes, negotiation may work well if the parties can make a realistic estimate of the likely results of litigation and where those results yield a result acceptable to both sides within the context of litigation.

Judge Randall Rader of the Court of Appeals for the Federal Circuit provides this explanation of a rational settlement process:

> So what produces a settlement? We'll plug some numbers in and I think you'll see the incentives for settlement in the system. Let's assume the plaintiff figures he's got a 60 percent chance of winning—better than even. He is going to win $100,000 dollars, and it's going to cost him $20,000 to litigate. If you multiply these out, and subtract the $20,000, you'll find that he figures he has got $40,000 at net value in this suit. Some economist is going to quickly jump on me and say there is a lot you're not counting in: what about the cost of settlement itself? Yes, there are those costs. I am making it simple and factoring those out. The defendant using the defendant's economic calculation will come up with a net cost to him of the suit he is likely to lose $80,000. So both parties are better off if they can settle for anywhere between $40,000 and $80,000—minus of course some settlement costs, but there is a margin for them to settle. Interestingly, the costs of the suit are a part of the incentive.[6]

[B] Early Neutral Evaluation

Early neutral evaluation is employed by some courts as a tool to provide an independent view of the dispute with the hope that an unbiased opinion will help the parties negotiate a resolution. A similar mechanism can be used outside the court system by having the parties seek a second opinion from an uninvolved attorney or expert. This strategy was employed in the early 1990s by two major food companies negotiating a stock purchase.

One of the issues in the transaction was the effect of preexisting agreements on the seller's ability to transfer certain trademark rights to the purchaser. Resolution depended on the application of French law to the original contracts written in French as the proper interpretation was not apparent from the English translations.

A large amount was at stake, and the parties were unable to reach agreement by themselves. Instead, they agreed to present the issue to a neutral, well-respected French law professor for a controlling opinion. With the

---

6. Rader, *supra* at Chapter 1 note 8.

benefit of the professor's advice, the remaining issues in the transaction were easily resolved. The same technique can be effective in other forms of disputes in which a neutral opinion may be all that is required to overcome conflicting views.

[C] Settlement Conference

A settlement conference is often part of the normal court adjudication process. The parties may meet together or in private caucus with the judge to discuss the possibility of settlement. If the judge assigned to the case is reluctant to play the role, the matter may be referred to a magistrate or to a judge who will not be hearing the case on the merits. Settlement conferences can be effective when the parties can be persuaded that the certainty of an immediate settlement is a greater benefit than the possibility of a positive result through trial. Settlement conferences usually focus on the costs of litigation, the weaknesses of each side's case, and the risk of an adverse result through litigation. Settlement in this form is perceived as a zero sum option. The judge will try to convince the parties that they each are likely to lose and, therefore, would be better off taking less than desired to avoid that greater risk. Settlement conferences usually do not focus on creative ways in which disputes may be resolved or in which the greater benefits can be achieved. In short, the settlement conference focuses on the possibility of negative results. It is said you can tell a good settlement if both sides are unhappy.

Top Ten Ways to Prevent Settlement
By U.S. Magistrate Judge Morton Denlow

I have found that parties successfully avoid settlement when they engage in the following behavior:

1. Insult opposing counsel and the client at the settlement conference (e.g., accuse them of lying and cheating).
2. Fail to bring a party representative with full settlement authority (e.g., bring a party representative who has no authority beyond existing offer).
3. Spend more in legal fees than is involved in the case (e.g., come to settlement conference having already spent $75,000 in fees to defend $30,000 claim).
4. Put your own interest in attorney's fees ahead of your client's interests.
5. Refuse to make any settlement demand or offer.
6. Pull your settlement demand out of thin air without a factual or legal basis for it (e.g., demand $1,000,000 in settlement when maximum statutory recovery is $300,000).
7. Raise your demand or lower your offer at the settlement conference (e.g., announce at the beginning of the settlement conference that your demand has now increased from $25,000 to $100,000).

8. Announce at the beginning of the settlement conference that you have no interest in discussing settlement until after judge has ruled on the summary judgment motion which you intend to file.
9. Show up at the settlement conference without first looking at the file.
10. Fail to show up at the scheduled settlement conference.

[D] Mediation

Mediation can often be the same as a settlement conference in the sense that the parties are weighing the risk of negative results against the certainty of a less negative resolution. However, mediation has the possibility of doing more. When effective, mediation can be a tool for finding better results based on balancing benefits rather than risks.

The first step in this process is exploration of creative ways in which the parties may achieve through settlement a result that is better than the best they could achieve through litigation. For example, imagine a company is sued by a supplier for passing off (i.e., when the company received orders for the supplier's product, it filled them with a competitor's product). During a five-year period, the total allegedly infringing sales amounted to $600,000 in purchases from competitors of the plaintiff. As the supplier enjoyed a 50 percent profit margin, it lost $300,000 in profit from the infringing sales. The supplier's best realistic result at trial was recovery of that amount in damages minus the legal fees incurred in seeking the result. If the focus were only on the negative, the case might settle for a payment of $150,000—an amount less than the risk faced by the defendant if it lost at trial and greater than what the plaintiff would receive if it lost at trial. Undoubtedly in this scenario, the relationship of the parties would end.

A creative alternative might be achieved through mediation by focusing on the possibility of the parties doing business together in the future. Suppose the defendant agreed to purchase its requirements from the plaintiff for a period of time. The plaintiff might receive orders yielding profits in excess of the amount lost. For example, if the defendant agreed through mediation to purchase $1,000,000 in product, the plaintiff would enjoy $500,000 in profits, faring much better than if it prevailed at trial.

Case Study

Two professors at a leading Eastern university published speculative technology articles about nanotechnology in which they coined a unique phrase for the process they intended to employ. Their articles appeared in academic journals and were excerpted in the popular media, which drew the attention of a western U.S. nanotechnology company operating under the same name used by the professors in their articles. The western company filed suit in its local district court for trademark infringement.

As no monetary damages were involved, the parties recognized that the cost of litigation could quickly exceed the value of the case. The plaintiff felt he could not allow his company name to become a generic phrase for another form of technology. The defendant university was compelled to protect the academic freedom of its professors, yet it was loathe to spend money on legal fees to defend in a distant forum.

The solution reached was mediation at an early stage, shortly after the complaint was filed but prior to the defendant's answer. Early mediation was desired as a way to reach an early solution and avoid the expense of discovery and other pretrial proceedings. Early mediation was appropriate under the circumstances as the basic facts were easily ascertained without need for further discovery. The conduct of the professors was clear from the published works. Similarly, the rights of the company could be determined from its marketing materials and federal trademark registration. The costs of the mediation process were further reduced by selecting a neutral with substantial experience in the trademark issues and by conducting the mediation sessions by telephone. The disadvantages arising from the lack of face-to-face contact were offset by significantly lower costs. This is a good example of the use of mediation as a means to finding an early solution to a dispute.

[E] Mini-Trial

Mini-trials typically take the form of a mock trial observed by decision makers of both sides. It may or may not involve the use of a mock jury. Counsel present argument, evidence, and possibly testimony before a panel of decision makers. A neutral will often be involved to conduct the hearing in keeping with the parties' intent. Upon hearing the presentation and the decision of the mock jury (if one is involved), the parties will be in a better position to settle upon a negotiated outcome. In some instances, the parties may agree that the result will be controlled by the decision of the mock jury. After the hearing, the neutral may facilitate negotiations, act as a mediator, or even render a nonbinding decision to assist the decision makers.

One important benefit of a mini-trial is that it brings executives into the process earlier than a full-blown trial. In complex cases, usually the dispute will not be given executive attention until immediately before trial after much time, money, and energy have been invested in discovery and pretrial practice. Thus, executives commonly aren't exposed to the merits of their opponent's position until they hear it at trial. The mini-trial process gives the executives an early opportunity to hear all sides of the disputes. In addition, actual presentation of a party's case in the mini-trial reduces the posturing that often occurs in settlement negotiations and mediation.

Perceived disadvantages of mini-trial include the early disclosure of evidence and strategy if the process fails to result in a resolution. However, in reality such disclosure will occur anyway during discovery and pretrial procedures. In any event, this concern is not a compelling reason to avoid the process.

Mini-trials give parties more control over the process and allow resolution to be reached at a lower cost than would be likely if the dispute proceeded through adjudication to trial. A mini-trial is a more structured form of ADR and involves more time, planning, and resources than negotiation or mediation. This fact makes it best suited for large, complex disputes that justify this higher commitment for resources, but it can be used for smaller disputes as well. The Cook County Illinois mandatory nonbinding arbitration program provides a similar dynamic in that the parties have an opportunity to present their case to a panel of neutrals who renders a decision. The parties may choose to reject the decision, but in practice the vast majority do not.

Harrie Samaras, formerly counsel for MCI and Elan, sees many benefits to the use of mini-trials:

> [Mini-trials are] less costly and timely than an actual trial; typically a confidential process; more structured than mediation but less formal than an actual trial; a flexible process that can be tailored to fit the parties' needs; likely to preserve business relationships more than arbitration or litigation; a means to provide an objective view of key evidence and arguments to decision makers; an opportunity (often times the first opportunity) for the parties to interact directly with one another; a means for considering how a third-party (the neutral) will perceive each party's case; apt to result in a settlement that is more creative and responsive to business needs than a court judgment or arbitration award; and a means for narrowing issues for trial, even if a settlement does not occur.[7]

[F] Summary Jury Trial

A summary jury trial is usually a private process involving a short presentation of trial proof to an impartial jury that renders a nonbinding verdict used as a basis for the attorneys and their clients to assess and settle the case. This type of trial will normally take a day or less. Given the demands of the process in terms of logistics and preparation, the procedure is most useful for complex cases that would otherwise require weeks or months of trial. The summary

7. Harrie Samara, *The Minitrial—A Sizeable Option for Resolving Disputes*, 17 Insight (Spring 2007).

jury trial will often be a court-annexed procedure conducted by the judge who will try the case or by another judge assigned solely for the purpose of the summary hearing. Federal court judges have the right to conduct summary jury trials both under Rule 16 of the Federal Rules of Civil Procedure and as a matter of the court's inherent power to manage its cases.[8] As a summary trial is a settlement tool, it is appropriate and acceptable for the proceedings to remain closed to the press and public.

[G] Arbitration

Arbitration is a process in which the neutral hears evidence and renders a decision on the merits in a manner similar to court adjudication. The principal similarities and differences between arbitration and court adjudication include:

- Both involve the presentation of evidence.
- Both involve a hearing.
- Both involve a decision on the merits.
- A court judge is a generalist, but a arbitrator may be selected based on special knowledge of the industry and/or applicable law.
- A court hearing is public, but arbitration is private and can be kept confidential.
- A court hearing in the United States involves extensive discovery; arbitration may limit discovery to reduce time and cost.
- A court hearing can be appealed, but arbitration awards normally are final and cannot be appealed on the merits.
- Court hearings are subject to jurisdictional limitations, but the parties in arbitration may agree upon the location and applicable law.
- Court proceedings are usually territorial in the sense that they will only resolve the dispute in one country; arbitrations may be used to resolve disputes on an international or global basis.
- The cost of court litigation is high, as already discussed; the cost of arbitration may rise to that level (if allowed by the parties and neutral), but normally the costs can be held to a lower level than court litigation.
- Court hearings are governed by the rules of civil procedure applicable to the relevant federal or state court; arbitration is governed by the applicable rules of the arbitration institution, such as the American Arbitration Association, the International Chamber of Commerce, the World Intellectual Property Association, etc.

---

8. Cincinnati Gas & Elec. Co. v. General Elec. Co., 854 F.2d 900 (6th Cir. 1988).

4.02 Making an Effective Choice for Using ADR

In making a choice among the various alternatives for ADR, it is useful for a party to consider several key factors involving perceived party autonomy, control, process, fairness, and formality—factors relating to the psychological dimension of dispute resolution. The psychology of dispute resolution has received substantial attention in the academic world. Attorneys can profit from some understanding of how parties respond to dispute resolution processes.

A variety of studies reveal that the most significant factor in satisfaction with dispute resolution processes is not the actual outcome or the cost, but instead the perception that the party has been heard and that the process has been fair. One study of actual litigants surveyed party attitudes to three types of dispute resolution experiences: trial, arbitration, and private settlement negotiations between the judge and counsel. In the first two categories, the parties participated in the hearing and were able to testify. In the latter, the dispute was resolved in chambers without direct participation by the parties. Regardless of the outcome, the researchers found that the parties were most satisfied when they were involved in a hearing that gave them a fair chance to present their case and be heard.

The results of these studies mirror my personal experience as an advocate and mediator in various disputes. For example, in one case involving a trademark infringement and cybersquatting dispute, the court scheduled a settlement conference with required attendance by decision makers from each side. We anticipated the judge would meet with the parties in a joint session to discuss the case and possibly in individual caucuses to hear their positions. Instead, the judge met only with counsel. The conference did not result in settlement. The client, who had traveled a long distance to attend the conference, was understandably dissatisfied with the process. He had no chance to be heard by the judge, no chance to express his position to the other side in the presence of the judge, and no chance to have feedback directly from the judge. While I don't believe the result would have changed had those opportunities been presented, I believe our client would have been satisfied with the process.

I contrast that experience with another dispute in which I served as mediator. The mediation session began with the parties' positions being far apart. During a day of joint sessions and individual caucuses, the positions came closer together through mutual compromise and exploration of alternative solutions. The process of offering a concession triggered a corresponding concession in response. At the end of the day, the parties agreed to a settlement that involved compromise by both that did not satisfy either party's starting point. Yet the president of one of the parties commented, "You know, I'm not completely happy with this result, but I am very happy with the process. I feel like I was heard." The lesson seems clear for both advocates and neutrals: process can be as or more important than the final result. These two experiences suggest the following keys to effective dispute resolution:

- Give the parties a chance to be heard.
- Engage in a process that involves active participation by the decision makers.
- Take time to let the process run its course.

When considering the options for ADR, the question often arises as to how corporations can capture the benefits of ADR and overcome internal resistance. The studies discussed in Chapter 1 identify the significant economic benefits to establishing effective ADR processes within a corporation. Companies that have taken a systematic approach have reduced internal legal budgets and outside litigation expenditures while increasing market value. However, the studies suggest that only a small percentage of companies have pursued the ADR path in a systematic way. They have not yet seen the benefits reported by others because they have not developed effective systems for dealing with disputes centered on ADR options.

Ad hoc use of ADR is unlikely to provide much change or improvement. Those who reap the most benefits are the companies that reinvent their methods of resolving disputes at an enterprise level. The key components of this reinvention involve commitment from management to the process, education of legal staff in ADR options, empowerment of legal staff to use ADR to resolve disputes, and creation of record-keeping systems to track success.

The AAA study identified the key characteristics of effective users of ADR.[9] The study found that the legal departments in such companies are more likely to be:

- Highly integrated into the general corporate planning process;
- Understanding of the broader business issues facing its company and industry;
- Spending a lot of time on highly complex and technical issues;
- Focused on preserving relationships and settling cases rather than just winning cases.

The legal departments in such companies were less likely to:

- Take an aggressive approach when disputes arise;
- Focus on reviewing contracts and agreements as opposed to higher level activities;
- Favor litigation over ADR.

9. AAA study, *supra*, Chapter 1 note 12.

The MACRO study discussed in Chapter 1 makes the following recommendations for turning a company into an effective user of ADR:[10]

- Ensure that the company's top-level employees are supportive of ADR efforts. This includes the CEOs, the senior level management, the general counsel's offices, and the human resources offices;
- Examine the types of disputes common within your organization and the frequency with which they occur;
- Design appropriate and productive ADR processes to apply in multiple areas (e.g., procurement, employee relations, etc.), and at various levels throughout the business (e.g., senior management, supervisors, "rank and file" employees, etc.);
- Ensure that at least one person is dedicated to monitoring the ADR program;
- Create an oversight body to support the visibility and credibility of the ADR program;
- Ensure that the pools of available and well-trained ADR neutrals are appropriate for the types of disputes at issue;
- Educate all levels of employees to recognize when ADR is appropriate and to know how to assess the corresponding tools and systems appropriately;
- Include successful use of the ADR program in the performance reviews of those accountable for implementing the programs.

By building on these results and recommendations, in-house counsel can create a transformation plan for the company to become an effective ADR user in a way that provides measurable results. In following the examples of those who have already successfully pursued this course, the company can improve its bottom line, increase its overall value, and reduce time lost to the prosecution of disputes.

Consider the following best practices:

1. Set a benchmark. Determine the company's current metrics with respect to dispute resolution. What is the internal legal budget for disputes? What is the outside expenditure for disputes? How much time is spent by legal staff and others on dispute resolution? How many open disputes exist within the company? What is the average time taken to resolve disputes?
2. Set a goal for improvement. Once the starting benchmark is known, establish a reasonable goal for improvement. Determine how success will be measured—by less lost time? Reduced expense? Fewer open

10. MACRO study, Chapter 1 note 15.

cases? Perhaps a 10 percent improvement each year is a reasonable goal. Articulate how this goal, if reached, will benefit the company as a whole.

3. Create a plan for shifting to ADR. In many companies, when a dispute arises, the first step is to send the problem to outside litigators who pursue the matter in court. Consider internal and external steps to change this practice. Internally, the company may adopt the practice of early case evaluation, and in appropriate cases, contact the opponent directly to discuss settlement, propose an executive level meeting to discuss the dispute, or explore mediation or early neutral evaluation. There may be several internal steps before the problem is submitted to outside counsel, and even then the company may instruct its lawyers to pursue appropriate forms of ADR at an early stage.
4. Seek management commitment to ADR plan. An ADR plan will not be effective if it is undermined by managers who want to focus on winning law suits. Certainly, there are some disputes that are a matter of principle and need to be resolved at trial, but the majority of disputes don't require trial and aren't likely to reach that point anyway. Management support for the ADR plan will help the legal team achieve the results seen by effective users of ADR.
5. Provide ADR training. In-house legal staff may not have sufficient experience or education in ADR to implement an effective plan without added training. Ongoing training will increase confidence in the ADR process and will likely lead to greater success.
6. Seek outside counsel with ADR experience. An ADR plan can also be undermined if not supported by outside counsel. Seek attorneys who understand the goal of ADR is to effectively resolve disputes, not merely to win lawsuits. Seek firms with attorneys who have a track record using ADR effectively as part of the litigation arsenal.
7. Measure and report results. Keep records on progress toward the established goals. Report these results so that stakeholders can see progress.

Case Study

A software developer was entitled to continued licensing royalties for the use of software developed for a client in the medical field. When challenged for nonpayment of the royalties, the client took the offensive by filing an action for breach of contract. The claim centered on whether the software delivered met the agreed-upon specifications, whether the developer had provided the required training and support, and whether the developer had improperly retained and used rights that should have been transferred to the client.

The parties attempted an early mediation of the case, but couldn't come to terms, largely due to factual uncertainties about the software and legal questions about the terms of the development agreement. The early mediation was terminated to allow the parties time for discovery and to file a motion for summary judgment. After substantial discovery and cross-briefing on a motion for summary judgment, but prior to a decision on the motion, the parties met again for mediation. The combination of discovery, further development of the law via briefing the summary judgment motion, and weight of ongoing legal fees led to a better understanding of the case for both sides and more realistic expectations for settlement. As a result, the second mediation resulted in a successful settlement that would not have been acceptable to either side earlier in the case.

Accordingly, early mediation is not always the best course. In some disputes the parties need to cool off, to suffer the expense of ongoing litigation, or to adduce more facts so that the dimensions of the dispute are better understood. There may be too much uncertainty early in the case for mediation to be effective. Thus, attempting mediation too early may be ineffective.

4.03 ADR in Action

The ADR process is generally handled by a private dispute resolution service. In some instances, arbitration and mediation are part of a court-annexed process such as the Cook County Illinois Mandatory Arbitration program or the Lanham Act mediation program in the Northern District of Illinois.

Examples of ADR in action include: NAD proceedings for false advertising claims, ICANN UDRP for cybersquatting disputes, Cook County Mandatory Arbitration, California Early Neural Evaluation, and Federal Circuit Appellate Mediation. The different forms of ADR can be categorized based on their various dimensions.

The first dimension is whether participation is mandatory or voluntary. Arbitration may be a mandatory process when required by a prior arbitration agreement. Mediation may also be mandatory if compelled by court order or procedures. Alternatively, either process may be voluntary if the parties are free to reject or accept participation.

The second dimension is whether the process is binding or nonbinding. One of the cited benefits of arbitration is that it offers a binding result in which the parties must comply with the decision of the arbitrator. Some arbitration schemes, however, produce a nonbinding result in which compliance with the decision depends on the cooperation of the losing party.

A third dimension is the level of judicial review. Mediation typically produces a result a disgruntled party may not challenge through such a review.

In arbitration under the Federal Arbitration Act, parties may obtain only very limited judicial review which is primarily with respect to the fairness of the process as opposed to arbitrator error. Other levels of review are possible, including abuse of discretion, errors of fact or law, or de novo. It is useful to bear these three dimensions in mind when selecting an ADR method.

The methods of ADR identified above have been used to create various ADR systems to address specific types of disputes. In the next section of this chapter, we will look at several examples of existing ADR systems and generate ideas as to how they may be utilized either as is or adapted to new situations.

[A] National Advertising Division (NAD)

The NAD is the National Advertising Division of the Better Business Bureau. It provides a forum for the voluntary, nonbinding arbitration of disputes involving national advertising claims.

The NAD has become the forum of choice for many sophisticated advertisers, such as S.C. Johnson & Son, Colgate Palmolive, Kimberly-Clark, and many others. As one observer notes:

> The NAD offers a faster, more cost-effective option for those seeking to challenge a competitor's claims. With its own extensive body of precedent, it is the ideal option for resolving most distortions and deceptions of the market.[11]

The NAD process begins with the filing of a complaint that sets forth the challenged claims in a letter. Normally the complaint is filed by a competitor, but members of the general public may also submit claims. The NAD staff reviews the complaint to determine if it meets the requirements for an investigation. If the staff decides an investigation is warranted, it sends a copy of the complaint to the advertiser that invites a response within fifteen business days. If the advertiser responds, the complainant has the opportunity to reply, or it may waive the right to do so to expedite the decision.

Once the file is complete, the matter is transferred to a panel of neutrals for decision. The panel may seek more information or proceed based solely on the submissions. In addition, the parties typically meet with the NAD to answer questions about their position. NAD's strict timetable can provide a written decision within sixty days. Compliance is voluntary. A party required to discontinue or modify its advertising may appeal the NAD's decision to the National Advertising Review Board (NARB). If the respondent defaults or does not comply with the decision, the process may be a prelude for court action by

---

11. Darren S. Cahr, *False Advertising Claims: Proceedings at the NAD*, Nat. L. J. (Feb. 20, 2006).

the complainant or by the Federal Trade Commission (FTC). However, the voluntary compliance rate is quite high: NAD reports that it has resolved over 3,700 disputes with an incredible 96 percent compliance rate.[12]

The benefits of the NAD process include confidentiality, no discovery, no evidentiary hearing, and timeliness. The parties to an NAD action are required to submit an agreement for participation that provides they will not publicize the dispute during the review. The process does not allow for the written discovery and depositions that are often the most costly and time-consuming aspects of litigation. Although the parties may meet with the NAD to address questions about their claims, there is no evidentiary hearing with witnesses and cross-examination. Finally, the NAD seeks to adhere to a timetable in which a decision is issued within sixty days after the proceeding begins—a far shorter period that typical litigation.

Disadvantages of the NAD process include the parties' inability to obtain emergency relief, the inability to take discovery regarding complicated claims, the lack of monetary relief, and the lack of coercive enforcement power. Although the NAD process goes quickly, it does not have a mechanism for seeking a temporary restraining order or preliminary injunction as is available through the courts. Although limiting discovery can be a benefit, it may prove disadvantageous in factually complex cases that require discovery for complete proof. The inability to obtain monetary awards means the process may be inappropriate in cases where significant damages are possible. Finally, the lack of coercive power to enforce awards may detract from the process, although compliance rates are exceptionally high and the NAD does have the ability to refer cases to the FTC if a party refuses to participate or comply with a decision.

For an example of a typical dispute by NAD consider this matter:

- Wal-Mart television and print advertising included an explicit claim that Wal-Mart saves the average family $2,500 per year. The implied claim was that shoppers saved more money at Wal-Mart than at other stores. Wal-Mart asserted that its advertising was supported by findings of an independent consulting company. The NAD reviewed the consulting reports and found the studies established that competitiveness and increased efficiencies resulted in general consumer savings whether people shopped at Wal-Mart or not. In the context of Wal-Mart's advertising, the claim was found to be misleading because it implied that shoppers would save more money at Wal-Mart than at other stores, when in fact the consulting reports did not support that message. NAD recommended that Wal-Mart discontinue the challenged advertising.

12. BBB website, *Andrea C. Levine, Senior VP and Director, National Advertising Division (NAD)*, http://us.bbb.org/WWWRoot/SitePage.aspx?site=113&id=01a45f12-5b9a-45ab-8d78-49100a077b92.

> Wal-Mart said it was "surprised by NAD's interpretation of an implied claim" and "would be proud" to take the recommendation into account in the future.[13]

[B] ICANN UDRP

The governing body for Internet domain names is the Internet Corporation for Assigned Names and Numbers (ICANN). It was formed in the late 1990s with one of its early initiatives being the incorporation of dispute resolution clauses in domain name registration contracts for generic top level domain names (gTLDs).

The ICANN Uniform Dispute Resolution Policy (UDRP) became effective on December 1, 1999, after a consultative process led by the World Intellectual Property Organization at the request of the U.S. government. The UDRP is a form of mandatory arbitration subject to de novo judicial review.[14]

The UDRP is addressed to resolving disputes concerning allegations of abusive domain name registration and use.[15] Accordingly, the jurisdiction is limited to providing a remedy in cases of "the abusive registration of domain names."[16]

A UDRP action is initiated by filing a complaint and evidence with one of the dispute resolution services providers (usually either the World Intellectual Property Organization or the National Arbitration Forum). The domain name registrant is given an opportunity to answer and submit evidence, and when appropriate, the complainant may reply.

Both providers have panels of independent arbitrators (usually IP practitioners or retired judges) to whom the cases are assigned for decision. Most cases are heard by a single panelist, although either party may elect to have the case decided by a panel of three arbitrators.

The panel makes its decision based on the submissions of the parties. There is no discovery, live testimony, or live hearing. Decisions are typically rendered within three months of the initial complaint, although extensions are possible for more complicated cases. Decisions may be appealed by filing a civil court action in an appropriate jurisdiction, although appeals have been relatively rare.

The most recently posted statistics (May 10, 2004) demonstrate the success of the UDRP as a tool for resolving disputes. Since the first decision was issued in early 2000, over 7,790 cases involving over 13,311 domain names

---

13. *NAD Reviews Advertising for Wal-Mart*, NAD NEWS (Mar. 31, 2008).
14. The ICANN UDRP Policy appears in the Appendix.
15. Milwaukee Elec. Tool Corp. v. Bay Verte Mach., Inc. d/b/a The Power Tool Store, WIPO Case No. D2002-0774.
16. Weber-Stephen Prod. Co. v. Armitage Hardware, WIPO Case No. D2000-0187. *See Report of the WIPO Internet Domain Name Process* 169–170.

have been resolved by decision. The complainant was the prevailing party in over 6,262 cases (with split decisions in 60 additional cases) resulting in over 10,779 domain names that have been transferred or cancelled. This means that about 80.4 percent of the cases have been decided in the complainant's favor. Multiple names can be recovered in a single action. For example, CNN recovered 325 domain names in one action in 2003, and in 2007 Ticketmaster prevailed against 108 in a single action.

Relief under the UDRP is limited to transfer or cancellation of the domain name. Accordingly, damages, fee shifting, and other monetary relief are not available.

One of the UDRP's most remarkable features is its ability to resolve disputes without regard to the limits of national jurisdictions. National boundaries do not limit the registration of gTLDs, so a registrant subject to the UDRP can be located virtually anywhere in the world. Indeed, in many instances in which false registration information is given, the registrant can't even be located. Yet the UDRP remains available for dealing quickly and cheaply with domain name disputes, often between nationals of different countries. For example, I participated in one case from my office in Chicago involving a registrant in the United Arab Emirates, a trademark owner in India, and my co-panelists in Australia and the United Kingdom.

The complainant is required to prove three elements to obtain a decision that a domain name should be either cancelled or transferred:

First, the complainant must show that the domain name at issue is identical or confusingly similar to a trade or service mark in which the complainant has rights. The question of similarity is normally established by direct comparison of the domain name and mark at issue, without regard to the manner in which they may be used on the offending Web site. The complainant's rights in the mark are typically shown by evidence of valid trademark registration or of use sufficient to establish common law rights. Personal names are only protectable if used commercially to establish trademark rights. Thus, celebrities such as Madonna, Julia Roberts, Spike Lee and soccer star Freddy Abu have obtained relief under the UDRP.

The second element is that the respondent has no rights or legitimate interest with respect to the domain name. The respondent may have a legitimate interest (for example, if it made bona fide use of the name before there was an objection, was previously known by the name, or is making noncommercial or fair use of the domain name).

The final element is proof that the domain name was registered and used in bad faith. This element is typically satisfied if the domain name is offered for sale at an unjustified premium, the registrant engages in a pattern of abusive domain name registration, the domain name is used to disrupt the business of a competitor, or the domain name is deliberately used to obtain commercial gain by misdirecting Internet traffic due to confusion with another's mark.

Given how cheap and easy it is for cybersquatters to obtain and profit from conflicting domain names, perhaps it is not surprising that many cases are not contested or that over 80 percent of the cases filed have been resolved in favor of the trademark owner.

Tips for UDRP Proceedings

Domain name conflicts affecting business are on the rise. Fortunately, victims of domain name abuse have an effective tool to fight cybersquatting. The Uniform Dispute Resolution Policy (UDRP) adopted in 1999 by the International Corporation for Assigned Names and Numbers (ICANN), the international body responsible for domain name governance, has been used to address thousands of domain name conflicts. As an ICANN UDRP panelist with over 150 reported decisions, I have read many submissions, some very good, many bad.

Here are six recommendations for UDRP submissions:

1. The complaint (or answer) should be a brief.

This is your only chance to argue your position. Treat it like a memorandum in support of a motion for preliminary injunction or summary judgment by presenting your case as an advocate. Mere notice pleading allowed in our federal system is not effective under the circumstances.

2. The pleadings should be brief.

Although the provider's limitations on length are largely ignored and exceeded, as a panelist I urge you to remember that effective legal writing is brief and to the point.

3. The pleadings should follow the UDRP.

Follow the elements of the Policy in stating your position. Remember the Panel must address each of these issues. Make it easy for the Panel to decide in your favor by organizing your argument around each element of the claim or defense.

4. Support your position with proof.

You need more than bald allegations to prove rights and bad faith, and you will find an increasing number of cases in which complainants are called upon to make additional submissions or lose their claim due to lack of proof. Strong submissions present evidence by way of exhibits and short affidavits. But don't merely shovel in piles of documents. Remember point 2.

5. Make good use of supporting authority.

Give cases to support your argument, and show why the cases are relevant. Avoid merely citing cases. There have been over ten thousand reported

UDRP decisions. Don't assume the panel knows the result and reasoning of each case you cite. Instead help the panel by providing at least a parenthetical on your cited cases.

6. Recognize the limits of the UDRP.

The Policy is designed to address cases of cybersquatting involving protectable trademarks. It is not intended for contract disputes, garden variety infringement cases, defamation claims, or issues arising from personal names that are not entitled to commercial protection. Adverse decisions are often the result of claims that obviously stretch beyond the scope of the Policy. Matters outside the scope of the Policy are better directed to appropriate civil courts.

A UDRP proceeding ends with a decision by the panel applying the Policy to the record presented in the dispute. Here is an example of a frequently cited decision in which I was the presiding panelist. It gives a flavor of a cybersquatting dispute, the way the panel views the submissions, and the general nature of this form of ADR:

Administrative Panel Decision

Madonna Ciccone, p/k/a Madonna v. Dan Parisi and "Madonna.com"
Case No. D2000-0847

1. The Parties
The Complainant is Madonna Ciccone, an individual professionally known as Madonna.

The Respondent is "Madonna.com," the registrant for the disputed domain name, located in New York, New York, U.S.A. or Dan Parisi, the listed contact for the domain name.

2. The Domain Name(s) and Registrar(s)
The disputed domain name is madonna.com.

The registrar is Network Solutions, Inc., 505 Huntmar Park Drive, Herndon, Virginia 20170, U.S.A.

3. Procedural History
This action was brought in accordance with the ICANN Uniform Domain Name Dispute Resolution Policy, dated October 24, 1999 ("the Policy") and the ICANN Rules for Uniform Domain Name Dispute Resolution Policy, dated October 24, 1999 ("the Rules").

The Complaint was received by the WIPO Arbitration and Mediation Center on July 21, 2000 (e-mail) and on July 24, 2000 (hardcopy). The Response was received on August 23, 2000 (e-mail) and on August 28, 2000 (hardcopy). Both parties are represented by Counsel. There have been no further submissions on the merits.

Respondent elected to have the case decided by a three-member panel. David E. Sorkin was appointed as the Respondent's nominee. James W. Dabney was selected as the Complainant's nominee. Mark V.B. Partridge was appointed as presiding panelist.

It appears that all requirements of the Policy and the Rules have been satisfied by the parties, WIPO, and the Panelists.

4. Factual Background

Complainant is the well-known entertainer Madonna. She is the owner of U.S. Trademark Registrations for the mark MADONNA for entertainment services and related goods (Reg. No. 1,473,554 and 1,463,601). She has used her name and mark MADONNA professionally for entertainment services since 1979. Complainant's music and other entertainment endeavors have often been controversial for featuring explicit sexual content. In addition, nude photographs of Madonna have appeared in *Penthouse* magazine, and Complainant has published a coffee-table book entitled *Sex* featuring sexually explicit photographs and text.

Respondent is in the business of developing Web sites. On or about May 29, 1998, Respondent, through its business, Whitehouse.com, Inc., purchased the registration for the disputed domain name from Pro Domains for $20,000. On June 4, 1998, Respondent registered MADONNA as a trademark in Tunisia. On or about June 8, 1998, Respondent began operating an "adult entertainment portal web site." The web site featured sexually explicit photographs and text, and contained a notice stating "Madonna.com is not affiliated or endorsed by the Catholic Church, Madonna College, Madonna Hospital or Madonna the singer." By March 4, 1999, it appears that Respondent removed the explicit sexual content from the Web site. By May 31, 1999, it appears that the site merely contained the above notice, the disputed domain name, and the statement "Coming soon Madonna Gaming and Sportsbook."

On June 9, 1999, Complainant, through her attorneys, objected to Respondent's use of the Madonna.com domain name. On June 14, 1999, Respondent through its counsel stated: "As I assume you also know, Mr. Parisi's website [sic] was effectively shut down before you sent your letter, and is now shut down altogether. He is in the process of donating his registration for the domain name."

The word *Madonna*, which has the current dictionary definition as the Virgin Mary or an artistic depiction of the Virgin Mary, is used by others as a trademark, trade name, and personal name. After Respondent's receipt of Complainant's objection, it appears that Respondent had communication with Madonna Rehabilitation Hospital regarding the transfer of the domain name to the Hospital. It further appears that Respondent has not identified all of its communications on this matter. Nevertheless, the transfer had not taken place at the time this proceeding was commenced.

By his own admission, Respondent has registered a large number of other domain names, including names that matched the trademarks of others. Other domain names registered by Respondent include <wallstreetjournal.com> and <edgaronline.com>. See Response, Exhibit A, ¶30, 35.

5. Parties' Contentions

A. Complainant

Complaint contends that the disputed domain name is identical to the registered and common law trademark MADONNA in which she owns rights. She further contends that Respondent has no legitimate interest or rights in the domain name. Finally, Complainant contends that Respondent obtained and used the disputed domain name with the intent to attract Internet users to a pornographic web site for commercial gain based on confusion with Complainant's name and mark.

B. Respondent

Respondent does not dispute that the disputed domain name is identical or confusingly similar to Complainant's trademark. Respondent, however, claims that Complainant cannot show a lack of legitimate interest in the domain name because Respondent (a) made demonstrable preparation to use the domain name for a bona fide business purpose; (b) holds a bona fide trademark in the word MADONNA; and (c) has attempted to make bona fide noncommercial use of the name by donating it to the Madonna Rehabilitation Hospital.

Respondent also contends that it has not registered and used the domain name in bad faith because (a) there is no evidence that its primary motivation was to sell the disputed domain name, (b) the domain name was not registered with an intent to prevent Complainant from using her mark as a domain name, (c) respondent is not engaged in a pattern of registering domain names to prevent others from doing so, (d) the use of a disclaimer on the Web site precludes a finding that Respondent intentionally seeks to attract users for commercial gain based on confusion with Complainant's mark, and (e) the use of a generic term to attract business is not bad faith as a matter of law. Finally, Respondent claims that Complainant cannot legitimately claim tarnishment because she has already associated herself with sexually explicit creative work.

6. Discussion and Findings

A. The Evidentiary Standard for Decision

Paragraph 4(a) of the Policy directs that the Complainant must prove each of the following:

(i) that the domain name registered by the Respondent is identical or confusingly similar to a trademark or service mark in which the Complainant has rights; and,

(ii) that the Respondent has no legitimate interests in respect of the domain name; and,
(iii) that the domain name has been registered and used in bad faith.

A threshold question in proceedings under the Policy is to identify the proper standard for reaching a decision on each of these issues. The limited submissions allowed under the Policy makes these proceedings somewhat akin to a summary judgment motion under the U.S. Federal Rules of Civil Procedure. On a summary judgment motion, the movant has the burden of showing that there are no disputes of material facts. All doubts are to be resolved in favor of the nonmoving party. If there are material disputes of fact, the motion must be denied and the case will advance to a hearing before a trier of fact, either judge or jury.

Although the nature of the record is similar to that found on a summary judgment motion, our role is different than that of the Court on a summary judgment motion. Paragraph 15 of the Rules states that the "Panel shall decide a complaint on the basis of the statements and documents submitted and in accordance with the Policy . . ." Paragraph 10 of the Rules provides that the "Panel shall determine the admissibility, relevance, materiality and weight of the evidence." Paragraph 4 of the Policy makes repeated reference to the Panel's role in making findings of fact based on the evidence.

Based on the Policy and the Rules, we disagree with the view that disputes over material facts should not be decided in these proceedings. Rather, it is clear to us that our role is to make findings of fact as best we can, based on the evidence presented, provided the matters at issue are within the scope of the Policy. There may be circumstances due to the inherent limitations of the dispute resolution process or for other reasons where it would be appropriate for a panel to decline to decide a factual dispute. However, the mere existence of a genuine dispute of material fact should not preclude a panel from weighing the evidence before it and reaching a decision.

Since these proceedings are civil, rather than criminal, in nature, we believe the appropriate standard for fact finding is the civil standard of a preponderance of the evidence (and not the higher standard of "clear and convincing evidence" or "evidence beyond a reasonable doubt"). Under the "preponderance of the evidence" standard, a fact is proved for the purpose of reaching a decision when it appears more likely than not to be true based on the evidence. We recognize that other standards may be employed in other jurisdictions. However, the standard of proof employed in the United States seems appropriate for these proceedings generally, and in particular for this proceeding which involves citizens of the United States, actions occurring in the United States and a domain name registered in the United States.

In this case, there are factual disputes over Respondent's intent in obtaining and using the disputed domain name. For the reasons just stated, these disputes do not preclude a decision. Instead, we reach a decision based on the preponderance of the evidence submitted by the parties on the basic issues under the Policy.

B. Similarity of the Disputed Domain Name and Complainant's Mark
As noted above, Respondent does not dispute that its domain name is identical or confusingly similar to a trademark in which the Complainant has rights. Accordingly, we find that Complainant has satisfied the requirements of Paragraph 4(c)(i) of the Policy.

C. Lack of Rights or Legitimate Interests in Domain Name
Complainant has presented evidence tending to show that Respondent lacks any rights or legitimate interest in the domain name. Respondent's claim of rights or legitimate interests is not persuasive.

First, Respondent contends that its use of the domain name for an adult entertainment Web site involved prior use of the domain name in connection with a bona fide offering of goods or services. The record supports Respondent's claim that it used the domain name in connection with commercial services prior to notice of the dispute. However, Respondent has failed to provide a reasonable explanation for the selection of Madonna as a domain name. Although the word *Madonna* has an ordinary dictionary meaning not associated with Complainant, nothing in the record supports a conclusion that Respondent adopted and used the term *Madonna* in good faith based on its ordinary dictionary meaning. We find instead that [the] name was selected and used by Respondent with the intent to attract for commercial gain Internet users to Respondent's Web site by trading on the fame of Complainant's mark. We see no other plausible explanation for Respondent's conduct and conclude that use which intentionally trades on the fame of another cannot constitute a "bona fide" offering of goods or services. To conclude otherwise would mean that a Respondent could rely on intentional infringement to demonstrate a legitimate interest, an interpretation that is obviously contrary to the intent of the Policy.

Second, Respondent contends that it has rights in the domain name because it registered MADONNA as a trademark in Tunisia prior to notice of this dispute. Certainly it is possible for a Respondent to rely on a valid trademark registration to show prior rights under the Policy. However, it would be a mistake to conclude that mere registration of a trademark creates a legitimate interest under the Policy. If an American-based Respondent could establish "rights," vis-à-vis an American Complainant through the expedient of securing a trademark registration in Tunisia, then the ICANN procedure would be rendered virtually useless. To establish cognizable rights, the overall circumstances should demonstrate that the registration was obtained in good faith for the purpose of making bona fide use of the mark in the jurisdiction where the mark is registered, and not obtained merely to circumvent the application of the Policy.

Here, Respondent admits that the Tunisia registration was obtained merely to protect his interests in the domain name. Respondent is not located in Tunisia and the registration was not obtained for the purpose of making bona fide use of the mark in commerce in Tunisia. A Tunisian trademark registration is issued upon application without any substantive examination. Although recognized by certain treaties, registration in Tunisia does not prevent a finding of infringement in jurisdictions outside Tunisia. Under the circumstances, some might view Respondent's Tunisian registration itself as evidence of bad faith because it appears to be a pretense to justify an abusive domain name registration. We find at a minimum that it does not evidence a legitimate interest in the disputed name under the circumstances of this case.

Third, Respondent claims that its offer to transfer the domain name to the Madonna Hospital in Lincoln, Nebraska, is a legitimate noncommercial use under Paragraph 4(c)(iii) of the Policy. We disagree. The record is incomplete on these negotiations. Respondent has failed to disclose the specifics of its proposed arrangement with Madonna Hospital. Complainant asserts that the terms of the transfer include a condition that Madonna Hospital not transfer the domain name registration to Complainant. It also appears that the negotiations started after Complainant objected to Respondent's registration and use of the domain name. These circumstances do not demonstrate a legitimate interest or right in the domain name, and instead suggest that Respondent lacks any real interest in the domain name apart from its association with Complainant. Further, we do not believe these circumstances satisfy the provisions of Paragraph 4(c)(iii), which applies to situations where the Respondent is actually making noncommercial or fair use of the domain name. That certainly was not the situation at the time this dispute arose and is not the situation now.

Respondent cites examples of other parties besides Complainant who also have rights in the mark MADONNA, but that does not aid its cause. The fact that others could demonstrate a legitimate right or interest in the domain name does nothing to demonstrate that Respondent has such right or interest.

Based on the record before us, we find that Complainant has satisfied the requirements of Paragraph 4(a)(ii) of the Policy.

D. Bad Faith Registration and Use

Under Paragraph 4(b)(iv) of the Policy, evidence of bad faith registration and use of a domain name includes the following circumstances:

> (iv) by using the domain name, you have intentionally attempted to attract, for commercial gain, Internet users to your Web site or other online location, by creating a likelihood of confusion with the Complainant's mark as to the source, sponsorship, affiliation, or endorsement of your Web site or location or of a product or service on your Web site or location.

The pleadings in this case are consistent with Respondent's having adopted <madonna.com> for the specific purpose of trading off the name and reputation of the Complainant, and Respondent has offered no alternative explanation for his adoption of the name despite his otherwise detailed and complete submissions. Respondent has not explained why <madonna.com> was worth $20,000 to him or why that name was thought to be valuable as an attraction for a sexually explicit Web site. Respondent notes that the complainant, identifying herself as Madonna, has appeared in *Penthouse* and has published a *Sex* book. The statement that *madonna* is a word in the English language, by itself, is no more of a defense than would be the similar statement made in reference to the word *coke*. Respondent has not even attempted to tie in his Web site to any dictionary definition of *madonna*. The only plausible explanation for Respondent's actions appears to be an intentional effort to trade upon the fame of Complainant's name and mark for commercial gain. That purpose is a violation of the Policy, as well as U.S. trademark law.

Respondent's use of a disclaimer on its Web site is insufficient to avoid a finding of bad faith. First, the disclaimer may be ignored or misunderstood by Internet users. Second, a disclaimer does nothing to dispel initial interest confusion that is inevitable from Respondent's actions. Such confusion is a basis for finding a violation of Complainant's rights. See *Brookfield Communications Inc. v. West Coast Entm't Corp.*, 174 F.3d 1036 (9th Cir. 1999).

The Policy requires a showing of bad faith registration and use. Here, although Respondent was not the original registrant, the record shows he acquired the registration in bad faith. The result is the equivalent of registration and is sufficient to fall within the Policy. Indeed, Paragraph 4(b)(i) of the Policy treats acquisition as the same as registration for the purposes of supporting a finding of bad faith registration. We, therefore, conclude that bad faith acquisition satisfies the requirement of bad faith registration under the Policy.

Respondent's reliance on a previous ICANN decision involving the domain name <sting.com> is misplaced. See *Gordon Sumner p/k/a/ Sting v. Michael Urvan*, Case No. 2000-0596 (WIPO July 24, 2000). In the *Sting* decision, there was evidence that the Respondent had made bona fide use of the name Sting prior to obtaining the domain name registration and there was no indication that he was seeking to trade on the goodwill of the well-known singer. Here, there is no similar evidence of prior use by Respondent, and the evidence demonstrates a deliberate intent to trade on the good will of Complainant. Where no plausible explanation has been provided for adopting a domain name that corresponds to the name of a famous entertainer, other panels have found a violation of the Policy. See *Julia Fiona Roberts v. Russell Boyd*, Case No. D2000-0210 (WIPO May 29, 2000); *Helen Folsade Adu p/k/a Sade v. Quantum Computer Serv. Inc.*, Case No. D2000-0794 (WIPO September 26, 2000).

There is also evidence in the record which tends to support Complainant's claim that Respondent's registration of the domain name prevents Complainant from reflecting her mark in the corresponding.com domain name and that Respondent has engaged in a pattern of such conduct. It is admitted that Respondent registers a large number of domain names and that some happen to correspond to the names or marks of others. We find, however, that the record is inconclusive on this basis for finding bad faith and do not rely on this evidence for our conclusion.

Respondent asserts that we should reject Complainant's claims because she has been disingenuous in claiming that her reputation could be tarnished by Respondent's actions. Respondent suggests that her reputation cannot be tarnished because she has already associated herself with sexually explicit creative work. That argument misses the point. Even though Complainant has produced sexually explicit content of her own, Respondent's actions may nevertheless tarnish her reputation because they resulted in association with sexually explicit content which Complainant did not control and which may be contrary to her creative intent and standards of quality. In any event, we do not rely on tarnishment as a basis for our decision.

Because the evidence shows a deliberate attempt by Respondent to trade on Complainant's fame for commercial purposes, we find that Complainant has satisfied the requirements of Paragraph 4(a)(iii) of the Policy.

7. Decision

Under Paragraph 4(i) of the Policy, we find in favor of the Complainant. The disputed domain name is identical or confusingly similar to a trademark in which Complainant has rights, Respondent lacks rights or legitimate interests in the domain name, and the domain name has been registered and used in bad faith. Therefore, we decide that the disputed domain name <madonna.com> should be transferred to the Complainant.

Mark V.B. Partridge, Presiding Panelist
James W. Dabney, Panelist
David E. Sorkin, Panelist
October 12, 2000

[C] Illinois Cook County Mandatory Arbitration

The Circuit Court of Cook County, Illinois, serving the Chicago area, is the largest unified court of general trial jurisdiction in the nation. In 1988, the Supreme Court of Illinois approved the implementation of an arbitration program for Cook County. The Cook County program is a mandatory non-binding arbitration process. All filed cases meeting the program criteria (a civil action involving less than $30,000) must go through arbitration before proceeding to trial. The cases are heard by a panel of certified lawyers serving as arbitrators. Usually the hearing is less than a half day. The hearings are evidentiary with the submission of evidence, live testimony, and argument. The panel issues a written award, but does not provide reasons in support of the decision. Any dissatisfied party may appeal the decision to the trial court. Remarkably, however, very few of the cases completing the arbitration process proceed to trial. In 2007, 12,517 cases were filed in the mandatory arbitration program. Of these, 10,916 cases were settled, 8,957 were arbitrated, and only 340 went on to trial (less than 3 percent).[17]

The Cook County program was part of a statewide initiative that began in 1987 in response to a heavy backlog in civil cases. The program has been effective in reducing the overall time for the resolution of civil disputes in Cook County. As a result of the program, the participating jurisdictions are able to dispose of 90 percent of the arbitration caseload within one year of filing, a substantial improvement over the situation before the program began.

The Illinois program created special evidentiary rules for certain types of evidence. Prior to the hearing, the parties can exchange evidence packages. If no objection is made, the evidence can be introduced at the hearing without counsel laying the type of foundation normally required for documentary evidence. This practice reduces the inefficiency of calling witnesses merely to authenticate documents, saving time and money for the parties. This feature is similar to the NAD and ICANN UDRP, in which evidence is submitted and considered without the formal rules of evidence needing to be followed.

[D] Northern District of Illinois Lanham Act Mediation

In 1996, the Federal District Court for the Northern District of Illinois adopted a voluntary mediation program for Lanham Act cases (i.e., cases under federal law involving trademark infringement, unfair competition, cybersquatting, false advertising, and trademark dilution). Under this program, all parties to a case filed in the Northern District involving a Lanham Act claim are required to file a joint statement indicating whether they wish to participate in the voluntary mediation program. If the parties do not wish to participate, they must provide a statement summarizing the reasons for that decision.

If the parties choose to participate, they may select a qualified neutral mediator from a list maintained by the Clerk of Court. The mediation sessions are confidential. They should be completed within thirty days, and

17. *Court-Annexed Mandatory Arbitration Annual Report 2007*, The Administrative Office of the Illinois Courts, Circuit Court of Cook County.

end with a report to the court indicating whether the matter was settled. The costs of the mediation are shared by the parties and depend on the rates charged by the mediator.

The requirement for certification of mediators is based on experience. Persons may qualify if they have a minimum of three years of experience as an ADR neutral or five years of practice with Lanham Act law. In practice, the list of mediators includes many of the most prominent trademark law practitioners in Illinois and the country. I've been a mediator in four cases under this program, all of which led to a mediated settlement after one or two days of mediation. Thus, from my personal experience, it is an effective process if . . . used. Unfortunately, the number of cases participating in the program is too small.

Case Study

A publisher of educational videos discovered that its licensor was violating the terms of an exclusive license by selling works in the licensee's exclusive market. The problem led to a federal complaint for copyright infringement and breach of contract, with the expense of defense being covered by the defendant's insurance. There being insurance at first seemed to be a positive development for the plaintiff as it indicated the presence of a deep pocket to pay damages. As the case proceeded, however, the presence of the insurance company became a detriment to resolution of the case. Efforts to settle between the licensor and licensee went nowhere as any settlement required insurance company approval. Moreover, once the licensor stopped the offending conduct it had little further interest in the outcome of the case as any award would be largely covered by the insurer.

The solution to this stagnant situation was court-annexed mediation with a magistrate judge who required the presence of decision makers for all parties, including the insurer. This gave the plaintiff an opportunity to present its argument and analysis of damages directly to the persons who needed to make a decision about settlement. As the risk of not settling was shown to be greater than the plaintiff's settlement demand, the defendant and the insurer recognized the better option, and the mediation resulted in a prompt settlement in a dispute that would likely have otherwise droned on to the point of frustration for all concerned.

This situation demonstrates the unique benefit obtainable in mediation in which counsel has an opportunity to speak directly to the opposing party's decision makers—one that does not readily arise elsewhere during litigation. This example also shows how insurance coverage can sometimes hinder resolution of a case by reducing the incentives on the insured party to seek a resolution. The attitude can often become "the insurance company is covering all the expenses, so I don't care what happens." Bringing a decision maker for the insurer into mediation can be a useful means to overcome that problem.

[E] Trademark Trial and Appeal Board (TTAB)

In many respects, the Trademark Trial and Appeal Board (TTAB) of the U.S. Patent and Trademark Office is a form of mandatory arbitration to adjudicate disputes over the registration of trademarks. Although a TTAB proceeding is created by statute, largely follows the Federal Rules of Civil Procedure, and is heard by Board members with the status of a federal judge, it involves streamlined procedures giving it an alternative character to court adjudication.

A party objecting to registration of a trademark may file a Notice of Opposition against a pending application or a Petition for Cancellation against an existing registration. The trademark applicant or registrant is required to respond or it will lose its registration through default. Once the case is initiated, the TTAB sets a schedule consisting of the following steps: (1) fact discovery, (2) testimony, (3) argument, and (4) decision. Extensive discovery is allowed using the same devices available in federal civil actions such as interrogatories, document requests, requests for admissions, and depositions.

The big difference lies in the taking of testimony. Unlike court adjudication, a TTAB proceeding does not involve a live evidentiary hearing. Instead, the parties may take testimony via deposition and submit documentary evidence for consideration by the Board. The parties may also request argument before the Board, which is a three-member panel of judges appointed under Article III of the Constitution. After the close of testimony and argument, if presented, the Board will render its decision regarding the registration. The relief available is limited to rejection or cancellation of the trademark registration. The Board does not have the authority to award monetary relief or sanctions or injunctive relief against use of the trademark. The Board's decision may be appealed to the Federal Circuit Court of Appeals or the matter may be brought to a federal district court for a trial de novo.

Despite the only limited relief available from the Board, TTAB proceedings can be a cost-effective alternative to infringement litigation in federal court and can be a good fit for disputes in which emergency injunctive relief is not needed.

Tips for Trademark Trial and Appeal Board Proceedings

TTAB cases present considerations common to all forms of litigation. They also present unique considerations, challenges, and concerns. Here are some key points to consider as an advocate in TTAB proceedings that are also applicable to advocacy in other forms of ADR and litigation.

1. Know your client's goals

As with all litigation, it is critical to start with an understanding of your client's goals. One size does not fit all. Although the stated purpose of TTAB litigation seems simple—obtain registration, oppose registration, cancel registration—the overall goals of your client can vary widely. From the client's point of view, the goals may include any of the following:

- Overcome an examiner's final rejection to registration.
- Remove a prior registration blocking the ability to obtain registration.
- Maintain or increase the distinctiveness of the client's mark on theregistry.
- Insure the ability to expand the client's business into new product lines or territories.
- Negotiate coexistence with a conflicting mark.
- Persuade the owner of a conflicting mark to discontinue use.
- Obtain an advantage in civil litigation.

The goals involve a mix of legal and business goals that will affect how you proceed with the TTAB case.

2. Insure your client understands the limits of the proceeding

Most clients will have some working knowledge of the civil court system, but are much less likely to have experienced Trademark Office proceedings. Unless told otherwise, they may assume the TTAB case will lead to an injunction or an award of damages. It is important to manage expectations about the proceeding. Some of the key aspects to discuss with your client include:

- The proceeding may take twelve to eighteen months or more.
- The decision will only involve the right to registration.
- The Panel does not have the authority to stop use.
- The Panel does not have the authority to award damages.
- The client may be required to produce documents, answer written questions, and testify at a deposition.
- There is no trial with live witnesses.
- The final decision can be appealed to a federal court or to the Court of Appeals for the Federal Circuit.

3. Understand the Rules

For attorneys fmiliar with federal litigation but new to TTAB proceedings, significant differences must be understood. These include:

- Limits on interrogatories (75)
- Set periods of time for discovery and testimony
- Lack of live evidentiary hearing
- Lack of monetary sanctions for discovery violations
- Notice of reliance for submission of evidence
- Argument before a three-member panel

Attorneys with past TTAB experience need to understand that familiar rules have changed. Be sure you know how these changes affect your preparation and case presentation. Some of the key changes to consider are:

- Service of complaint
- Early discovery and settlement conference
- Initial disclosures
- Expert disclosures
- Pretrial disclosures
- Standard protective order

4. Remember your audience

Civil litigators are accustomed to presenting cases to generalist judges who may have little or no prior experience with trademark infringement disputes. Careful education may be needed to overcome a judge's initial reaction based merely on a side-by-side in-court comparison.

In contrast, a TTAB case is presented to a panel of trademark experts—judges who have seen and heard hundreds of cases involving similar issues. This has several key effects:

- It is unnecessary and unproductive to spend time and effort to educate the Panel on the basics of trademark law.
- The Panel is likely to be impatient with a superficial or erroneous presentation of the law. In contrast, the Panel is likely to have greater patience with the nuances of applicable case law, especially prior TTAB and Federal Circuit decisions.
- Although the Panelists know the law, they may not know the industry involved, so it is productive to present helpful evidence about the nature of the products and the relevant industry.
- Effective argument focuses on the correct application of proven legal principles to the specific facts of your case.

5. Keep your briefs brief

Whatever happened to the idea that briefs should be . . . well, brief? Too often lawyers function as if they are paid by the word. When told that a memorandum in support of a motion has a fifteen-page limit, lawyers feel deficient if they haven't filed a lengthy motion explaining why they need ten more pages.

The need for briefer briefs is evident in civil litigation. Judges frequently comment that brevity is more persuasive—and more likely to be read. This principle applies with even more force in TTAB proceedings, where the Panel has expert knowledge of trademark law and the legal issues are narrow. Little good is served by length. Less *is* more.

6. Make it easy to decide in your favor

Here are two ideas that will help the Panel decide in your favor. The first is psychological; the second is structural.

When judges are asked what they would change about legal argument, their common refrain is that lawyers should use less hyperbole, as judges know when they see inflated, overly argumentative language designed only to slam the opponent's position. The problem with hyperbole as a persuasive tool is that it backfires. The psychological response to hyperbole is: "Oh yeah? Prove it." This sets the reader against you.

A more persuasive approach is this: present the facts or legal principles first. Let your story do the persuasive work. If done right, your "plain" statement will cause the reader to side with your position. The reader will reach the conclusion you want before you state your point. When you finally state your conclusion, the reader will think, "Oh yeah! Exactly." That's the psychological response you want.

You can also help yourself through the structure of your written presentation. TTAB decisions tend to follow a pattern: discussion of facts, legal analysis involving priority, legal analysis involving likelihood of confusion. The latter issue tends to follow an analysis of the relevant factors. The decisions rely on TTAB and Federal Circuit decisions, whenever possible, rather than district court decisions that rest on different tests and considerations.

When writing your brief, make it easy for the Panel to decide in your favor by covering the factual and legal issues in the order likely to be followed in the decision, and use relevant authority.

7. Focus

The final thought for litigation tips and strategies is the need for focus.

Begin with the end in mind. Know what you need to prove. Find model decisions that provide a roadmap for your discovery, evidence and argument. Create a plan. Follow it.

Given the high cost of litigation, it is time to put the days of uncovering every stone without a focused plan behind us.

[F] Federal Circuit Court of Appeals Mediation

The Federal Circuit Court of Appeals initiated an appellate mediation program in 2005. The Federal Circuit is the exclusive court of appeals for patent disputes. It also may hear disputes arising in various federal agencies, including the Trademark Office, etc. The panel of mediators includes a distinguished roster of experienced attorneys mediating cases on a pro bono basis. The guidelines for selection of mediators are as follows:

In appropriate cases, the Chief Circuit Mediator, the Circuit Mediation Officer, or both may serve as mediator. In other cases, the mediator is an outside volunteer. The court has created a roster of outside mediators. The court's mediators include distinguished, experienced attorneys and academicians with expertise in the substantive areas of the court's jurisdiction as well as attorneys with experience mediating. The court invites more applicants with the application being available on the Federal Circuit Bar Association and the court's Web sites. Candidates are encouraged but not required to be members of the bar of the court.

Mediators and applicants to be mediators must not be in active practice. For purposes of these guidelines, *not be in active practice* means that the applicant or mediator is not appearing, and will not appear while a member of the court's mediation panel (1) as counsel for a party or amicus in any matter that would or could be appealed to this court, or (2) as counsel for a party or amicus in any appeal to this court.

Mediators are not paid for their services, but are reimbursed by the court for minor out-of-pocket expenses such as photocopying costs, telephone charges, facsimile charges, and transportation to the courthouse. Mediation proceedings may be held in the courthouse if desired. If the mediator must travel to conduct the mediation, reimbursement for the mediator's reasonable travel and lodging expenses is assumed by the litigants.

If the circuit mediation officers do not conduct the mediation, the circuit mediation officers select a mediator from the court's list with one exception. If counsel under the program jointly propose a mediator not on the list, then the circuit mediation officers have the option of appointing that mediator, provided the parties agree to pay any travel, lodging, and out-of-pocket expenses of the mediator and the mediator agrees to serve pro bono. Whether or not the case is selected for mediation under the court program, parties are of course free to participate in mediation outside the court's program under terms to which they agree.

If the mediator is affiliated with a law firm, and that law firm represents or has represented a party to an appeal within the last five years, if the mediator is appointed to any case involving that party, the mediator will recuse him- or herself. Before final selection of a mediator, the circuit mediation officers inquire about conflicts of interest. The mediator must not presently represent either party or any amicus for any purpose; must disclose any past relationships he or she has had with counsel, counsels' firms, and the parties; and must disclose any potential issues conflicts. Mediators are required to decline from participating in any cases in which there is a conflict of interest, in which they perceive a conflict, or in which a reasonable person would perceive a conflict.[18]

As of December 31, 2007, 39 appeals had been resolved through mediation with a success rate of 42 percent.[19]

18. http://www.cafc.uscourts.gov/pdf/mediationguidelines5-1-08.pdf.
19. http://www.cafc.uscourts.gov/pdf/mediationstats_december_31_07.pdf.

[G] Court-Annexed ADR

In addition to the programs discussed above dealing with special types of situations, various jurisdictions around the country have developed creative programs annexed to the court itself. Some leading examples are discussed below.

[1] Non-Binding Arbitration

The Northern District of California provides an option for nonbinding arbitration at no charge to the litigants. The goal of the court-sponsored arbitration is to provide adjudication that is earlier, faster, less formal, and less expensive than trial. The award in the nonbinding arbitration may become the judgment in the case if accepted by the parties or may serve as a starting point for settlement discussions. The arbitration award is not admissible at a subsequent trial de novo unless stipulated by the parties and is not disclosed to the trial judge until the case is terminated. The request for arbitration may occur at any time. The arbitration hearing is normally made within ninety days after referral for arbitration. The court's ADR staff appoints an arbitrator or panel of arbitrators with expertise in the substantive legal area of the lawsuit.

[2] Early Neutral Evaluation

The Northern District of California also offers litigants another option for dispute resolution known as early neutral evaluation. The goal of this process is to enhance direct communication between the parties about their claims and to provide an assessment of the merits of the dispute by a neutral with subject matter expertise. All civil cases are eligible. The neutral evaluators volunteer preparation time and four hours of the early neutral evaluation sessions. Additional time may be provided voluntarily or at an hourly rate of $200 to be split between the parties as they agree. After eight hours, the neutral may charge his or her usual hourly rate or such other rate as agreed to by the parties.

[3] Settlement Week

The Southern District of Ohio encourages settlement by holding a week of mediation conferences each quarter known as *settlement week*. The process began during the initial Rule 16 conference in which the parties are asked to indicate in the Rule 26(f) report whether they would like to participate in settlement week. The conferences are conducted by a neutral mediator who is a federal litigator with training or experience in mediation. The neutrals provide this service as unpaid volunteers. The settlement week conferences occur at the federal courthouse and usually last one-and-a-half to two hours. At the conclusion of the conference, the neutral advises the court if the case has settled or if further proceedings are necessary. The program has been successful in resolving disputes. According to Terry Kemp, Magistrate Judge and Settlement Week Coordinator, about half of the cases going through the process settle as a result of the conference.[20]

[4] Michigan Mediation

The Western District of Michigan has adopted a version of a Michigan state court program known as "Michigan Mediation" or case evaluation. Although called mediation, the program is a form of arbitration. It has become the most popular form of ADR in the Western District of Michigan. In cases referred to the program, counsel present their case to a panel of three neutrals who render an evaluation based on counsels' arguments and evidence. Referral is mandatory for medical malpractice cases under the Michigan Medical Malpractice Mediation Act and tort disputes under the Michigan Tort Mediation Act. The ADR administrator selects the neutrals. Each party sends each neutral $100 for a total cost of $300 per party. The award is typically rendered at the conclusion of the hearing, but in extraordinary cases the award may be issued no later than seven days after the hearing.

[5] Settlement Conference

Many if not all of the federal courts use magistrate judges for the purpose of conducting settlement conferences. The nature of the conferences may range from an in camera discussion with counsel about the possibilities of settlement to an extended formal mediation. Some magistrates are extremely experienced and skilled at the mediation process. However, it should be recognized magistrates may lack subject matter expertise relating to particular disputes, and may also tend to focus on technical issues of law to resolve the disputes as opposed to placing importance on the business aspects and objectives of both parties.

These various court-annexed programs offer a sampling of the possibilities used by the courts.

---

20. Interview with Terry Kemp, April 8, 2008, *available at* http://www.fjc.gov/public/home.nsfpp764.

Steps to an Effective Settlement Conference: Before You Come to the Table By U.S. Magistrate Judge Morton Denlow, Northern District of Illinois

I. Introduction

Judges and lawyers participate in numerous settlement conferences each year. Oftentimes, the participants depart the conference feeling that they have wasted their time and the clients' money without making progress. Why? Based on my twenty-four years in private practice and five years on the bench, I see three major reasons why settlement con ferences fail: 1) failure of the court and counsel to treat a settlement conference as a serious and integral part of the litigation process; 2) lack of preparation on the part of counsel and their clients prior to participating in the settlement conference; and 3) the unwillingness of participants to use the negotiation process as a method of resolving their dispute. Because over 95 percent of all civil cases terminate without a trial, it is imperative that bench and bar consider how to maximize their efforts when utilizing judicial settlement conferences. This article will discuss steps which I take prior to the settlement conference to insure that everyone's time is well spent.

II. When to Initiate Topic of Settlement

I make it a practice to raise the topic of settlement at almost every court appearance. While I would prefer that counsel initiate settlement discussions on their own, this rarely happens. I find that I enable both sides to save face with their clients if I initiate the topic and allow the attorneys to report back to their clients that "the judge has asked us to consider settlement." Some lawyers are reluctant to initiate settlement talks out of fear that either their clients or their opponents may perceive such a discussion as a sign of weakness. I never felt that way because I always wanted to know which direction I should devote my efforts. If the case was going to settle, I focused my efforts to insure that I had enough information from which to discuss settlement. On the other hand, if there was no interest in settlement, I could devote my efforts to preparing the case for trial.

What is the proper time to set a settlement conference?

There is no one magic moment in time. The key is that the parties must have a sincere interest in seeking a negotiated resolution and enough information from which to make an intelligent decision. As a result, I have been involved in successful settlement talks shortly after a case has been filed, before and after discovery has been completed, before and after rulings on dispositive motions, before and after final pretrial orders have been prepared, and before and after trials have been held. The key factor has been well-prepared parties committed to a negotiated resolution.

From a judicial perspective, settlement conferences are more effective when parties face a less desirable alternative. For example, setting a settlement conference with a looming discovery cut-off date, date for filing of dispositive motions, final pretrial order or firm trial date is more effective than setting a settlement conference without other dates looming. The presence of firm dates enables counsel to discuss with their clients the likely expense and litigation risks which each of those dates hold and imposes a reality check into the settlement process. Parties will generally act more realistically and responsibly in settlement conferences when they have firm dates staring back at them.

III. Written Settlement Demand and Offer

Prior to the settlement conference, I require the plaintiff to deliver to defendant a written itemization of damages and settlement demand. I require defendant to respond with a written settlement offer. This is an extremely important exercise because it requires the parties to become actively involved in the settlement process, it crystallizes positions, and it changes the psychology of the litigation, if only for a brief period, to a focus on settlement. At this point, parties may realize that they do not have enough information with which to itemize damages or to evaluate the case. If that is the case, the parties can focus their energies and discovery in gathering the necessary information to enable them to exchange written demands and offers.

Requiring the parties to exchange their demands and offers in writing adds a level of seriousness and precision which is often lacking when demands and offers are conveyed orally. Absent a writing, parties can disagree as to what the actual settlement proposals were. This can lead to confusion, distrust, and delay in negotiations. A written proposal will generally be more inclusive of all proposed terms and can easily be transmitted to clients for their input. I require the parties to provide me with copies of their written demands and offers two days before the settlement conference.

IV. Requiring the Personal Appearance of Clients with Full Authority

I insist that a client with full authority appear at the settlement conference. It is essential that clients with full authority be present for a number of reasons. First, it is their case and they should be given the opportunity to see and understand the alternatives they face and to hear presentations made by the other side. I find that many clients do not understand or appreciate the complexities of the litigation process. At a settlement conference they have the opportunity to observe, ask questions, and participate in decisions which affect them. Second, what transpires in a settlement conference can oftentimes make a difference to a party's perception of a case. This cannot be adequately captured by a telephone report to a client who is available by phone. Third, if a client is unwilling to attend, the client is probably not interested in settling. I take the view that if it is important enough for the court to set aside several hours to engage in this process, it should be important enough to the client. Finally, client participation in this process gives them a better understanding and appreciation for our system of justice.

Clients are grateful for the opportunity to discuss their problems with a judge in the more informal and relaxed atmosphere of a settlement conference. When they successfully work out a solution to a thorny problem, they walk away with a positive feeling towards the court and their counsel.

V. Avoid Surprises by Means of a Standing Order

Each judge has [his or her] own way of conducting a settlement conference. Although many judges or courts have standing orders for final pretrial orders, very few have adopted such orders for settlement conferences. I have found that the distribution of a standing order, which outlines my procedures and expectations of counsel and their clients, results in a savings of time for all concerned and more effective settlement conferences. A copy of my standing order setting settlement conference is attached.

VI. Conclusion

Settlement plays an important role in the disposition of cases. Courts and lawyers can make the settlement conference more useful and effective if the necessary preparation takes place before the parties come to the table. A standing order which explains the court's procedures and requirements will facilitate the process and result in more efficient and satisfying settlements.

4.04 Dispute Resolutions Service Providers

The service providers for ADR include organizations that are public or private and that can be categorized as local, national, or international. A brief overview of some leading organizations appears below:

International Institute for Conflict Prevention & Resolution (CPR), 575 Lexington Avenue, 21st floor, New York, New York 10022. www.cpradr.org.

> CPR was founded in 1979 as the Center for Public Resources from a coalition of leading General Counsel dedicated to identifying and applying appropriate alternative solutions to disputes, thereby mitigating the extraordinary costs of lengthy court trials. That determination is still at the basis of CPR's activities today. CPR is an all-purpose resource for lawyers seeking arbitrators and mediators; ADR case decisions and practice guides; and CLE courses, publications, and conferences.

World Intellectual Property Organization, Arbitration Dispute Resolution Center (WIPO), www.wipo.int.

> Based in Geneva, Switzerland, the WIPO Arbitration and Mediation Center was established in 1994 to offer ADR options, in particular arbitration and mediation, for the resolution of international commercial disputes between private parties. Developed by leading experts in cross-border dispute settlement, the procedures offered by the Center are widely recognized as appropriate for technology, entertainment, and other disputes involving intellectual property.

American Arbitration Association (AAA). www.adr.org.

> The AAA is a not-for-profit organization that administers ADR cases from filing to closing. The AAA was founded in 1926 shortly after the Federal Arbitration Act (FAA) became effective.

National Arbitration Forum (NAF), P.O. Box 50191, Minneapolis, MN 55401-0191. www.arb-forum.com.

> NAF is a private ADR provider focused on various types of commercial disputes, including commercial finance, construction, consumer, employment, healthcare, insurance, intellectual property, and real estate.

JAMS, 1920 Main Street, Suite 300, Irvine, CA 92614. www.jamsadr.com.

> JAMS was founded in 1979, and has since grown into the largest private ADR provider in the world. It provides mediators and arbitrators for complex, multiparty, and business and commercial cases. JAMS also holds seminars, workshops, and external education programs for dispute resolution.

International Mediation Institute (IMI), Lange Vijverberg 12, 2513 AC The Hague, the Netherlands. www.imimediation.org.

The IMI's stated mission is: "Generate confidence in and much enhanced understanding and usage of the mediation process among businesses and other disputants by encouraging high standards of training, by certifying high competency standards of mediators throughout the world, and by aiding users to find suitable competent mediators quickly and easily in the most transparent ways." It is pursuing this mission by establishing mediator certification on a global basis. The IMI does not provide end-user ADR services, but does plan to include a directory of IMI-certified mediators.

CHAPTER 5

Arbitration

In 1985, Chief Justice Warren E. Burger endorsed the use of arbitration at a meeting of the Minnesota Bar Association and the American Arbitration Association: "My own experience persuades me that in terms of cost, time and human wear and tear, arbitration is vastly better than conventional litigation for many kinds of cases."[1]

Part of the essential competency advocated by this book includes a working knowledge of arbitration. Yet, the process remains unfamiliar to many. This hypothetical tale is presented to dispel some of the mystery of arbitration for those new to the procedure.

---

1. *AAA Looks At The Next Century*, AMERICAN ARBITRATION ASSOCIATION HANDBOOK ON COMMERCIAL ARBITRATION 8–9 (Thomas E. Carbonneau et al., eds., 2006).

5.01 *Lakeside Informatics v. Northshore Housecall*: A Hypothetical Case Study

Lakeside Informatics is a software developer for the medical industry located in Skokie, Illinois. Several years ago, Lakeside accepted a development contract with Northshore Housecall, a medical service provider of home visit physician services. Lakeside's task was to develop integrated scheduling, medical record, and billing software for use by both physicians in the field and back-office personnel. The specifications for the program involved the following components:

- The software would be hosted on Northshore's server and maintained by Northshore personnel.
- Northshore physicians could access the system via the Internet using laptop computers with cell phone cards.
- Physicians in the field would be able to check and update their appointment schedule as well as review and update patient records.
- Back-office personnel would be able to schedule new appointments for the physicians; receive information on the services provided through a physician's visit; and prepare the appropriate electronic invoice for submission to government payors, insurance providers, or patients (depending on who had responsibility for payment).

Lakeside completed the software according to specification and delivered the product to Northshore in 2004. The software was designed to operate on an existing database platform owned by Lakeside and licensed to Northshore for an annual user fee of $25,000. Northshore was the owner of the rights in the new software created to its specifications and for which it paid $600,000. After the initial sixty-day warranty period, Lakeside continued to provide support and training as requested on an hourly basis.

Northshore had difficulty operating the software, but Lakeside asserted that it operated according to specification. At the end of 2004, Northshore failed to pay the royalty payment for the coming year and also did not pay invoices due for support and training. The amount owed was $25,000 for the licensing fee plus $75,000 for support and training. When Lakeside demanded payment, Northshore claimed breach of contract and sought reimbursement of all payments made for the software.

The contract between the parties included an AAA arbitration clause. Lakeside had insisted on including an arbitration clause based on its experience in other litigation. In one prior incident, a customer had claimed ownership rights in the licensed software and sued Lakeside for copyright infringement based on Lakeside's continued use and licensing of the software platform to others. Ultimately, Lakeside prevailed in the dispute, but only after two years of discovery and motions that were accompanied by legal expenses exceeding $1,000,000. As a result, the CEO of Lakeside insisted that its attorney find a better way to resolve disputes. Counsel recommended that all future contracts include an AAA arbitration clause.

When Lakeside received Northshore's response to its request for payment, the CEO's heart sank as he contemplated another drawn-out legal battle. However, he hoped that this time Lakeside might through arbitration avoid the headaches and expense of the past. The CEO turned the letter over to Lakeside's counsel with instructions to recover the money owed as efficiently as possible.

[A] The Arbitration Demand

The first step in initiating the arbitration process is the making of an arbitration demand. As the contract provided for arbitration through the AAA, Lakeside's counsel went to the AAA website, www.adr.org, to obtain the Commercial Arbitration Rules Demand Form, a single page document used by AAA to start the process.[2] In addition to contact details, the form covers a few simple and easy to answer questions and requests for information:

- What is the date of the arbitration agreement?
- State the nature of the dispute.
- What is the amount of the claim?
- What other relief is sought?
- Describe the appropriate qualifications for the arbitrators.
- Identify the hearing locale and indicate if it is specified in the agreement or merely requested by the complainant.
- Estimate the time needed for hearing.
- State the nature of the businesses of the parties.
- Identify if the dispute is between a business and consumer, or arises from an employee relationship.

The form is filed with the appropriate filing fee, which depends on the amount of the claim. In Lakeside's case, the amount claimed was $100,000, which meant a $1800 filing fee.[3] Two copies of the completed form and the arbitration agreement were sent to the AAA, and the original was sent to the respondent.

Recalling Lakeside's prior litigation, Lakeside's CEO was pleased that it was so easy to initiate the proceeding compared to federal court litigation.

---

2. http://www.adr.org/si.asp?id=3771.
3. http://www.adr.org/sp.asp?id=22440#Fees.

Instead of a carefully crafted, multiple page complaint used in the federal court, the AAA proceeding required only a single page form. The savings in time and legal expense far outweighed the higher filing fee—$250 for federal court versus $1800 for AAA.

[B] Confirmatory Notice and Answering Statement

Once the demand is filed, the next step is for the AAA to send the respondent a confirmatory notice of the proceeding. The respondent then has fifteen days to file an answering statement. This may include a counterclaim, but if so the appropriate filing fee must accompany it.

Northshore had threatened to seek full recovery of all money paid so far for the software, which amounted to $650,000. The filing fee for that counterclaim would have been $6000. As it turned out, Northshore did not include a counterclaim with its answering statement, a turn of events that pleased Lakeside's CEO, who had expected the worst. Northshore's failure to assert a counterclaim sent a signal to Lakeside that the demand for full recovery was merely a negotiating tactic that lacked sufficient merit to justify the added expense. Lakeside's CEO believed things would have been different if the case had proceeded in federal court where there would have been no added cost for Northshore to include a counterclaim in its answer to the complaint. The potential added expense of filing a counterclaim had already flushed out and removed a weak but potentially distracting claim.

[C] Arbitrator Selection

Shortly after Northshore submitted its answering statement, the AAA sent each party a list of ten potential arbitrators. Lakeside's arbitration demand stated that the arbitrator should be an attorney with at least ten years of legal experience dealing with software contracts and ten years of experience as an arbitrator. This requirement had been included in the arbitration contract. The AAA turned to its national roster of arbitrators to provide a list of ten who were qualified and located in the Chicago area where the arbitration was set to proceed.

Lakeside, with the help of its counsel, selected three candidates from the list based on qualifications and recommendations. However, Lakeside felt the selection process had a weakness: it was not possible to obtain a prior history of arbitration decisions by those included on the AAA's list. Nevertheless, Lakeside was satisfied that it had settled upon qualified, objective choices. To aid in the selection process, Lakeside's counsel reviewed the information available about the background of the proposed arbitrators, but did not contact any of the proposed arbitrators directly.

Although Lakeside would have liked more information about prior decisions by the arbitrators, it recognized that the process provided more information and control than a federal court proceeding. In federal court, Lakeside's case would have been randomly assigned to a generalist judge handling a full plate of wide-ranging disputes from discrimination cases to criminal prosecutions. Lakeside benefitted from being able to select an arbitrator with experience in the software field.

When considering the addition of an arbitration clause to its development agreements, Lakeside had discussed with counsel the risk of having one arbitrator versus three. While three arbitrators could result in more careful consideration of all issues and lessen the chance of extreme results, the expense would increase because the parties would be responsible for paying three people instead of one. It could also be more difficult to coordinate schedules to arrange hearings.

On balance, Lakeside expected that the amount in controversy was unlikely to exceed $1 million. In addition, as withheld payments during contract disputes would stretch Lakeside's resources, cost and timing were critical issues. Lakeside satisfied itself that the risk of a renegade arbitrator was reduced by AAA's arbitrator roster being well vetted. Therefore, Lakeside's preferred arbitration clause—the one found in its agreement with Northshore—called for only a single arbitrator. Lakeside's initial expectations about arbitrator selection were further satisfied in the Northshore proceeding when all the arbitrators proposed by the AAA appeared to be well suited to hear the dispute in terms of both their arbitration and relevant legal experience.

Lakeside attempted to reach agreement with Northshore on the selection of an arbitrator. Northshore, however, did not agree to accept any of the three arbitrators favored by Lakeside. After fifteen days, in accordance with the AAA rules, Lakeside returned the original list of ten to the AAA with all but its three favored arbitrators stricken. Northshore ignored the fifteen-day deadline and failed to return the original list to the AAA. As a result, the AAA appointed one of the arbitrators remaining on Lakeside's list.

[D] Disclosure

The AAA case administrator advised the proposed arbitrator of the selection to determine availability and potential conflicts. The AAA arbitrator appointment process involves detailed guidelines for disclosure of potential conflicts. Arbitrator bias is a critical concern that may be a basis for vacating an award. Thus, the disclosure process is extremely important. The AAA poses these questions to help the proposed arbitrator with his or her disclosures:

1. Do you or your law firm presently represent any person in a proceeding involving any party to the arbitration?

2. Have you represented any person against any party to the arbitration?
3. Have you had any professional or social relationship with counsel for any party in this proceeding or the firms for which they work?
4. Have you had any professional or social relationship with any parties or witnesses identified to date in this proceeding or the entities for which they work?
5. Have you had any professional or social relationship of which you are aware with any relative of any of the parties to this proceeding, or any relative of counsel to this proceeding, or any of the witnesses identified to date in the proceeding?
6. Have you, any member of your family, or any close social or business associate ever served as an arbitrator in a proceeding in which any of the identified witnesses or named individual parties gave testimony?
7. Have you, any member of your family, or any close social or business associate been involved in the last five years in a dispute involving the subject matter contained in the case, which you are assigned?
8. Have you ever served as an expert witness or consultant to any party, attorney, witness, or other arbitrator identified in this case?
9. Have any of the party representatives, law firms, or parties appeared before you in past arbitration cases?
10. Are you a member of any organization that is not listed on your panel biography that may be relevant to this arbitration?
11. Have you ever sued or been sued by either party or its representative?
12. Do you or your spouse own stock in any of the companies involved in this arbitration?
13. If there is more than one arbitrator appointed to this case, have you had any professional or social relationships with any of the other arbitrators?
14. Are there any connections, direct or indirect, with any of the case participants that have not been covered by the above questions?

Potential arbitrators are directed to make a disclosure if they are aware of any information that may lead to a justifiable doubt as to their impartiality or independence, including creating an appearance of partiality.

Sarah Jackson, the proposed arbitrator, was an attorney in private practice with a small firm in Chicago. When she received the invitation to serve as an arbitrator, she conducted a standard conflict check through her firm's docket system and sent an e-mail inquiry to all members of the firm. The conflict check found no formal conflicts. However, one of Jackson's partners advised her that he had served as an expert witness in a case in which Jason Smith, Lakeside's outside counsel, represented the opposing party. Jackson considered the disclosure questions stated above and decided that her partner's relationship with Lakeside's counsel did not require disclosure. She returned the Notice of Appointment stating "I have conducted a check for conflicts and have nothing to disclose."

[E] Prehearing

Next, the AAA case administrator scheduled a prehearing conference. The arbitrator and counsel agreed to conduct the conference by telephone. The conference participants included the arbitrator, the case administrator, Lakeside's counsel and CEO, and Northshore's counsel. The arbitrator questioned the parties about the procedural aspects of the case and set deadlines for the following matters:

- Serving and responding to document requests;
- Submitting discovery disputes to the arbitrator;
- Exchanging expert reports, witness lists, and exhibits;
- Filing prehearing memoranda.

The arbitrator and parties also agreed on a two-day hearing to begin ninety days from the initial prehearing conference. Although both sides stated the hearing would take no more than two days, the arbitrator scheduled two additional days the week afterwards "just in case." She also noted that changes to the schedule would only be permitted upon a showing of good cause. Finally, she got the parties to agree that they would not take depositions, file any dispositive motions, or subpoena third party witnesses.

Lakeside's CEO was pleased that he was part of the initial prehearing conference. The arbitrator seemed fair, well organized, and decisive. He was also glad to have discovery and pretrial proceedings limited. In prior litigation, he learned that depositions were time consuming and expensive, and that summary judgment motions could significantly delay a case. Such motions were also expensive in terms of legal fees. The arbitration seemed to be moving smoothly in a direction that would reduce cost and result in a prompt decision.

However, before long the smooth path to decision became bumpier. Two weeks before the scheduled date of the arbitration, Northshore retained new counsel who filed a motion for a continuance, a demand for depositions, and a motion to dismiss the arbitration on the grounds that the arbitration clause was unenforceable. For a time, Lakeside's CEO feared Northshore's new counsel would be able to send the case to court or at least delay the proceedings for several months. The arbitrator scheduled a telephone conference to address the motions. She concluded that Northshore had failed to demonstrate any true need for depositions and therefore denied that request. She also denied the motion to dismiss the arbitration, concluding that the arbitration clause was valid and enforceable. As a courtesy to new counsel, however, she agreed to a two-week extension of the date for the arbitration hearing.

Northshore took advantage of the delay by filing a motion in federal court to stay the arbitration and requesting a ruling on the validity of the arbitration agreement. Along with the stay of arbitration, Northshore asked for a thirty-day briefing schedule. However, the federal judge addressed the motion immediately. He concluded that the court had jurisdiction to determine the validity of the arbitration agreement, but further concluded this arbitration clause was valid. Thus, the court denied Northshore's request for a stay of the arbitration.

[F] The Arbitration Hearing

The arbitration hearing proceeded on the reset date. Both sides presented opening statements about their position in the dispute. Lakeside followed that by calling several witnesses, including the CEO. Each was cross-examined by Northshore's counsel. Lakeside also presented various documents that were accepted into evidence over Northshore's objection. Northshore presented one witness, its president, who was cross-examined by Lakeside. Both sides made closing arguments. Anticipating that Northshore's counsel might attempt to challenge the conduct of the arbitration after the hearing, Lakeside's counsel arranged for a stenographer to make a transcript of the arbitration.

At the hearing, Northshore's counsel vigorously objected to the admission of evidence and sought an extension to present additional evidence. The arbitrator was firm at the hearing, ruling fairly on the evidentiary issues. She closed the hearing at the end of two days after each party acknowledged it had no further evidence to present at that time and after Northshore acknowledged that it was unable to specify any newly discovered evidence.

[G] Ruling

The arbitrator issued her ruling soon after the close of the hearing, finding in Lakeside's favor but awarding less than demanded. Nevertheless, Lakeside's CEO was satisfied and relieved that the cost and time involved had been far less than his prior experience with court litigation.

The dispute was not over, however: Northshore filed another action in federal court asking the court to overturn the arbitral decision. Northshore argued that the arbitrator had erred by refusing Northshore a fair opportunity to present its case. The court reviewed the hearing transcript and denied the claim, concluding that the arbitrator had exercised appropriate discretion and that the award did not violate the Federal Arbitration Act (FAA). The court's decision was upheld on appeal, ending the dispute.

5.02 The Facets of a Successful Arbitration

As this case study illustrates, there are many facets to conducting a successful arbitration. Some parties turn to arbitration after bad litigation experiences, hoping for a faster, cheaper procedure. Others who have had unhappy experiences with arbitration are quick to return to court adjudication.

One in-house counsel with a Fortune 500 company voiced dissatisfaction with arbitration based on his experiences with the process in major disputes in Canada and the United Kingdom. He found that both proceedings took at least as long and cost at least as much as court litigation, and said that next time he would turn to the courts to handle the disputes he managed. His experience is echoed by others who give very mixed reviews overall for arbitration, especially in terms of time and cost. Nevertheless, arbitration is often required by contract and remains an important option for certain types of disputes. Experienced counsel M. Scott Donahey and Tom Sikora provide valuable insights about using arbitration to best advantage.

[A] Valuable Arbitration Insights

Donahey focuses exclusively on domestic and international arbitration, mediation, and domain names under the Uniform Domain Name Dispute Resolution Policy (UDRP).[4] Donahey has more than twenty years experience in complex commercial, intellectual property, and international commercial disputes; he has decided more than 150 commercial arbitration cases and more than 200 disputes under the UDRP. One example involved a claim for breach of contract between an American company and a Russian scientist residing in America. The contract concerned the assignment and ownership of patents concerning the use of single-molecule Raman spectroscopy for direct DNA sequencing. and of patents concerning the use of a "nanolens" to directly identify each individual subunit in a single strand of DNA as the subunit is encountered. The claim was for the assignment of the patents at issue, which were valued in excess of US $10 million.

It is hard to imagine a federal court dealing effectively with a claim of this type. How does a generalist federal judge learn the complex technical background necessary to understand the dispute while managing a full caseload of

4. M. Scott Donahey, mediator and arbitrator. *See* http://www.scottdonahey.com.

criminal and civil cases? How does the court effectively manage discovery? Arbitrators such as Donahey come to the table with the technical background and industry experience needed to deal with such complex disputes, including having a background in biotechnology and patent law.

Donahey also sees benefits in the power of the parties to control the arbitration process in ways that are not possible in court adjudication:

> What is frequently overlooked when people discuss the advantages of alternative dispute resolution is the ability of the parties to control the process. Where they choose arbitration, they may choose their arbitrator or define the qualifications that he or she must possess. They can give the arbitrator broad powers, beyond those available to national courts, or they can strictly limit what he or she can decide. They can agree on how much time each side will have to present its case and how soon a decision must be rendered after the close of the hearing. They can define exactly what issues an arbitrator is to decide. They can exclude certain areas entirely from the arbitrator's discretion, such as the award of punitive damages or the issuance of injunctive relief. The parties can dictate the form the award must take, whether it be a one liner or a reasoned opinion, setting forth the facts found and the application of the law the parties have chosen to those facts. They can require that the arbitrator prepare a draft award for the parties review and comment before the arbitrator can prepare a final award. They can agree upon the issues, and each party can specify a finding and a remedy for each issue defined and require that the arbitrator select the finding and remedy of one of the parties as to each issue, without modification. In short, the parties can tailor the procedure to their particular dispute, rather than take the one size fits all procedure of the court's rules of civil procedure. In the court, the judge is the master of all he assays, and the parties are required to follow his or her script. In arbitration, the arbitrator is the servant of the parties. The source of all of the arbitrator's powers is the agreement of the parties. In arbitration, as in mediation, the parties are in control. When those who use the process control the process, they can use it in an efficient and effective way, if only they take the time to fit the process to their particular dispute.[5]

Sikora, who is Senior Counsel for Arbitration, Complex Litigation, and E-Discovery for the El Paso Corporation, has years of international arbitration experience.[6] He takes a flexible approach to using arbitration clauses in contracts. Sikora identifies three circumstances in which he prefers arbitration over litigating in the courts:

1. International contracts where there may be a bias toward the foreign counterpart or where there is a lack of sophistication in the local judiciary or court system. Also, he may not have sufficient information

5. M. Scott Donahey, correspondence, December 9, 2008.
6. International Dispute Negotiation podcast interview by Michael McIlwrath, October 5, 2007.

to feel comfortable about resorting to the local courts, particularly in the developing world.

2. Large complex commercial contracts for which a jury in a desirable jurisdiction may have difficulty understanding the economics or technology of the transaction. Arbitration allows the parties to have the dispute decided by a panel of experts.
3. Forums in which the court procedures are burdensome, such as the U.S. federal district courts where U.S. rules for electronic discovery introduced December 2006 apply. Arbitration is a way to opt out of the expense of the U.S. court system. Such discovery can be very intrusive, complex, and expensive for the average company that may have hundreds of legacy computer systems with backup records.

In arbitration clauses, Sikora wants as much certainty and predictability as possible; therefore, he tries to pin down as many details as he can, such as situs, number of arbitrators, governing law, restrictions on awards of certain types of damages, etc. Sikora prefers locations for arbitration where there is well-developed arbitration law and a court system that will assist but not interfere with the arbitration process. Sikora usually prefers a three-member panel for larger disputes (even though this can lead to delay and increase cost) because decisions by three-arbitrator panels appear to be more carefully considered, typically will be less extreme, and provide a better-reasoned result. However, he will use only one arbitrator in smaller disputes.

Sikora tries to mediate as often as he can, and believes that the wave of the future will be to include mediation clauses in contracts. He also predicts that mediation will often be done in conjunction with arbitration.

[B] Questions to Consider

When making a decision to use arbitration as an alternative to court adjudication, counsel should carefully consider three additional questions:

1. How can you avoid arbitrary results in arbitration?
2. How do you require another party to engage in arbitration?
3. Should party-appointed neutrals be advocates for the party appointing them?

The questions are explored more fully below.

[1] How Do You Avoid Arbitrary Results in Arbitration?

One criticism directed at arbitration is that it leads to arbitrary results—results that are not tied to the facts or law but merely "split the baby." This risk, coupled with the fact that traditional arbitration is final and nonappealable, leads some to reject arbitration as a dispute resolution option. However, arbitrary results can be avoided through effective use of the arbitration process, which according to Larry Engel, former chair of the ABA Business Law Section, involves three steps.[7] Parties who desire to reduce the risks of arbitrary results should:

1. Specify qualifications to insure that the potential arbitrators have the expertise and personal qualities necessary to render a decision on the merits.
2. Require three arbitrators so that the party-nominated arbitrators can assure quality control of the decision-making process. (Three heads are better than one.)
3. Require arbitrators to follow the applicable law and to prepare findings of fact and conclusions of law.

Each of these steps may be included in the arbitration agreement, whether it be as a clause in the underlying agreement from which the claim arises or an agreement reached after the dispute arises. The failure to implement these steps can obliterate much of the value of selecting arbitration, particularly the first step. One of the key benefits of arbitration is the ability to have the matter heard by a person with expertise in both the relevant law and commercial field—a benefit not obtainable in court where matters are heard by a generalist judge. Utilizing arbitrators with relevant expertise can expedite the proceeding and lead to a decision that better reflects the reality of the commercial situation.

Here is an example of a clause that might be appropriate for an arbitration agreement in a trademark license:

> Arbitrators must be active members of the State Bar with expertise in regularly representing trademark licensors or licensees in comparable transactions, either in negotiating or documenting such transactions or in litigating disputes involving such agreements. Such arbitrators shall have no less than 10 years' experience in so representing parties to such transactions as a material portion of the law practices. Such arbitrators shall also be recognized by selection to the American Arbitration Association's National Panel of Commercial Arbitrators.[8]

A clause of this type requires a potential arbitrator to have legal expertise in trademark and licensing law from practice as a lawyer in that field,

---

7. *See* Larry Engel, *Commercial Arbitration: Winning Over the Skeptics*, AMERICAN ARBITRATION ASSOCIATION HANDBOOK ON COMMERCIAL ARBITRATION (2006).
8. Based on clause from Engle, *supra* note 6.

commercial experience in licensing transactions based on specific experience, and personal characteristics of temperament and integrity demonstrated by selection to a distinguished arbitration panel. In other words, a clause of this type seeks to use objective criteria to aid what is otherwise a largely subjective judgment.

[2] How Do You Require Another Party to Engage in Arbitration?

Once you determine that arbitration is a desirable option for resolving a dispute, the question arises as to how you require or induce your opponent to engage in arbitration. One option of course is for the parties to the dispute to agree after the dispute arises to use arbitration as the means of resolution.

Another possibility is that a court may require court-annexed arbitration. The mandatory arbitration procedure in the Illinois state courts discussed in Chapter 4 is an example of this.

The remaining options depend on the existence of a prior arbitration agreement, such as a clause in a licensing agreement, a services contract, or a domain name registration agreement. If the parties are signatories to a prior arbitration agreement, the party who desires arbitration may initiate an arbitration proceeding in accordance with the terms of the arbitration clause. If a case filed in court is covered by a prior arbitration agreement, the party seeking to arbitrate may file a motion to compel arbitration. Because of the strong public policy favoring resolution of disputes by arbitration, the court will normally grant the motion.

Under some circumstances, nonsignatories may be compelled to arbitrate as well. Five theories have been recognized by the court to compel arbitration: (1) alter ego or piercing the corporate veil, (2) incorporation by reference, (3) assumption, (4) agency, and (5) equitable estoppel.

Alter ego. A claimant may compel arbitration with a corporate parent or related company if it can demonstrate that the other company is an alter ego for the signatory to the arbitration agreement. Assume for example that the claimant has a dispute with a corporation that has defaulted on the terms of a contract containing an arbitration clause, and the corporation has become judgment proof. It may be possible to compel arbitration by the owner or officers if the corporate veil can be pierced. This may be the case where there has been fraud or the affairs of the corporation and owner are such that the corporation and owner are no longer separated.

Incorporation by reference. A claimant may compel arbitration with a nonsignatory if the opposing party is a signatory to a contract that incorporates the agreement with the arbitration clause. Assume, for example, that company A and company B are parties to an arbitration agreement. Company C later agrees with company A to perform the obligations of company B and references the agreement between A and B. Company C's incorporation by reference of the agreement between A and B may require A and C to arbitrate.

Assumption. A claimant may require arbitration if a nonsignatory's conduct demonstrates that it has assumed the benefits and obligations of the contract containing an arbitration clause. Assume that company A participates through counsel in arbitration with company B even though company A is not a signatory to any agreement with B. As a result of this conduct, company A may be bound to the arbitration decision and may not avoid the results of the arbitration on the grounds that it never agreed to be bound by arbitration results. Thus by virtue of its conduct, company A may be held to have assumed the obligation to arbitrate.

Agency. Agents may be bound to an arbitration agreement they have not signed. Assume for example that company A and company B are parties to a services contract. Company B has the services performed by its agent company C, which results in damage to company A. Company A may compel company C to arbitrate the damage claim even though company C is not a signatory to the arbitration agreement. Similarly, company C may rely on the arbitration clause it did not sign to compel A to arbitrate.

Equitable estoppel. Finally, equitable estoppel may be used to compel a party to arbitrate. Assume for example that company A and company B are parties to a license agreement containing an arbitration clause. Company B is subsequently acquired by Company C. A dispute arises over the license. Although there was no intent by company A to arbitrate with company C, and company C is not a signatory to the arbitration agreement, company C may nevertheless compel company A to arbitrate the dispute. Under these circumstances, company A may be equitably estopped from avoiding arbitration.

[3] Should Party-Appointed Neutrals Be Advocates for the Party that Appointed Them?

Some arbitration schemes call for the appointment of one arbitrator by each party. The appointed arbitrators or the arbitration institution then appoints the final arbitrator. The question thus arises as to whether the arbitrator appointed by a party should be an advocate in the arbitration process. The answer may vary by field, institution, and country. On a spectrum of lowest to highest degree of advocacy, the starting point would be arbitrary selection of neutrals without consideration of their leanings on controlling issues, without expectation that the neutral would be an advocate for the appointing party and without prior ex parte contact with the neutral. This lowest degree of selection is close to a completely arbitrary appointment similar to what occurs regarding assignment of cases to judges in federal court. The next degree of advocacy might involve consideration of the neutral's leanings or prior positions on controlling issues, but the parties would have no prior contact with the neutral and would not have any expectation that the neutral would be an advocate.

This degree of selection is what occurs, for example, in ICANN UDRP dispute proceedings in which the record of a panelist's prior decisions are available and it is relatively easy to gauge the panelist's likely leanings as such a limited range of issues are involved. Although prior decisions of the panelist are available for review, the rules prohibit direct contact with the panelist and require the panelist to submit a statement of neutrality. In traditional arbitration, however, parties are not likely to be able to review a potential neutral's prior record of decisions because decisions are not public record.

A greater degree of transparency is available where potential neutrals have public records independent of their role as arbitrators—for example, one based on the published decisions of a retired judge or the positions advocated by practicing attorneys—but a public record in other circumstances will not be a wholly reliable basis for gauging future positions. The prior positions of arbitrators may also be gleaned by consulting parties and counsel who have previously appeared before the potential arbitrator. Whatever the case, diligent party counsel will naturally seek as much background information as possible about the potential neutral as part of their preparation and representation of their client.

The next degree of selection occurs when it is possible to interview the potential neutral on substantive positions prior to selection. This may or not be permitted, considered ethical, or welcomed by the potential neutral. Some arbitration schemes do not allow such questions. Finally, some potential neutrals may not be willing to engage in a substantive discussion of the case. On the other hand, some arbitration cultures expect this to occur.

The final degree would be selection of a neutral who serves as an advocate for the party—a person who would be expected to promote the party's position at hearings and during panel deliberations. The level of advocacy could range from mild and subtle to outspoken and extreme. In extreme cases, the neutral may become part of the party's team during the arbitration by participating in direct ex parte communication or meetings with the party.

U.S. courts have expressed mixed views on the propriety of neutrals serving as advocates of the party appointing them. Judge Pound of the New York Court of Appeals stated in 1925:

> [T]he practice of arbitrators conducting themselves as champions of their nominators is to be condemned as contrary to the purpose of arbitrations, and as calculated to bring the system of enforced arbitrations into disrepute.[9]

9. Am. Eagle Fire Ins. Co. v. New Jersey Ins. Co., 240 N.Y. 398, 405 (1925).

In contrast, a later decision of the New York Court of Appeals reflects a different point of view:

> In short, usage and experience indicate that, in the type of tripartite arbitration envisaged by the contract before us, each party's arbitrator "is not individually expected to be neutral."[10]

The California courts echo this view: "There is no statutory requirement that the arbitrators appointed by the parties must be neutral or impartial."[11]

The FAA touches on this issue without being specific when it provides for vacatur of arbitration awards "[w]here the award is procured by corruption, fraud, or undue means" or "[w]here there was evident partiality or corruption in the arbitrators, or either of them."[12] But how should this be interpreted? Does it mean that evident partiality by a party-appointed arbitrator would be grounds for vacating the decision? Compare this language with the Uniform Arbitration Act that provides for vacatur in a case of "evident partiality by an arbitrator appointed as a neutral." Does this imply that party-designated arbitrators are not neutral and may display evident partiality? Court interpretations seem to vary widely.

Further guidance is provided by the Code of Ethics for Arbitrators in Commercial Disputes approved by the American Bar Association House of Delegates on February 9, 2004, and approved by the Executive Committee of the board of Directors of the AAA. The preamble to the Code takes the position that neutrality is the rule unless otherwise provided. The Code states:

> In some types of commercial arbitration, the parties or the administering institution provide for three or more arbitrators. In some such proceedings, it is the practice for each party, acting along, to appoint one arbitrator ("a party-appointed arbitrator") and for one additional arbitrator to be designated by the party-appointed arbitrators, or by the parties, or by an independent institution or individual. The sponsors of this Code believe that it is preferable for all arbitrators—including any party-appointed arbitrators—to be neutral, that is, independent and impartial, and to comply with the same ethical standards . . .. However, parties in certain domestic arbitrations in the United States may prefer that party-appointed arbitrators be non-neutral and governed by special ethical considerations . . .. This Code establishes a presumption of neutrality for all arbitrators, including party-appointed arbitrators, which applies unless the parties' agreement, the arbitration rules agreed to by the parties or applicable laws provide otherwise. This Code requires all party-appointed arbitrators, whether neutral or not, to make pre-appointment disclosures of any facts which might affect their neutrality, independence, or impartiality. This Code requires

---

10. Astoria Med. Group v. Health Ins. Plan of Greater N.Y., 11 N.Y.2d 128, 134 (1962).
11. Tipton v. Systron Donner Corp., 99 Cal. App.3d 501, 505 (1979).
12. 9 U.S.C. § 10(a)(1) and (2).

> all party-appointed arbitrators to ascertain and disclose as soon as practicable whether the parties intended for them to serve as neutral or not. If any doubt or uncertainty exists, the party-appointed arbitrators should serve as neutrals unless and until such doubt or uncertainty is resolved . . .

Canon IX of the Code imposes several significant obligations, stating that party appointed arbitrators:

- Shall ascertain as early as possible but not later than the first meeting of the arbitrators and parties whether the parties have agreed that the party-appointed arbitrators will serve as neutrals or not;
- Shall provide a timely report of their conclusions regarding neutrality to the parties and other arbitrators;
- Should review the agreement of the parties, the applicable rules, and any applicable law bearing upon arbitrator neutrality; and
- Shall remain neutral and observe all obligations of neutrality until they conclude that party-appointed arbitrators were not intended to serve as neutrals.

CHAPTER 6

Mediation

6.01 Why Mediation?

Mediation is a process of facilitated negotiation. The mediator does not decide the case; instead, the parties are in control of the result. The mediator's role is to assist the parties in reaching a negotiated resolution.

My partner David C. Hilliard is a veteran mediator of complicated disputes, including a widely publicized dispute involving the Terra Museum, discussed more fully in Chapter 7. Hilliard believes the first task of a mediator in any dispute is to develop trust among the litigants. In the Terra dispute, he did this by meeting privately with each of the board members before beginning the mediation sessions.

Hilliard notes that mediation "ferrets our issues and solutions that go beyond the pleadings in the complaint." Thus, trust, flexibility, and creativity become dynamic characteristics of a productive mediation.

Mediation is a powerful process for several reasons:

- It affords the parties the satisfaction of having "their day in court" without the expense of going to court. Many litigants want the opportunity to tell their story to a neutral, to be heard, and to be validated in their concerns. Once this is done, it becomes easier to compromise and reach a settlement.
- It provides the opportunity to explore options that could not be achieved as the result of a court decision. The mediator can explore options for "win-win" solutions, options for "expanding the pie," and options for nuanced outcomes.
- It can give the parties a chance to speak directly to one another.

6.02 Mediation Process: Understanding the Standard Steps

Because mediation is an unusual strategy for many litigants, it is useful to understand the standard steps in the process. The mediation process typically involves three stages: preliminary coordination, the hearing, and post-hearing actions.

[A] Preliminary Coordination

First, the parties select a neutral to mediate the dispute. They normally have wide latitude in making this selection. Court-annexed programs will have lists of approved or certified neutrals available to mediate. Professional organizations such as the American Intellectual Property Organization, the International Trademark Association, and bar associations maintain lists of neutrals. ADR institutions such as the American Arbitration Association, the National Arbitration Forum, and the World Intellectual Property Organization also have rosters of neutrals and will also provide a case manager and case management infrastructure. Parties may also rely on referrals and word of mouth.

One issue in selecting a mediator is to assess the person's mediation ability. Experience as a great lawyer, sitting judge, or legal expert does not necessarily equate to being a good mediator. The role of mediator demands particular aptitudes, training, experience, and skills—and it is often hard to determine if those skills are present. One solution to this problem is provided by the International Mediation Institute in The Hague, The Netherlands, which certifies competency standards for mediators.[1]

The second step in the typical mediation process is the mediation agreement. This is normally provided by the mediator to establish the terms of engagement, the general procedures to be followed, and the rules of confidentiality and privacy.

The final preliminary step is for the parties to provide position statements. These may be in the form of demands exchanged between the parties or more detailed statements of the claim provided to the mediator that may or may not be exchangedbetween the parties. In some complicated cases, the mediator may meet individually with parties and witnesses to gather information prior to the hearing.

[B] The Hearing

When the preliminary steps are completed, the parties and mediator proceed to the hearing. Again, there can be variations in how the mediator approaches the hearing, and mediators may vary their own approach from case to case depending on how they perceive the dynamics of the parties and the dispute. However, a typical mediation follows this format:

- *Introduction.* Usually the mediator will begin with comments to explain the procedure. Key points in the introduction will be the fact that everything is confidential and that the mediator will not decide the case.
- *Opening statements.* The parties usually have an opportunity to make a statement to the mediator and their opponent.
- *Caucus.* Following the opening statements, the mediator will usually separate the parties and meet with each side individually. There can be several rounds of back-and-forth discussions as the mediator explores the nature of the claims, the interests of the parties, and the options for settlement.
- *Group discussion.* After or during the caucus rounds, the mediator may bring the parties back together to discuss positions on settlement.
- *Counsel conference.* The mediator may meet solely with counsel to discuss certain issues and roadblocks.

---

1. More information about IMI can be found at www.imimediation.org.

- *Conclusion.* At the end of the mediation session, the mediator will summarize the settlement or positions of the parties. If settlement is reached, it is usually desirable to conclude the mediation with a written agreement or term sheet signed by the parties. If settlement is not reached, it is useful to leave all parties with a clear understanding of the best position offered by each side as there may or may not be further meetings or negotiations after the mediation session.

[C] Post-Mediation Activities

After the mediation session is completed, there can be various post-mediation activities. These may include:

- In a court-annexed mediation, the mediator will normally provide a brief report to the court on the results of the mediation.
- The mediator may be retained to facilitate preparation of a formal settlement agreement.
- The mediator may continue to facilitate negotiations between the parties via phone or in-person meetings.
- The mediator may be retained to provide an advisory opinion on the merits of the dispute.
- The mediator may be retained to provide recommendations to the parties on a fair settlement.

[D] Mediation Example

The mediation process is extremely flexible, as illustrated by the following example. The dispute involved a trademark infringement claim between two health care service providers. The parties met in my offices for a day of mediation. We followed the usual procedure outlined above. At the end of the day, the parties hadn't reached a settlement, but believed they were making progress. They wanted to continue mediation, but were caught on their different views on the merits of a few key legal issues. They asked me to switch roles and provide an advisory opinion on the disputed legal issues. We agreed each side would provide a brief on their position, and that I would issue an opinion.

As I reviewed the merits of the dispute, I found I was able to render an opinion that clarified the issue, but I chose not to reach a final conclusion, as I thought doing so would be more likely to hinder than help settlement. I was concerned the opinion would harden positions. Instead I issued my analysis, leaving the final weighing of the evidence to a private discussion with each side. We met several weeks after the first session for me to share my opinion and continue negotiations. At that point we were able to reach a conclusion on settlement in a few hours.

6.03 Mediation Styles

Commentators recognize several different approaches to mediation.[2] The principal ones are:

- Evaluative Mediation
- Facilitative Mediation
- Transformative Mediation

Understanding these different approaches is an important part of selecting the right mediator for your dispute and a key component in achieving a successful result through mediation.

[A] Evaluative Mediation

Evaluative mediation focuses on the strengths and weaknesses of the case. This method is commonly used by judges. Current judges will typically employ the method in settlement conferences, and retired judges retained by parties as mediators often carry over that judicial point of view to their mediation assignments.

The evaluative mediation process often begins with the mediator providing an analysis of the merits of the dispute in terms of the strengths and weaknesses of each side. This will probably be done in private caucuses rather than the group setting. The evaluation will sometimes include a prediction of the likely outcome of the case, often as a percentage chance of success. Specifically, the evaluative mediator may use *litigation risk analysis* to estimate the probabilities of different litigation outcomes. This evaluation and prediction will be used to encourage one or both parties to compromise and move closer to the other party's position. Through thoughtful evaluation and prediction, a respected mediator can lead the parties to modify their positions sufficiently so that they arrive at a settlement position somewhere between the opening offers.

The thought process of evaluative mediation is similar to the analysis typically employed by attorneys to advise their clients. Thus, the approach seems

---

2. Stephen B. Goldberg & Frank E.A. Sander, *Selecting a Mediator: An Alternative (Sometimes) to a Former Judge*, 33 Litig. (Summer 2007).

understandable and natural to the attorneys. When they mesh their evaluation with that of the mediator, counsel appear to be more savvy and in control, and face less surprise.

However, this method has several shortcomings. First, the parties may not accept the mediator's evaluation, instead believing they will be more successful at trial. Second, counsel may conclude the evaluation fails to account for their superior advocacy skills at trial. Finally, by focusing on the likelihood of success at trial, the approach may fail to uncover creative solutions that go beyond the strict confines of the legal claims.

[B] Facilitative Mediation

Instead of evaluating the odds of success at trial, facilitative mediation focuses on the interests of the parties. This process may reveal settlement possibilities not considered by the parties. Often the new possibilities involve a result that would not have been achieved through the narrow, bipolar lens of adjudication under which one party wins and the other loses.

The facilitative process typically begins by the mediator seeking an understanding of the wants of each party. The mediator then explores the reasoning behind each side's desired result. With this information, the mediator may help the parties focus on outcomes independent of who has the better case, the better advocate, or the greater entitlement.

However, this process is not natural to most lawyers or judges, at least to those whose training and experience has focused on litigation, as the litigation mind-set is better suited to the evaluative mediation process. The mind-set for facilitative mediation seems to come more easily to those with experience in business negotiations in which it is often the case that neither side is right or wrong. By focusing on interests and concerns rather than legal rights and wrongs, facilitative mediators can help craft a solution that best accommodates the strongest interests of the parties to the point the outcome is viewed as more desirable than continued litigation.

[C] Transformative Mediation

Transformative mediation focuses on the interpersonal relationship between the parties. Although it seems more fitting to disputes between individuals, it can also be a powerful tool in commercial disputes where emotions are high. Commercial disputes are not limited to those where the only considerations are cold, hard numbers. Indeed, most disputes involve emotional content, with each side believing it has been wronged by the other. These strong emotions can interfere with the resolution of the dispute.

Transformative mediation often proceeds with direct discussion between the parties. Given the emotions involved, the mediator needs to facilitate understanding through discussion of the parties' feelings and perceptions. If emotions are strong, it may be impossible to get to solutions until the emotional component is diffused. Experience teaches this is unlikely to occur in private caucuses. Instead, it may take a setting where each side has the chance to explain itself to the other. Once emotions are cooled, the parties may be better able to focus on solutions.

For this reason, transformative mediation will usually begin with the mediator asking questions to understand the emotions of the parties. After the emotions are addressed, the mediator may focus on interests. In some cases, once the emotions are addressed, the interests of the parties may be easy to reconcile.

6.04 Selecting a Mediator

Understanding the different approaches commonly taken to mediation will help parties select an appropriate mediator. The choice depends on considerations of legal strength, interests, and emotions. Depending on its evaluation of these considerations, a party's best choice may not be a former judge. For most business disputes, a party will want more than merely a discussion facilitator, and it will also want someone who does more than merely evaluate claims. Instead, it will be desirable to have a mediator who can facilitate discussion, evaluate claims, *and* identify and build on party interests. Within the framework discussed above, a party will be seeking a hybrid of the evaluative and facilitative approaches.

Yet the starting point for locating a mediator for ad hoc mediation is often a former judge. In court-annexed mediation, the initial option often involves a sitting judge or magistrate judge. Of course there are other options. Many courts and ADR institutions maintain rosters of mediators. Some attorneys and trained facilitators maintain a full-time practice as mediators and ADR specialists. Many law firms have ADR or dispute resolution groups or specialists, and many experienced attorneys include mediation as part of their larger practice. There are many choices, which can make selection puzzling or confusing.

One of the benefits of mediation is the ability to control the selection of mediator. Barry Weiner of Ruberto, Israel & Weiner PC in Boston urges parties to give adequate attention to the selection process:

> [I]f the mediator is not right, the mediation may well be a waste of time. Accordingly, counsel should take the time to carefully review the background, experience, reputation, and availability of potential mediators. . . . [D]on't shortcut your due diligence in selecting the right mediator. Carefully think through how the candidate matches up with the issues and the parties involved, and don't be afraid to ask questions and seek commitments. If, however, the

candidate is unavailable to respond to your questions, move on to someone else. If he or she is busy, the odds are that your case will not be given the kind of attention it warrants.[3]

Here are some of the key factors to consider when selecting a mediator:

- The mediator's training and experience with the mediation process.
- The mediator's experience with the type and nature of dispute in the particular case.
- The mediator's style and approach.
- The mediator's experience and knowledge of the trial process.
- The mediator's willingness to adapt the process to circumstances, parties, and counsel.
- The mediator's availability on the dates selected for the session with the parties.

Robert Hassould is a veteran mediator from South Carolina. Reflecting on the characteristics of a great mediator in his article "Establishing A Mediation Practice: Advice For Lawyers," Hassould suggests that much depends on innate ability flowing from the kind of personality that inspires confidence, including the ability to persuade others that resolution of the dispute is better than taking the case through litigation or arbitration.[4] A good personality helps to establish rapport. A reputation as a good negotiator suggests the mediator may have the right temperament, while a reputation as a hardball litigator may not. Great mediators have a passionate belief in mediation as a dispute resolution tool. Great mediators also usually have good communications skills allowing them to communicate in clear, understandable terms. They are good listeners who can "hear" verbal and nonverbal communication and read between the lines. These traits are useful to look for when selecting a mediator, but they are not always present in persons who are exceptional litigators, arbitrators, or judges.

6.05 Selecting Disputes for Mediation

Not all disputes are well suited to mediation.[5] Mediation may not be appropriate in situations (1) where one or both of the parties need a precedent for

3. Barry Y. Weiner, *Mediation and the Business Divorce*, Bus. L. Today (Jan.–Feb. 2008).
4. Robert W. Hassould, Jr., *Establishing A Mediation Practice: Advice for Lawyers*, Dispute Resolution J. 30 (Aug.–Oct. 2007).
5. Roger J. Peters & Deborah Bovarnick Mastin, *To Mediate or Not to Mediate: That is the Question*, Dispute Resolution J. (May–July 2007) (discussing mediation for construction disputes).

similar disputes with other parties, (2) where the dispute is a matter of principle for one of the parties, (3) where it is impossible to bring an indispensable party to the mediation table, or (4) where a reckless party is forcing a frivolous claim.

In contrast, mediation is well suited to disputes in which the parties are motivated to settle by virtue of an existing relationship, the economics of litigation, the possibility of a future business relationship, or the likelihood that a court decision will not provide an optimum solution to the litigated problem.

6.06 Mediation Sample Documents and Language

[A] Mediation Clause

Mediation may be triggered by court rules, a prior contract between the parties, or agreement of the parties after the dispute arises. The American Arbitration Association recommends the following clause for inclusion in contracts in which parties wish to use mediation to resolve future disputes. This may be used alone or in conjunction with a standard arbitration clause:

> If a dispute arises out of or relates to this contract, or the breach thereof, and if the dispute cannot be settled through negotiation, the parties agree first to try in good faith to settle the dispute by mediation administered by the American Arbitration Association under its Commercial Mediation Procedures before resorting to arbitration, litigation, or some other dispute resolution procedure.

[B] Court-Annexed Mediation

Mediation annexed to courts may be initiated by the court clerk in accord with the rules and procedures of the relevant court. Here is the letter used by the Northern District of Illinois to invite participation in mediation in trademark disputes.

Northern District of Illinois Lanham Act Mediation Letter

Dear Counsel:

Mediation frequently aids in settling trademark disputes and other Lanham Act cases. For that reason, the District Court for the Northern District of Illinois established its voluntary mediation program in 1996 for Lanham

Act cases. The program is Lanham Act case specific and draws on mediators who are specialists in such cases. Since its establishment, the Northern District mediation program has assisted many parties in resolving their disputes without expending the large amounts of time, effort and resources normally involved in full scale litigation.

You will find enclosed materials describing the Court's Lanham Act mediation program. They include a description of the program, the Local Rules and procedures governing it, and a current list of mediators that have been qualified by the Court to mediate Lanham Act disputes. The program has often delivered prompt and economical resolutions to disputes, and the Court strongly encourages you and your client to take advantage of it.

The docket indicates that you are appearing as counsel for one of the parties in this litigation. Pursuant to this Court's Rules and procedures, you are required to provide copies of this letter and all enclosures to each party you represent. If you represent a plaintiff, you also must provide copies of these papers to the attorney for each defendant. The attorney for each defendant then must provide these materials to each party that attorney represents. Within 20 days of the date of receipt of this letter, each attorney is required to file a Certificate with the Court stating that copies of these documents have been provided to the appropriate parties and attorneys.

The Rules also require that the parties file a Notice with the Court stating whether they will participate in the Court's Lanham Act mediation program. This Notice must be filed at the earlier of the first scheduling conference, or 60 days after this case was filed. The Judge to whom this case has been assigned has been notified that you have been sent this letter, and will expect you timely to file the Certificate and Notice.

The experience of the Court shows that the program provides tangible benefits to parties in resolving their disputes. Many lawyers and their clients have expressed satisfaction with the program, and many routinely encourage their clients to submit their disputes to mediation. We urge you and your client to proceed with mediation in this case. The best interests of your client would be served thereby.

Sincerely,
Deputy Clerk

[C] The Mediation Agreement

The starting point for the mediation relationship will often be a private agreement between the parties and mediator. Here is a sample mediator's agreement in the form I have used for commercial mediations initiated during litigation by agreement of the parties.

Mediator Retention Agreement

Plaintiff, the Acme Corporation, and defendant, North American University, ("the Parties") have agreed to participate in a mediation ("the Mediation") in an attempt to resolve the above-captioned civil action. The parties have agreed to retain Mark V.B. Partridge of the law firm of Pattishall, McAuliffe, Newbury, Hilliard and Geraldson LLP, 311 South Wacker Drive, Suite 5000, Chicago, Illinois, 60606, as the mediator ("the Mediator") for this Mediation. To enable the Parties to discuss all aspects of their dispute freely and to enable the Mediator to assist the Parties in reaching a voluntary resolution of their dispute, the Parties and the Mediator ("the Participants") agree to the Mediation Rules and Procedures attached hereto and to the additional terms as follows:

A. Confidentiality and Immunity

1. Conferences and discussions which occur in connection with mediation services provided pursuant to this Agreement shall be deemed settlement discussions, and nothing said or disclosed, nor any document produced, which is not otherwise discovered, shall be offered or received as evidence or used for impeachment or for any other purpose in any current or future litigation, administrative proceeding, arbitration proceeding, or in any other dispute resolution forum, regardless of the law of the forum. Should disclosure of such information to the Court be necessary in enforcing this Agreement, such disclosure shall be made under seal.

In particular, except in enforcing this Agreement, the Participants will not disclose any information or documents related to or disclosed in the Mediation, including offers, promises, conduct, statements, or settlement terms whether oral or written, made by any of the Parties, their agents, employees, experts, and attorneys. Such information and documents are confidential and privileged under any applicable state or federal privileges, and any state confidentiality statutes, rules, or doctrine.

2. This Agreement covers all communications made in the course of the Mediation, including all telephone calls and meetings of either or both Parties with the Mediator and all telephone calls and meetings between the Parties in the absence of the Mediator so long as done under the auspices of the Mediation.

3. Except for pleadings and other court filings, the Mediator will not disclose to another Party or its attorneys any briefing papers, materials, or other information submitted by a Party or its attorney to the Mediator without the consent of the submitting Party or its attorney.

4. The Parties agree, on behalf of themselves and their attorneys, that none of them will call or subpoena the Mediator in any proceeding of any

kind to produce any notes or documents related to the Mediation or to testify concerning any such notes or documents or his thoughts or impressions. If any Party attempts to compel such testimony or production, such Party shall be liable for and shall indemnify the Mediator for any liabilities, costs, and expenses, including attorney's fees and lost professional time, which he may incur in resisting such compulsion.

5. Each Participant agrees to notify the other Participants of the receipt of any subpoenas or any request for information that is related to the Mediation.

6. Except for claims to enforce this Agreement, the Mediator shall not be liable to any Party for any act or omission in connection with the Mediation. The Mediator shall have the same common law immunity as judges and arbitrators from suit for damages or equitable relief and from compulsory process to testify or produce evidence based on or concerning any action, statement, or communication in or concerning the Mediation.

B. No Attorney-Client Relationship

The Parties understand that there is no attorney-client relationship between the Mediator and any Party, and each Party acknowledges that it will seek and rely on legal advice solely from its own counsel and not from the Mediator.

C. Disclosure of Prior Relationships

1. The Mediator has made a reasonable effort to identify and has disclosed to the Parties: (a) all business or professional relationships the Mediator has had with the Parties or their law firms within the past five years, including all instances in which the Mediator served as an attorney for any Party or adverse to any Party; (b) any financial interest the Mediator has in any Party; (c) any significant social, business, or professional relationship the Mediator has had with an officer or employee of a Party or with an individual representing a Party in the Proceeding; and (d) any other circumstances that may create doubt regarding the Mediator's impartiality in the Mediation.

2. Each Party and its law firm have made a reasonable effort to identify and has disclosed to the other Party and the Mediator any relationships of a nature in paragraph C.1. not previously identified and disclosed by the Mediator.

3. The Parties and the Mediator are satisfied that any relationships disclosed pursuant to paragraphs C.1. and C.2. do not affect the Mediator's independence or impartiality. Notwithstanding any such relationships, the

Parties wish the Mediator to serve in the Mediation and the Mediator agrees to so serve.

D. Future Relationships

1. The Mediator shall not undertake any work for or against a Party regarding the dispute which is the subject matter of the Mediation.

2. Neither the Mediator nor any person assisting the Mediator shall personally work on any matter for or against a Party, regardless of subject matter, prior to six months after the termination of his services in this Mediation.

3. Other members of the Mediator's firm may work on matters against a party during the Mediation proceeding if such matters are unrelated to the Mediation. The Mediator shall establish appropriate safeguards to ensure that members and employees of the firm working on any such matters do not have access to any confidential information obtained by the Mediator during the course of the Mediation.

E. Compensation

The Mediator shall be compensated for time expended in connection with the Mediation at the rate of $XXX per hour, plus reasonable travel and other out-of-pocket expenses. The Mediator may utilize members and employees of the firm to assist in connection with the Mediation and may bill the parties for the time expended by such person in accordance with the standard billing practices and rates employed by the Mediator's firm. The Mediator's fee shall be shared by the Parties, so that one half (1/2) shall be paid by the plaintiff and one half (1/2) shall be paid by the defendants.

F. Conclusion

This Agreement is made on between the Mediator and the following parties: This Agreement may be executed in one or more counterparts, each of which shall be deemed an original, but all of which together shall constitute one and the same instrument, once all Participants have executed a counterpart.

IN WITNESS WHEREFORE, the Participants have entered into this Agreement.

[D] Demand Letters and Statement of Position

Mediators will typically call upon the parties to exchange demand letters or provide statements of position prior to the mediation session. In some instances, these letters are exchanged between the parties with copies to the mediator. In other instances, the statement of position will be provided on a confidential basis to the mediator only.

Sample Mediation Demand Letter Directed to Counsel

Dear Alice:

New MPV, Inc. ("New MPV") and BRIGHTLINE/eav, Inc. ("Brightline") provide the following settlement proposal in advance of our mediation conference on September 24, 2003.

As you know, our clients' dispute concerns ABC's unauthorized distribution and sale of certain New MPV and Brightline works through distributors and wholesalers and in the educational market ("Unauthorized Customers"). Sales to Unauthorized Customers are outside the scope of the License Agreements between the parties, and, therefore, constitute copyright infringement.

Due to ABC's copyright infringements, and because New MPV's and Brightline's works are subject to federal copyright registrations, New MPV and Brightline are entitled to (a) actual damages and ABC's additional profits or (b) statutory damages. *See* 17 U.S.C. § 504. Pursuant to 17 U.S.C. § 504(c), a copyright owner may elect to recover statutory damages in the amount of $750 to $30,000 per work infringed. The court may increase the award of statutory damages to a sum of $150,000 per work for willful infringements. *See id.* The relevant unit in calculating potential statutory damages in this case is each copyrighted work identified in MPV's and Brightline's complaints. *See MCA Television Ltd. v. Feltner*, 89 F.3d 766, 769 (11th Cir. 1996); *Gamma Audio & Video, Inc. v. Ean-Chea*, 11 F.3d 1106, 1117 (1st Cir. 1993). MPV is also entitled to an award of attorneys fees under 17 U.S.C. § 505. Attorneys' fees are routinely awarded to successful copyright claimants, regardless of the amount of actual damages. *See Gonzales v. Transfer Tech., Inc.*, 301 F.3d 608, 610 (7th Cir. 2002). Our clients' current attorneys' fees and costs are $156,713.

The evidence at trial will establish that ABC's infringements were willful. An infringement is willful if the infringer knows that its conduct is an infringement or acts in reckless disregard of the copyright owner's rights. *See Wildlife Express Corp. v. Carol Wright Sales, Inc.*, 18 F.3d 502, 511 (7th Cir. 1994). Violation of written notice is "perhaps the most persuasive evidence of willfulness." *Chi-Boy Music v. Charlie Club, Inc.*, 930 F.2d 1224, 1227 (7th Cir. 1991).

The record here shows an egregious history of willful infringement. The Agreements entered in 1999 specifically state that sales to Unauthorized Customers are not permitted. In October 2000, New MPV became aware that ABC was making unauthorized sales and sent ABC written notice. ABC stated it would comply, but it is now apparent that ABC continued its unauthorized sales. MPV again gave notice on February 28, 2003, and filed suit for copyright infringement. Even then, according to the sales records provided by ABC in connection with the case, ABC continued to make unauthorized sales as recently as April 2003. These actions clearly constitute willful infringement and justify a heightened award of statutory damages.

Accordingly, due to ABC's willful infringements, New MPV is entitled to a statutory damages award of up to $150,000 per each of the 10 copyrighted works identified in its complaint, totaling $1,500,000. Brightline is entitled to a statutory damages award of up to $150,000 per each of the 21 copyrighted works identified in its complaint, totaling $3,150,000. ABC, therefore, faces total liability for statutory damages of $4,650,000.

Instead of proceeding with its claims and seeking statutory damages, which do not require proof of *any* actual damages, New MPV and Brightline are willing to consider settling their disputes with ABC for a figure approximating their actual damages resulting from ABC's copyright infringement and breach of contract. We have been attempting for many months to obtain complete sales data from ABC so that we can make accurate calculations of actual damages and are disappointed that we did not receive the allegedly complete information for 2003 until two days ago. Even that information appears to be incomplete since there are substantial discrepancies between the sales information recently provided and the totals appearing on the royalty reports ABC previously submitted to New MPV and Brightline. We fear that the sales information understates the actual damages to New MPV and Brightline, and that an audit will be necessary to obtain accurate figures and to explain the discrepancies between the reports.

Nevertheless, for the purposes of settlement, New MPV and Brightline have used the sales information provided by ABC and prepared the calculations of actual damages shown in the enclosed spreadsheets. Based on the sales data you have provided, we conclude that actual damages in lost profits are $70,187 for Brightline and $361,113 for New MPV for a total of $431,300. In addition, your sales reports show that the royalties reported to Brightline were underreported by $34,506. This results in a total of $465,806. We believe even this amount understates the actual damages suffered by New MPV and Brightline as a result of ABC's actions.

In addition to damages, Brightline and New MPV have the right to terminate the license agreements with ABC due to ABC's repeated breach of the agreements. ABC induced New MPV to broaden its license by guaranteeing to release additional titles within the ninety day period required under the agreement, but never did so. ABC also continued to make infringing sales to Unauthorized Customers despite repeated notice. In addition to these acts of default, ABC's performance makes termination a business necessity.

ABC's minimal sales have produced no royalties in the past nine months and ABC's royalty payments and reports have frequently been late and sent only after ABC was issued a default notice. And ABC unreasonably filed suit against New MPV in South Carolina. ABC's performance under its contracts is totally unsatisfactory and its conduct in initiating litigation against New MPV in South Carolina is highly objectionable. Therefore, New MPV and Brightline are not willing to continue in an ongoing business relationship with ABC as its licensee.

Summary of Settlement Demand

In summary, New MPV and Brightline demand the following terms of settlement:

I. ABC shall pay New MPV and Brightline $622,519.
II. The court will enter judgment ordering the License Agreements between New MPV and ABC, and Brightline and ABC, to be completely and immediately terminated.
III. ABC shall dismiss and provide a full release of all claims and counter claims asserted in the cases pending between the parties in South Carolina and Illinois.

Sincerely,

Sample Mediation Demand Letter Submitted to the Mediator Only

Confidential

Dear Mr. Nelson:

A. Nature of the Case

This is a case for trademark infringement, unfair competition and deceptive trade practices. The Complaint asserts that plaintiff's federally registered trademark rights in the name and mark PRACTICAL FORENSICS for engineering services are infringed by the defendant's subsequent use of the PRACTICAL FORENSICS mark for similar services. Plaintiff seeks an injunction, damages and recovery of attorneys fees, as provided under Federal Trademark Law and under the laws of various states, including Minnesota.

More specifically, Plaintiff, Practical Forensics Corporation ("PFC"), has been using the trade name and mark PRACTICAL FORENSICS in connection with its engineering company since 1993. It has provided various types of engineering services to an array of business sectors since its inception. PFC owns U.S. trademark registrations for PRACTICAL FORENSICS, including incontestable Reg. No. XXX for "forensic engineering services" for PRACTICAL

FORENSICS and Design, issued in 1995, and Reg. No. XXX for "mechanical engineering consulting services" for PRACTICAL FORENSICS CORPORATION, issued in 2002. PFC also owns a domain name registration for <practical-forensics.com> issued in 1997. Over the years, PFC has developed a great deal of goodwill in the PRACTICAL FORENSICS trademark, relying in large part on its strong reputation to develop new business.

PFC's federal trademark registrations provide PFC with nationwide constructive use of the mark from the date of application (15 U.S.C. § 1057), provide other parties with constructive notice as a matter of law of PFC's prior rights (15 U.S.C. § 1072), and are evidence of the validity, ownership and PFC's exclusive rights in the mark (15 U.S.C. § 1057).

In 1998, long after PFC established rights in the PRACTICAL FORENSICS mark, Defendant, Practical Forensics, Incorporated ("PFI"), started to use the trade name and mark PRACTICAL FORENSICS for engineering goods and services. PFI adopted this mark despite having constructive notice of PFC's rights. In addition, PFC understands that PFI received actual notice of PFC's rights when PFI attempted to register the domain name <www.appliedkinetics.com>, which was already owned by PFC. Upon realizing that the domain name was taken, PFI instead registered the confusingly similar domain name <www.practicalforensics.com>.

PFC first learned of PFI as a result of an instance of actual confusion when a vendor confused the companies. In addition, PFC has learned of at least one additional instance of confusion involving an employee of a potential customer who mistook PFI for PFC. Further instances of confusion are inevitable as PFC's business continues to grow.

After learning about the confusion resulting from PFI's name, PFC contacted PFI in an effort to resolve the dispute and avoid confusion between the parties. PFI refused to take any corrective action. Instead, in October 2003, after the parties had numerous conversations about this dispute, PFI filed a trademark application to register the mark PRACTICAL FORENSICS for "automated process and test equipment and systems, optical inspection apparatuses for industrial use, automation software, measurement sensors, and automated process and test equipment components, all for use in the manufacture of disk drives or components of disk drives." An Examiner of the U.S. Patent and Trademark Office ("PTO") refused to register the mark, stating that PFI's application is likely to cause confusion with both of PFC's registrations. PFI has tried to avoid that refusal by narrowing the scope of goods it seeks to cover by its registration. To date, the PTO has not made a final ruling. Nevertheless, the initial refusal of the Trademark Examiner further demonstrates the merit of PFC's concerns about the confusion and damage caused by PFI's actual use.

B. Settlement Positions

The parties have discussed settlement possibilities on several occasions, including a recent meeting of counsel by telephone in accordance with this Court's Notice.

Prior to the recent meeting of counsel, it has been PFC's position that this matter should be resolved by PFI ceasing its use of the name and mark PRACTICAL FORENSICS. Because PFI is using a mark that is identical to PFC's registered trademark, it is PFC's position that the only way to prevent confusion is for PFI to change its name. For the purpose of settlement, PFC has offered to allow PFI a reasonable phase out period if PFI agrees to stop using the trade name and mark PRACTICAL FORENSICS.

In contrast, PFI refuses PFC's offer, representing that it is not willing to change its name at this time. PFI instead proposes to limit the goods and services it offers under the PRACTICAL FORENSICS mark. That position is not acceptable to PFC. Given the overlap with PFC's services and the fact that the marks are identical (and are being confused), PFI's proposal is not an adequate resolution. PFI's continued use of PRACTICAL FORENSICS as a name, mark and domain name for a Web site and business related to engineering services will continue to cause confusion and interfere with PFC's growing business.

PFC remains interested in finding an amicable resolution. At this time, before the parties incur further expense, PFC is willing to forego recovery of damages and profits, if PFI agrees to the following:

- Cease all use of the mark PRACTICAL FORENSICS as a trade name and trademark within six months; his matter.
- Abandon with prejudice trademark application.
- Assign its domain name registration for <www.practicalforensics.com> to PFC
- Never again use a mark that is confusingly similar to the mark PRACTICAL FORENSICS;
- Destroy or remove the PRACTICAL FORENSICS mark from all advertising and promotional materials in its possession;
- Send overlays with instructions to cover the PRACTICAL FORENSICS mark to all customers who have equipment bearing the mark; and
- Reimburse PFC $30,000, a portion of the attorney's fees it has incurred in this matter.

C. Remaining Liability Issues

The remaining liability issues against PFI are (1) trademark infringement in violation of Sections 32 and 43 of the Lanham Act, 15 U.S.C. §§ 1114 and 1125(a), and the common laws of various states, including Minnesota; (2) unfair competition in violation of Section 43 of the Lanham Act, 15 U.S.C. § 1125(a), and the common laws of the various states, including Minnesota; and (3) deceptive trade practices in violation of the Minnesota Uniform Deceptive Trade Practices Act, §§ 325D.43–325D.48.

1. *Trademark Infringemen*

PFC's federal registration of its PRACTICAL FORENSICS trade name and mark functions as prima facie evidence of the validity of the name and mark, PFC's ownership of the name and mark, and of PFC's exclusive right to use the name and mark in commerce. 15 U.S.C. § 1057(b). As such, defendant bears the burden of overcoming these presumptions arising from plaintiff's registration. *Iowa Farmers Union v. Farmers' Educational & Co-op Union*, 247 F.2d 809, 818 (8th Cir. 1957).

The crux of a claim for relief under Federal Trademark Law is the likelihood of confusion, deception, or mistake. The Eighth Circuit has enumerated six factors relevant to determination of the likelihood of confusion: (1) the strength of the mark; (2) the similarity between the plaintiff and defendant's marks; (3) the competitive proximity of the parties' products; (4) the alleged infringer's intent to confuse the public; (5) evidence of any actual confusion; and (6) the degree of care reasonably expected of plaintiff's potential customers. None of these factors is determinative. *Anhueser Busch, Inc. v. Balducci Publ'ns*, 28 F.3d 769, 774 (8th Cir. 1994).

The facts here establish PFC's right to relief. The marks are identical and the goods and services are related. There have already been instances of actual confusion and the U.S. Trademark Office concluded that confusion is likely. PFI currently markets its services on the Internet using the domain name <practicalforensics.com>, which is virtually identical to PFC's domain name <practical-forensics.com> and PFC's registered PRACTICAL FORENSICS marks. There is an overlap in potential customers for the parties' services. Finally, PFI proceeded with constructive and actual notice of PFC's prior use and rights in the PRACTICAL FORENSICS mark.

2. *Unfair Competition*

Likelihood of confusion, mistake, or deceit as to affiliation, connection, or association is also the issue in a claim for unfair competition. 15 U.S.C. § 1125(a). The Eighth Circuit has noted that the "facts supporting a suit for [trademark] infringement and one for unfair competition are substantially identical." *Heaton Distrib. Co. v. Union Tank Car Co.*, 387 F.2d 477 (8th Cir. 1967)(citations omitted). Based on the facts outlined above, PFI has also engaged in unfair competition.

3. *Deceptive Trade Practices*

The Minnesota Uniform Deceptive Trade Practices Act provides relief against any party who engages in an act that causes likelihood of confusion or of misunderstanding as to the source, sponsorship, approval or certification of goods and services; or causes likelihood of confusion or of misunderstanding as to affiliation, connection, or association with, or certification, by another. Minn. Stat. §§ 325D.44–325D.45 (2003). "In the context of trademark infringement, the Minnesota Deceptive Trade Practices Act creates claims that mirror those under the Lanham Act." *Hellerich & Bradsby Co. v. Christian Brothers, Inc.*, 943 F. Supp. 1136, 1140 (D. Minn. 1996).

The discussion above establishes that PFI has created a likelihood of confusion as a result of its use of PFC's PRACTICAL FORENSICS name and mark. Therefore, in addition to violating Federal Trademark Law, PFI has also violated the Minnesota Uniform Deceptive Trade Practices Act.

D. Computation of Damages

As a result of PFI's knowing and deliberate infringement of PFC's registered trade name and mark, PFC is entitled to PFI's profits and PFC's damages. 15 U.S.C. § 1117. Because of the nature of PFI's infringing activity, it is particularly difficult to calculate a specific damage amount. According to 15 U.S.C. § 1117, in seeking recovery of profits, PFC bears only the burden of proving the amount of PFI's sales. The burden of proof then shifts to PFI, who must prove all elements of cost or deduction from this overall amount in order to arrive at a final calculation of damages. PFC has not yet had suffi-cient discovery to establish the amount of PFI's profits that it can recover at trial.

Under the Federal Trademark Law, a prevailing plaintiff is also entitled to recover attorneys fees in an exceptional case. 15 U.S.C. § 1117. Exceptional cases occur when the infringement is "deliberate or willful." *Stephen W. Boney, Inc. Boney Service*, 127 F.3d 821, 826 (9th Cir. 1997). Here, PFC is entitled to recover attorneys' fees because PFI's infringement was deliberate and willful. PFI had constructive and actual notice of PFC's prior rights and use of PRACTICAL FORENSICS, yet it proceeded to use the identical mark for similar services. PFC's attorneys fees and expenses through August 2004, are approximately $58,000.

E. Analysis of Practical Forensics Corporation's Last Settlement Position

PFC's last settlement position is exceedingly generous. PFC's prior rights in the PRACTICAL FORENSICS mark and the likelihood of confusion created by PFI's use of PRACTICAL FORENSICS are not subject to reasonable dispute.

PFC's prior rights are established by its prior federal registration of the mark and use of the mark in commerce for an engineering company since 1993. PFI adopted the same mark in bad faith, since it had constructive and actual notice of PFC's prior rights and use of PRACTICAL FORENSICS for engineering services. Importantly, PFI's use of PRACTICAL FORENSICS has resulted in actual confusion, and a Trademark Examiner for the United States Patent and Trademark Office has already found that PFI's subsequent use of the mark is likely to cause confusion, mistake or deception with PFC's mark.

At trial, PFC has a high likelihood of proving infringement and entitlement to injunctive relief, an accounting of profits and recovery of attorneys fees, given PFI's adoption of an identical mark for similar services in the face of its constructive and actual knowledge of PFC's rights. We expect that the amount sought in recovery, if this matter proceeds to trial, will be in excess of $250,000.

Respectfully submitted,

[E] Sample Preparation Outline for Mediation

Preparation is key for effective participation in mediation. Here is a sample preparation outline used by counsel to brief client representatives before a mediation involving a domain name and Web site infringement dispute.

Sample Preparation Outline

Acme Machinery v. Jones Machine
Mediation Preparation Outline
November 17, 2004

I. JONES Response

A. Admissions

1. JONES has used ACME's marks without permission since September, 2003.
2. JONES used meta tags and attraction pages (AKA spider food) to attract Internet traffic to its Web site.
3. JONES did so with full knowledge of ACME's long use of its marks.
4. JONES deliberately used the marks of its principal competitor to mislead Internet users for its commercial gain.
5. JONES did not obtain any prior opinion of counsel that its conduct was permitted.
6. JONES does not deny that it made false statements in the attraction pages about it relationship with ACME.
7. ACME is the victim and has responded appropriately to protect its rights.

B. JONES's Key Points

1. JONES has an ongoing relationship with ACME.
   1) RESPONSE:
      (1) that relationship does not justify the false statements made by JONES about that relationship.
      (2) that relationship does justify unauthorized use ACME's marks in advertising.
2. Traffic Power never submitted text of meta tags to JONES for approval.
   1) RESPONSE:
      (1) That has not been proved.
      (2) JONES admittedly provided the key words and is still responsible for that selection.
3. ACME engages in use of OEM names as meta tags.
   1) RESPONSE:
      (1) Is this true?
      (2) ACME uses OEM names in a fair manner.
      (3) RP's conduct is not the same and exceeds that allowed as fair use by the cases it relies upon.

4. JONES placement report shows Web site placements did not result from use of ACME MACHINERY or WIDGET TECH.
   1) RESPONSE:
      (1) JONES has only produced one early report, yet suggests there were more.
      (2) P's list of services indicates that more information is available.
      (3) JONES has failed to produce more information, giving rise to an inference that additional reports would be adverse to RP's position.
5. JONES has been damaged by OEM response to ACME letters.
   1) RESPONSE
      (1) ACME's letters were true and privileged.
      (2) JONES has presented no evidence.
6. ACME pursued this claim as harassment even though JONES said the conduct had stopped.
   1) RESPONSE:
      (1) JONES did not stop the online misuse prior to the filing of this suit.
      (2) JONES failed to take any action to correct the problem online.
      (3) JONES continued to use the WIDGET TECH mark
      (4) JONES threatened to take action against ACME's letters, justifying defensive action
7. ACME does not have trademark registrations covering its claimed marks.
   1) RESPONSE:
      (1) ACME and Meyer both have common law rights based on used.
      (2) JONES was clearly aware of the ACME and Meyer marks since it was a competitor and the parties had done business together.

C. JONES Legal Position Is Erroneous

1. JONES argues that full disclosure is all that is required, citing *Champion* and *Nitro*
   1) RESPONSE:
      (1) JONES's cases are inapposite to the current situation.
      (2) JONES relied on false statements and failed to mark full disclosure.
2. JONES argues that OEM meta tags are permitted, citing *Bijur.*
   1) RESPONSE:
      (1) Bijur is inapposite to the current situation.
      (2) JONES did not make fair nominative use of ACME's marks.
3. JONES argues that there are no rights in disclaimed features, citing *Oakwood.*
   1) RESPONSE:
      (1) RP's reliance on *Oakwood* is misplaced.
      (2) *Oakwood* relies on 1939 case.

(3) That case specific recognizes that claim for unfair competition remains available despite disclaimer.
(4) Current trademark statute specifically says disclaimer does not affect common law rights.

4. JONES argues that ACME cannot recover monetary damages, citing *Web Printing*.
   1) RESPONSE:
      (1) JONES states the holding of *Web Printing*.
      (2) *Web Printing* specifically recognizes that other forms of relief are available including recovery of attorney's fees and an accounting of defendant's profits.

IV. ACME Position

A. Key Points

1. JONES admits it intentionally used ACME's marks to attract Internet users to its Web site for over six months. Its purpose was to take business from ACME, not merely to describe the nature of its goods.
   1) They used "attraction pages" or "spider food" to mislead Internet users.
   2) Those pages contained repeated false representations about ACME.
   3) RP's deceit is highlighted by its contradictory explanation of its conduct.
      (1) JONES claims in on instance that it used ACME in a nominative sense to describe its relationship with ACME.
      (2) Then JONES claims it used ACME in a nominative sense to identify Acme Lathe.
      (3) They can't have it both ways.
2. ACME has strong common law rights in the ACME MACHINERY and WIDGET TECH marks based on long use and advertising.
3. JONES did not fairly use ACME MACHINERY's marks, but instead misrepresented its relationship with ACME for profit.
4. ACME letters are true and are not any basis for a damage claim.
5. ACME is entitled to recover attorneys' fees and an accounting of profits based on RP's deliberate infringement of its rights, even if ACME is unable to show actual deception.

V. Settlement Process

A. Steps

1. Demand
2. Joint Presentations
3. Party Caucus
4. Agreement

B. Magistrate

1. Balance of likely outcome against expense
2. Press for compromise
3. Search for creative solutions

VI. Settlement Strategy

A. ACME initial demand

B. JONES initial demand

C. Settlement Assessment

1. ACME desired outcome (Why did we bring this suit and what more do we want to achieve?)
2. Most likely outcome from litigation (What can we expect to accomplish through litigation and at what cost?)
3. ACME best alternative to litigation (What would be are better outcome than litigation?)
4. Least acceptable alternative to litigation (What is the least you will accept at the settlement conference before continuing with litigation?)
5. What is the least JONES will accept as an alternative to litigation (What do you think JONES would be willing to do to settle the litigation?)
6. Are there any opportunities for better results?
   1) Continued relationships
   2) Expanded pie
   3) Cooperation
   4) Low cost benefits to opponent

D. Concession Patterns

JONES refrains from all misuse of ACME and Meyer marks and:

1) JONES pays percentage of its profits (10 percent?) plus expenses.
2) JONES pays for corrective advertisements.
3) JONES pays for six months of keyword advertisements
4) JONES pays equal amount to ACME for search optimization ($6000?)
5) JONES pays expenses only.
6) Each party pays own expenses.

E. Establish Final Position

[F] Sample Outline for Mediation Hearing

Organization and preparation for the presentation of a client's position at the mediation is also critical. Here is a sample outline used to facilitate presentation of a party's position at the mediation session.

Sample Outline for Mediation Hearing

Acme Machinery v. Online Strategies
Outline for Settlement Conference

A. Plaintiff and its rights in WIDGET STORAGE

- Plaintiff is one of the leading resellers of gear manufacturing equipment in the country.
- The principal means to market and promote its products has traditionally been the use of product catalogs.
- Plaintiff has used the WIDGET STORAGE mark as the name of its product catalog for twenty years.
- The catalogs are mailed to Plaintiff's list of customers and potential customers, distributed at industry tradeshows, and mailed to the DNA mailing list.
- Plaintiff's related business is Partridge Publishing, which publishes the gear industry magazine WIDGET TECH.

B. Defendant and its use of WIDGET STORAGE

- Defendant also publishes a magazine for the gear industry in competition with Partridge Publishing and is partly owned by one of Plaintiff's principal competitors.
- Defendant started its magazine publishing business in 2003. Defendant's magazine is directed to the same people to whom plaintiff sends its catalogs and features advertising by plaintiff's competitors.
- In October 2003, defendant's principals attended the GMA tradeshow, where Plaintiff displayed and distributed its catalog.
- In early 2004, both Online Strategies and RS Equipment, used plaintiff's marks to redirect people to their Web site. RS Equipment used the ACME MACHINERY mark. This resulted in a separate lawsuit, which has been settled.
- At about the same time, Online Strategies selected the WIDGET STORAGE mark for its Web site. The mark was featured in full page ads in defendant's magazine in May, June and July, and continues to be used in those ads on Online Strategies' Web site today.

- The mark was also used for a forum page, which included links to defendant's principal site featuring advertisements for plaintiff's competitors.

C. Harm caused by defendant's use of WIDGET STORAGE

1. The people who receive plaintiff's WIDGET STORAGE catalog also receive defendant's magazine.
2. In May, June, July those people were exposed to advertisements for the WIDGET STORAGE Web site.
3. It is likely that persons familiar with plaintiff's use of WIDGET STORAGE were confused by defendant's ad and went online to find the site.
4. It is also likely that persons familiar with plaintiff's use of WIDGET STORAGE would try to find that name online even without seeing the ads.
5. Once at defendant's site, they would be taken via links to defendant's principal site which features ads and links for businesses in direct competition with plaintiff, including the business of defendant's co-owner, RS Equipment.
6. Thus, it is likely that defendant's use of WIDGET STORAGE resulted in lost sales to plaintiff by diverting potential customers to competitive businesses. The potential loss of sales is significant. A typical sale is $50,000 to $100,000 or more.

   - Defendant profits from the use of WIDGET STORAGE by selling advertising on its Web sites.
   - The law recognizes that actual confusion and actual damages are difficult or impossible to prove in these cases. Thus, the trademark laws provide for statutory damages or up to $100,000 per domain name and recovery of attorneys fees.

D. Infringement Analysis

1. The WIDGET STORAGE mark has been used for twenty years and is entitled to protection.
2. The marks are identical.
3. The nature of the uses is closely related. Plaintiff provides a catalog for gear manufacturing equipment. Defendant offered a forum relating to gear manufacturing equipment with links to sellers of gear manufacturing equipment.
4. The relevant customers are the same: potential purchasers of gear manufacturing equipment.

5. Nature of the use results in diversion of potential customers to plaintiff's competitors.
6. Actual confusion has not come to plaintiff's attention, but is not required.
7. Intent is not required, but is apparent from the circumstances of adoption.
8. The expense of the purchase does not avoid confusion, since persons familiar with WIDGET STORAGE are likely to find what they need at the competitor's business and not be concerned about the identity of the reseller of the equipment.

E. Cybersquatting Analysis

1. Defendant had no prior use of WIDGET STORAGE.
2. Defendant had no prior rights in WIDGET STORAGE.
3. WIDGET STORAGE is not the legal name of defendant's business.
4. The circumstances indicate that Defendant knew of plaintiff and its use of WIDGET STORAGE.
5. Defendant's conduct is similar to that in *Sporty's Farm v. Sportsman's Market, Inc.*, 202 F.3d 489 (2d Cir. 2000), where the defendant adopted the mark of a competitor for an unrelated business.

F. Circumstances Demonstrating Bad Faith

1. Defendant attended a tradeshow where plaintiff distributed its catalog.
2. Plaintiff's principal competitor is a co-owner of defendant's business.
3. Competitor also used plaintiff's mark to divert business to its Web site.
4. Defendant admits it checked plaintiff's Web site for use of WIDGET STORAGE.
5. Defendant failed to consult with counsel about use of WIDGET STORAGE.
6. Defendant failed to check trademark office records.
7. Defendant failed to contact plaintiff.

G. Defendant's Lack of Credibility

1. Morrison claims he searched plaintiff's site in March but did not find WIDGET STORAGE. If he had done so, he would have found it used in a letter on the site.
2. Morrison again claims he searched plaintiff's site after the lawsuit was filed, but did not find WIDGET STORAGE. If he had done so, he would found use on the site.

3. Morrison says the first time he saw the ACME MACHINERY logo was when he looked at the Web site in 2004. But it was prominently displayed at the 2003 trade show.
4. Morrison admits he stood in front of the ACME MACHINERY booth in 2003, but says he did not see WIDGET STORAGE. It was prominently displayed.
5. Defendant's alleged lack of knowledge about the mark is not credible.

H. Settlement Position

1. Plaintiff has a claim against defendant for about $230,000 for statutory damages and attorneys' fees.
2. For the purpose of settlement. we are prepared to accept $175,000.

I. Factual Support

1. CM has used WIDGET STORAGE for its catalog for twenty years.
2. CM customers refer to WIDGET STORAGE by name and use it to place orders (CAD 1031 etc.).
3. CM displays its catalogs at tradeshows (see photos).
4. Smith admits he has seen the ACME MACHINERY catalog. He admits he may have seen it a few times.
5. Smith admits he has visited the ACME MACHInery booth at trade shows "once in a while" (36:23) and was across the aisle from the CM booth at a China trade show (39:21).
6. Smith speaks to Cooper regularly, sometimes once a week (55:6).
7. Clark admits he visited the CM booth in 2003 and spoke with CM sales manager Tom Khadha (27:8). He may have gone by the booth "quite a few times" (28:12).
8. Clark claims he went to CM Web site to see if CM used WIDGET STORAGE (50:9–22).
9. Widget Storage included full page ads for WIGESTSTORAGE.COM in May, June, and July.
10. Widget Storage traffic report shows over 34,000 requests during May, June, and July 2004 (OSI 0061).
11. WIDGETSTORAGE.COM includes a link to GEARSONLINE.COM (OSI 0066 etc.).
12. GEARSONLINE.COM features ads for CM competitors that link to sites selling gear manufacturing equipment in competition with CM.
13. The Gear Solutions media kit shows defendant targets potential customers of CM.

[G] Sample Term Sheet Developed During Mediation

During mediation, the parties or the mediator may find it useful to work from a specific set of terms or recommendations to facilitate progress toward resolution. Here is a sample based on a term sheet developed during a trademark dispute mediation involving competing health-care services providers. If a resolution is reached, the best course is to have the parties agree upon and sign a term sheet at the conclusion of the mediation session to avoid disputes when preparing a formal agreement.

Sample Term Sheet Developed During Mediation

ABC Healthcare Services v. ABC Health Services
Settlement Options

Mediator's Recommendation

A. ABC-Illinois changes name

1. ABC-I discontinues use of ABC
2. ABC-I assigns common law rights in ABC to ABC-W
3. ABC-W pays $55,000; paid in seven days
4. ABC-W makes no incorrect, misleading, or deceptive statements about ABC-I; if asked for, ABC-W has to explain
5. Mutual release
6. Phase out until Dec. 31, 2001
7. Reciprocal attorneys' fee to enforce agreement
8. Jurisdiction Cook County or N.D.Ill. (Eastern Division)

B. ABC-Wisconsin changes name

1. ABC-W discontinues use of ABC in Illinois
2. ABC-W adopts new name in settlement area
3. ABC-W assigns concurrent federal rights to ABC-I for settlement area.
4. ABC-I pays $60,000
5. ABC-I grants right of first refusal to sell back registration and name.
6. Parties agree to cure problems relating to use of name.

[H] Sample Settlement Agreement Based on Mediation

The resolution should be documented as soon as possible after the mediation session. Here is a sample settlement agreement formalizing a resolution reached during mediation:

Settlement Agreement

This SETTLEMENT AGREEMENT is entered into by and between ONLINE STRATEGIES, INC. a corporation duly organized and existing under the laws of the State of Alabama (hereinafter "OSI"), and ACME MACHINERY CO., INC., a corporation duly organized and existing under the laws of the State of Illinois (hereinafter "ACME").

WHEREAS, ACME filed a lawsuit against OSI in the U. S. District Court for the Northern District of Illinois, captioned *Acme Machinery Co., Inc. v. Online Strategies, Inc.*, for alleged cybersquatting, unfair competition, and deceptive trade practices (hereinafter "the CIVIL ACTION");

WHEREAS, OSI denies that it has engaged in any unlawful acts; and

WHEREAS, after consulting with independent legal counsel, and after participating in a judicial settlement conference on April 5, 2005, ACME and OSI have agreed upon the terms and conditions of final settlement.

NOW, THEREFORE, in consideration of the mutual covenants herein, the Parties agree as follows:

1. Within thirty (30) days of execution of this SETTLEMENT AGREEMENT, or no later than May 5, 2005, OSI shall pay to ACME an amount of fifty-five thousand U. S. Dollars ($55,000), subject to the provisions in this paragraph.
2. OSI agrees to transfer to ACME ownership of the domain name <widgetstorage.com> within thirty (30) days of execution of this SETTLEMENT AGREEMENT, or no later than May 5, 2005.
3. OSI agrees to refrain hereafter from engaging in all uses of the phrases "WIDGET STORAGE," "WIDGET STORAGE industry forum," and "widgetstorage.com." The Parties expressly agree that this provision of the SETTLEMENT AGREEMENT does not apply to situations referencing a type of gear, a gear function, or a technical property a gear(s).
4. OSI acknowledges the validity of ACME's trademark rights in the mark WIDGET STORAGE, and OSI agrees not to challenge, object to, or contest in any way ACME's rights in this mark.
5. Within seven (7) days of receipt of the payment set forth in Paragraph 1 by counsel for ACME, ACME shall dismiss its claims in the CIVIL ACTION by filing the Agreed Order of Dismissal in the CIVIL ACTION in the form attached hereto as Exhibit 1. Such dismissal shall be with prejudice.
6. ACME hereby releases OSI and its officers, directors, employees, and agents against any and all existing or potential claims or causes of action as of the effective date of the SETTLEMENT AGREEMENT, whether now known or hereafter discovered, including but not limited to all claims or causes of action that were or could have been asserted in the CIVIL ACTION.
7. OSI hereby releases ACME, Partridge Publishing, Inc., and their officers, directors, employees, and agents against any and all existing or potential claims, counterclaims or causes of action as of the effective

date of the SETTLEMENT AGREEMENT, whether now known or hereafter discovered, including but not limited to all claims, counterclaims or causes of action that were or could have been asserted in the CIVIL ACTION.

8. The Parties agree that no press releases regarding the CIVIL ACTION or its settlement will be issued unless mutually agreed upon. All questions as to the CIVIL ACTION or the claims therein, shall be answered by the corporate officers, employees, their attorneys, accountants, agents and successors with only the following statement: "*THIS MATTER HAS BEEN CONCLUDED TO THE SATISFACTION OF ALL PARTIES.*"
9. This SETTLEMENT AGREEMENT and the dismissal of the CIVIL ACTION are the result of the compromise of disputed claims and shall not be construed as an admission of liability or fault by any of the Parties.
10. This SETTLEMENT AGREEMENT shall be governed by and construed in accordance with the laws of the State of Illinois.
11. This SETTLEMENT AGREEMENT represents the entire agreement between OSI and ACME, and supersedes all understandings that may have been reached by the Parties prior to this time. Any amendments to this SETTLEMENT AGREEMENT shall be in a writing signed by all Parties, and there shall be no oral amendments.
12. This SETTLEMENT AGREEMENT shall be binding upon and shall inure to the benefit of the Parties, their employees, agents, representatives, servants, heirs, assigns and successors-in-interest.
13. The Parties agree that the Magistrate Judge of the United States District Court for the Northern District of Illinois shall retain exclusive jurisdiction over the Parties and this CIVIL ACTION for the purpose of enforcing the terms of this SETTLEMENT AGREEMENT through July 31, 2005. *See* Exhibit 1.
14. The Parties hereby mutually acknowledge and represent that they have been fully advised by their respective legal counsel of their rights and responsibilities under this SETTLEMENT AGREEMENT, that they have read, know and understand completely the contents hereof, and they have voluntarily executed the same.
15. Each of the Parties represents and warrants that the person signing this SETTLEMENT AGREEMENT on its behalf is fully authorized to execute this SETTLEMENT AGREEMENT on its behalf.
16. This SETTLEMENT AGREEMENT may be executed in counterparts, each of which shall be deemed an original, but all of which together shall constitute one and the same instrument. The Parties agree that the SETTLEMENT AGREEMENT may be executed by facsimile signature and that each such signature shall be deemed an original.
17. In the event that any part of this SETTLEMENT AGREEMENT shall be found to be illegal or in violation of public policy, or for any reason unenforceable at law, such finding shall not invalidate any other part hereof.

IN WITNESS WHEREOF, this SETTLEMENT AGREEMENT has been duly executed by OSI and ACME.

United States District Court Northern District of Illinois Eastern Division

ACME MACHINERY CO., INC.	)	
	)	
Plaintiff,	)	
v.	)	Civil Action No:
	)	
ONLINE STRATEGIES, INC.	)	
	)	
Defendant.	)	

Agreed Order of dismissal

The parties hereby agree that this case has been settled and that all issues and controversies have been resolved to their mutual satisfaction. The parties request the Court to retain jurisdiction to enforce the terms of their settlement agreement under the authority of *Kokkonen v. Guardian Life Insurance Company of America*, 511 U.S. 375, 381–82 (1994):
IT IS HEREBY ORDERED:

1. The parties shall comply with the terms of their settlement agreement entered into on April 5, 2005.
2. By consent of the parties, the Court shall retain jurisdiction for the purpose of enforcing the terms of the settlement agreement through July 31, 2005.
3. Except as provided for in paragraphs 1 and 2 above, this case is dismissed, with prejudice, each party shall bear its own attorney's fees and costs.

ENTER:

Dated:

United States Magistrate Judge

CHAPTER

7

Legal Trends

When ADR Goes to Court

Principal legal trends involving ADR include waiver of right to arbitrate, challenges to arbitration provisions and awards, right of third parties to invoke arbitration, enforcement of mediated settlement agreements, and the confidentiality of ADR proceedings.

The court decisions regarding each of these issues can significantly impact the value of ADR as a low cost, efficient dispute resolution tool.

There is a school of thought that courts should not hear these issues because doing do undermines the utility of ADR as an efficient, cost-effective mechanism for dispute resolution. According to this school, the systems should be separate. If the parties choose arbitration, leave it at that. Don't allow litigation over the arbitration. Consideration of these issues by the courts yields a body of decisions that in turn creates more litigation over the exceptions to the decisions. Rather than providing clear guidelines, the courts provide more fodder for dispute.

Conversely, litigators and clients by nature push the courts to consider these issues, adding layers of litigation to ADR. As one observer puts it, "Cautious litigators and risk adverse clients are seeking more judicial review, expanded document protection and more depositions . . . Once you do all that, it begins to look a little less like the animal it was intended to be."[1] As a result, ADR (especially arbitration) begins to function more like general litigation. In fact, what was once a streamlined procedure becomes even more cumbersome than traditional litigation. Not only do we have arbitration and court litigation procedures to deal with but a whole body of law and related litigation over the interface between arbitration and litigation regarding issues such as the right to litigate, the scope of judicial review of litigation, and the enforcement of awards.

Ultimately, the natural consequence of these developments is that arbitration ceases to provide the desired benefits of fast, efficient, low-cost dispute resolution and become less popular for commercial applications.

7.01 Litigation Involving Arbitration

[A] Waiver of the Right to Arbitrate

[1] *Zimmer v. CooperNeff*

An example of a dispute over the obligation or right to arbitrate as mandated by a contract clause is *Zimmer v. CooperNeff Advisors, Inc.*, decided by the Third Circuit in 2008.[2]

Zimmer, who held a Ph.D in economics from Harvard, had worked in the financial industry since 1988. In late 2002, Zimmer interviewed with

---

1. Marci Coyle, *Justices Take Critical Look at Arbitration,* 30 NAT. L. J. 9 (Oct. 29, 2007).
2. Zimmer v. CooperNeff Advisors, Inc., 86 U.S.P.Q.2d 1254 (3d Cir. 2008).

CooperNeff Advisors, Inc., a hedge fund. During his interview, Zimmer offered an explanation of a stock trading model of his own creation that he hoped to use in his new job. Zimmer ultimately accepted an offer of employment from CooperNeff. On March 3, 2003, the first day of his employment, CooperNeff provided Zimmer with an employment contract that included an arbitration clause covering:

> any and all legal or contractual disputes of any nature arising at any time (including after termination of employment) between [the employee] on the one hand and the Company and its affiliates on the other . . .

The employment contract further stated:

> The types of claims and disputes that will be resolved under these procedures include all claims and disputes arising under this agreement or in connection with your employment by the Company; all claims arising from the terms and conditions of your employment; all claims arising from the termination of your employment . . . . However, the Company retains the right to bring any claims to enforce any of its rights in paragraph 6 of this agreement directly in a court of competent jurisdiction and the Company need not arbitrate any such claims.

Paragraph 6 of the employment contract related to "exclusivity of services, non-solicitation, confidentiality, intellectual property, return of documents and property upon termination and enforcement provisions." The effect of the provision was to allow CooperNeff to file a lawsuit against an employee on any of those issues.

Zimmer expressed concern about the impact of the agreement on his rights in his stock trading model. He was told the agreement was not negotiable and that he would be terminated if he did not sign the agreement. Ultimately, Zimmer relented and signed the employment contract.

During his employment, Zimmer implemented his stock trading model, but attempted to isolate it from the company's other systems. For example, he did not install it on CooperNeff's system, instead bringing it to work with him every day on a portable hard drive.

In June 2004, Zimmer gave notice to CooperNeff of his resignation and intent to go to another hedge fund. At his exit interview, he was handed a complaint that CooperNeff filed the day after he left. The complaint sought an injunction and other remedies on six different theories: inadequacy of legal relief, breach of contract, misappropriation of trade secrets, breach of fiduciary duty, conversion, and unfair competition. On July 1, 2004, the state court granted a TRO enjoining Zimmer from disclosing or using his model.

Zimmer responded by filing a federal court action and seeking to remove the state court action. His complaint, however, was dismissed for lack of subject matter jurisdiction because Zimmer had not yet registered the copyright in his model. Zimmer did register the copyright on August 11, 2008, and then obtained a TRO in federal court ordering CooperNeff to "cease all use of Plaintiff's computer model and any copies, derivatives, modifications, or adaptations of the computer model" pending further court action. More filings occurred back and forth.

On September 20, 2004, the day before a preliminary injunction hearing, CooperNeff filed a motion to compel arbitration and stay further proceedings that the district court denied on the grounds that the arbitration agreement was procedurally and substantively unconscionable and that CooperNeff had waived its right to compel arbitration.

Although there was no final order, the Court of Appeals took jurisdiction under the Federal Arbitration Act (FAA), 9 U.S.C. Section 1 et. seq., which permits appeal from an order denying a motion to compel arbitration.[3]

As explained by the Court of Appeals, an arbitration clause may be unenforceable if it is procedurally or substantively unconscionable. *Procedural unconscionability* refers to "the process by which an agreement is reached and the form of an agreement, including the use therein of fine print and convoluted or unclear language." *Substantive unconscionability* refers to whether the arbitration provision "unreasonably favors the party asserting it."[4]

The court reversed the lower court holding that the arbitration clause was unenforceable by reason of procedural unconscionability, noting that Zimmer had a meaningful choice in accepting or rejecting the contract. He accepted the job with full knowledge that an employment agreement had not yet been reached. When he signed the agreement, he was able to question its terms, and he was free to leave CooperNeff and take other employment opportunities instead of accepting the employment contract terms.

The court also rejected the argument that the agreement was substantively unconscionable, finding that CooperNeff had plausible reasons for reserving to itself an exclusive right of access to the court for certain legal disputes.

On the waiver issue, the first question was whether that was a matter for the arbitrator or the court to decide. The court held the the issue of waiver is properly before the court where waiver is based on litigation conduct.

The second question was whether CooperNeff waived its right to compel arbitration by virtue of its litigation conduct. The primary argument against CooperNeff was the fact that it first initiated a state court action, then later moved to compel arbitration. Such conduct by CooperNeff is one of several

3. 9 U.S.C. § 16(a)(1).
4. Zimmer v. CooperNeff Advisors, Inc., 86 U.S.P.Q.2d 1254, 1258 (3d Cir. 2008).

nonexclusive factors to be considered in determining whether a waiver has occurred. The key consideration of this argument is whether the party claiming waiver was prejudiced by the other party's conduct. As the district court had not adequately considered the full scope of this issue, the decision was vacated and remanded for further proceedings.

The final result is frustrating The motion to compel arbitration was a last minute, ultimately unsuccessful effort to delay a hearing on a preliminary injunction motion. The district court's decision on the motion to compel arbitration was issued December 20, 2004. The Court of Appeals decision wasn't issued until April 14, 2008, and it doesn't dispose of the matter, but merely sends it back to the District Court for a further hearing on the motion to compel arbitration. Whatever it decides may again be appealable. In short, the employment dispute has gone on for years, and we still don't know if it will proceed as an arbitration or court hearing.

Who is benefitting from this circumstance? During this time, is Zimmer able to use his stock trading model? Does CooperNeff continue to use Zimmer's model? How has the ability to seek arbitration benefitted the parties in terms of cost and time efficiency? In this situation, is it fair to conclude that the ability to seek arbitration has primarily served as a procedural roadblock to efficient litigation? In the end, we learn that litigation over the right or obligation to arbitrate can overwhelm the goal of efficient dispute resolution.

[2] *Glazer's Distributor's of Illinois, Inc. v. NWS-Illinois LLC*

The question of waiver was also addressed by *Glazer's Distributor's of Illinois, Inc. v. NWS Illinois LLC*, decided by the Illinois Appellate Court in 2007. NWS, the owner of distribution rights to Grolsch and Goose Island Beer, entered into both a management services agreement and a conditional sales agreement with Glazer's, including an option for Glazer's to purchase certain NWS assets. The conditional sales agreement included an arbitration clause, and both agreements provided for Illinois law to be applicable.

The dispute arose when NWS entered negotiations to sell its distribution rights to Anheuser-Busch. Glazer's responded by filling suit in state court seeking declaratory judgment, injunctive relief, and compensatory damages. When its motions for a temporary restraining order and preliminary injunction failed, Glazer's amended its complaint to demand arbitration, which the trial court denied.

The appeal centered on whether Glazer's had waived its right to arbitration. First, the appellate court determined it had the right to review the denial of arbitration. Second, the appellate court evaluated whether federal or state law applied. Although both litigants were owned by out-of-state companies, the contracts provided for the application of Illinois law. In circumstances where parties to a contract have agreed to arbitrate in accordance with state law, the court concluded that the FAA does not apply, even where interstate commerce is involved.[5]

The next question was whether the state court had authority to decide the issue of waiver or whether it should have reserved the decision for an arbitration panel. Although the U.S. Supreme Court has indicated that such decisions are presumptively reserved for the arbitrator, the issue of waiver is treated differently when raised by the party opposing arbitration.[6]

Finally, the court considered the question of waiver itself. The court noted that Illinois favors resolution of disputes by arbitration and disfavors a finding that a party has waived its right to arbitrate. Nevertheless, the contractual right to arbitrate can be waived when the party's inconsistent conduct indicates that the party has abandoned that right. Here, Glazer's took many steps that were inconsistent with the right to arbitrate: (1) it filed the original complaint without mentioning arbitration, (2) it sought complete relief in state court, and (3) it sought arbitration only after it lost its initial motions for injunctive relief. According to the court, these circumstances suggest (as NWS argued) that Glazer's was engaging in impermissible forum shopping by filing a demand for arbitration after unsuccessfully seeking relief before the Circuit Court.

Accordingly, the court concluded that Glazer's waived its right to arbitrate so the Circuit Court did not abuse its discretion in reaching the same conclusion.

[3] *Good Samaritan Coffee v. LaRue Distributing Inc.*

Who should decide the questions of waiver, the arbitrator or the court? The Nebraska Supreme Court addressed this issue in *Good Samaritan Coffee v. LaRue Distributing Inc.* Good Samaritan contracted with LaRue to supply green coffee beans. The supply contract included an arbitration agreement. LaRue ended the relationship, and on December 16, 2003, Good Samaritan sued LaRue for breach of contract. Over the next few years, LaRue filed an answer and counterclaims. On January 5, 2007, LaRue moved to compel arbitration and stay trial. The trial court concluded that LaRue had waived its right to arbitrate.

The Nebraska Supreme Court agreed that the issue of waiver was best decided by the court rather than the arbitrator because the court was familiar with the proceedings in the case. Thus, sending the issue to an arbitrator would delay resolution.

---

5. Citing Yates v. Doctor's Assoc., Inc., 193 Ill.App.3d 431, 438 (1990) and Volt Info. Sciences Inc. v. Board of Trustees of Stanford University, 489 U.S. 468 (1989).
6. *See* Howsam v. Dean Witter Reynolds Inc., 537 U.S. 79 (2002).

[4] *Woods v. Patterson Law Firm*

The Illinois Appellate Court also addressed the issue of waiver in connection with actions taken by a defendant in *Woods v. Patterson Law Firm*. The Patterson Law Firm was engaged by several clients under a contract that called for AAA arbitration. When the clients sued the law firm for malpractice, the firm took initial steps in court to defend against the claim, including filing two motions to dismiss, serving interrogatories, and subpoenaing documents. Then the firm requested arbitration. The trial court denied the request, and an appeal followed.

The American Arbitration Association rules applicable to the Patterson contract purport to impose a no waiver rule. AAA Rule 48(a) states: "No judicial proceeding by a party relating to the subject matter of the arbitration shall be deemed a waiver of the party's right to arbitrate." If the litigants are parties to an arbitration agreement that calls for AAA arbitration, will the no waiver rule prevail over the waiver doctrine as applied in the cases cited above?

The Illinois Appellate Court decided that the AAA Rule does not trump traditional waiver doctrine.[7] The majority opinion recognized that Illinois courts disfavor waiver. Nevertheless, the right to compel arbitration is a created by contract and can be waived like any other contractual right. The right to arbitrate may be waived when a party's conduct is inconsistent with the arbitration clause (for example, the party submits arbitratable issues to the court for decision or engages in prejudicial delay in asserting the right to arbitrate).

While "limited legal maneuverings" in court may not be enough to effect a waiver, the Illinois court concluded that the actions of the law firm crossed the line.[8] They gave particular weight to the fact that interrogatories and subpoenas are not readily available in AAA arbitration (their use requires an agreement of the parties or the discretion of the arbitrator). The court expressed concern that the courts might be misused to gain unfair advantages:

> [I]t would provide a party with the option of obtaining or attempting to obtain discovery in the courthouse, when discovery is not a matter of right under the arbitration process, and then when the discovery process has been concluded request arbitration. Arbitration was designed as an efficient and relatively inexpensive method of settling dispute. It is an alternate dispute resolution process. If we allow a party to file or defend a court action with the intent to obtain discovery, the entire alternative dispute resolution process loses its major objective. The costs and the time parameters for the party litigants become prohibitive.

---

7. Woods v. Patterson Law Firm, 2008 WL 901160 (Mar. 31, 2008).
8. Compare Atlas v. 7101 Partnership, 109 Ill. App.3d 236 (1982) and Kostakos v. KSN Joint Venture No. 1, 142 Ill.App.3d 553 (1986).

The court uses a parade of horribles—the destruction of the ADR process, prohibitive expense, misuse of the judicial system—as a reason for denying the parties the benefit of ADR. It is an interesting argument, as recognized in a dissenting opinion. Given the stated policy of favoring arbitration as a method of settling disputes, waiver should not be lightly inferred. But according to the dissent, that is exactly what the majority was doing. The legal maneuverings were essentially the same as those found to be "limited" in prior cases rejecting waiver. "In short," dissenting Justice Wolfson states,

> the plaintiffs are trying to slip out of their contractual duty to arbitrate. We should not let it happen. I believe the trial court abused its discretion when it denied the defendants' motion to compel arbitration.
>
> The majority envisions dire consequences should the "logic of the dissent" be followed. I do not see how requiring parties to fulfill their contractual obligations would produce the calamitous scenario spun by the majority.
>
> We should hew to the line, undeterred by visions of horrific discovery tactics. Even where those tactics include (gasp!) the filing of interrogatories.[9]

[5] Best Course for a Doctrine of Waiver?

Given this collection of cases, what is the best course with respect to the doctrine of waiver? First, we should recognize that waiver is an equitable concept. How far a case is allowed to proceed in court may well depend on whether a party takes any actions suggesting it's trying to "game" the system. However, when a defendant appears in court, is it surprising that it might respond with motions to dismiss before bringing a motion to compel arbitration? Defendants operate under court-imposed deadlines, and various defenses can be lost if not raised in a motion to dismiss at the time of answering. Moreover, might it not be reasonable for a party to attempt to dispose of the case completely on a motion to dismiss and then seek arbitration if the motion fails? Might this not be the kind of limited legal maneuvering that would be acceptable? Is the analysis different when the party is a plaintiff? When is it reasonable to allow a plaintiff to take advantage of the courts before filing a motion to compel? Might it not be reasonable for a plaintiff to file for emergency relief—a TRO or preliminary injunction, for example—and then seek arbitration rather than a trial on the merits? Although emergency relief can be sought in some arbitration schemes, it is not as common or may not be as expeditious as through a court.

These questions pose both policy and tactical concerns. On the policy level, it appears we need to balance the policy favoring arbitration against a desire to prevent unfairness in the court. We favor arbitration, but find it unfair for parties to seek an advantage in court and then switch to arbitration.

9. Woods, *supra* note 6 at 15 (dissent).

As a tactical matter, litigants may desire the immediate results that may be obtained in court—dismissal or preliminary injunction—while reserving the right to proceed with arbitration on the merits.

[B] Challenges to Arbitration Provisions

Some of the litigation over arbitration focuses on the validity of arbitration clauses. This issue was faced by an Illinois Appellate Court in *Bess v. DirecTV Inc.*, a consumer dispute over a satellite television service contract.[10] The plaintiff, Charlotte Bess, brought a class action suit to attack a $5.00 late fee charged by DirecTV. The service contract included an arbitration provision that DirectTV relied upon in requesting an order to compel arbitration. Bess challenged the validity of the arbitration clause.

The court recognized that the validity of the arbitration clause was a question for it to decide. In contrast, the court noted an attack on the agreement as a whole would have been a question for the arbitrators. Next the court recognized an arbitration clause could be attacked if it was unconscionable, and that unconscionability could be found on either procedural or substantive grounds. Bess argued the clause was procedurally unconscionable because she wasn't presented with the agreement until after the transaction was completed, giving her no meaningful choice regarding acceptance of the terms. The court's majority rejected this position, finding that Bess could have cancelled the service without penalty when she received the agreement. As she did not, the terms were accepted, and therefore the agreement wasn't procedurally unconscionable.

Bess also argued the agreement was substantively unconscionable because the cost of bringing a class action in arbitration would be prohibitive. The court ruled that to prove this point, Bess would have to present individualized evidence to show that she was financially incapable of meeting the cost of arbitration. The majority found she had failed to do so and therefore had failed to prove that the arbitration clause was substantively unconscionable.

However, one judge dissented:

> In this case, it is undisputed that DirecTV did not mail Bess a copy of the customer agreement containing the arbitration provision until after she had already acquired the satellite television equipment and after she had contracted to receive DirecTV service. Therefore, Bess did not see, and could not have seen, the arbitration provision before entering into the contract with DirecTV . . . . [W]hatever other context there might be in which a contractual provision would be found to be procedurally unconscionable, that label must apply to a

10. Bess v. DirecTV, Inc., 2008 WL 740344 (Ill. App. Ct. Mar. 18, 2008).

situation such as the case at bar, where Bess did not see and could not have seen the arbitration provision before entering into the contract.[11]

The Bess decision illustrates the principle of unconscionability as applied to arbitration clauses. The issue is more likely to arise with consumer and employment contracts than with business contracts. Nevertheless, attacks on the validity of arbitration contracts generate litigation in the courts that can derail the benefits of arbitration. Therefore, unconscionability is a question to raise during the drafting stage. Counsel should query whether there is anything about the arbitration provision, procedurally or substantively, that could give rise to a future challenge. If so, counsel should decide if anything can be done at the drafting stage to avoid that problem.

[C] Challenges to Arbitral Awards

The Federal Arbitration Act provides only narrow grounds for vacating, modifying, or correcting an arbitral award. The policy behind this is to encourage arbitration as an efficient, inexpensive alternative to litigation for parties who contractually choose to arbitrate. By limiting the grounds for challenge, the FAA seeks to limit the scope of litigation over arbitral awards.

Section 10(a) of the FAA specifies the statutory grounds on which a court may vacate an arbitrator's award:

1. Where the award was procured by corruption, fraud, or undue means.
2. Where there was evident partiality or corruption in the arbitrators, or either of them.
3. Where the arbitrators were guilty of misconduct in refusing to postpone the hearing, upon sufficient cause shown, or in refusing to hear evidence pertinent and material to the controversy, or of any other misbehavior by which the rights of any party have been prejudiced.
4. Where the arbitrators exceeded their powers, or so imperfectly executed them that a mutual, final, and definite award upon the subject matter submitted was not made.
5. Where an award is vacated and the time within which the agreement required the award to be made has not expired the court may, in its discretion, direct a rehearing by the arbitrators.

But what if the parties agree to supplement the basis for challenge, adding additional grounds? This issue was recently addressed by the U.S. Supreme Court in *Hall Street Associates LLC v. Mattel Inc.*[12]

---

11. *Id. supra* note at 9
12. Hall Street Associates LLC v. Mattel Inc., 2008 WL 762537 (2008).

[1] *Hall Street Associates LLC v. Mattel Inc.*

Hall Street Associates LLC was a real estate lessor, and Mattel was its lessee. The leased property was used for many years as a manufacturing site with the leases providing that the tenant would indemnify the landlord for any costs resulting from the tenant's failure to follow environmental laws. A dispute over the property landed the parties in federal court. During the litigation, the parties agreed to arbitrate certain issues with de novo judicial review of the arbitrator's legal rulings. The arbitration agreement stated:

> The United States District Court for the District of Oregon may enter judgment upon any award, wither by confirming the award or by vacating, modifying or correcting the award. The Court shall vacate, modify or correct any award: (i) where the arbitrator's finds of facts are not supported by substantial evidence, or (ii) where the arbitrator's conclusions of law are erroneous.

Hall Street lost before the arbitrator, but prevailed in the de novo judicial review by the trial court. The Ninth Circuit reversed, and the case went to the U.S. Supreme Court to resolve a split in the circuits. Several circuits had allowed parties to an arbitration agreement to agree to supplement the FAA with additional nonstatutory grounds for vacating arbitration awards. The Ninth and Tenth Circuits, however, held that parties were limited by the grounds stated in the FAA.

Hall Street's argument to the Court was that the FAA allowed flexibility, consistent with goals of the statute and the interests of judicial economy. The flexibility to challenge legally erroneous rulings promotes arbitration as an option for parties who might otherwise avoid the process. Mattel's response was that the FAA grounds are the limits for challenging an arbitral award, and that allowing parties to agree to grounds outside the FAA would undermine the FAA's purpose and goals. Mattel further argued that the court's role should be limited to enforcing the FAA and the arbitral award; accordingly, it should not review the merits of the arbitrator's decision.

Justice Souter issued the decision for the court. Justice Souter noted that the Court's prior decision in *Wilko v. Swan*, 346 U.S. 427 (1953) included language that some courts had used as a basis beyond the FAA to vacate arbitral awards. *Wilko* stated: "Interpretations of the law by the arbitrators in contrast to manifest disregard of the law are not subject, in the federal courts, to judicial review for error in interpretation."

This wording informs us that federal courts will not review for errors in interpretation. However, some have gone further in their analysis to conclude the language means that federal courts may review for "manifest disregard of the law," a basis for review that goes beyond the FAA. If the courts may go beyond the terms of the FAA, Hall Street argued that contracting parties such as Hall Street and Mattel should be able to go beyond those terms as well and contract a judicial review of legal error. However, Souter rejects this position, inviting attention to the entire statement quoted from Wilko, which specifically states that interpretations of law by arbitrators are not subject to judicial review for error. Wilko, therefore, does not provide the support Hall Street seeks.

Hall Street next sought support from *Dean Witter Reynolds Inc. v. Byrd*, 470 U.S. 213 (1985), which states the FAA is "motivated, first and foremost, by a congressional desire to enforce agreements into which parties have entered." Therefore, Hall Street argues, the court should uphold the parties' agreement for review beyond the scope of the FAA. Again, Souter concludes this argument goes too far. Indeed, parties have leeway within the FAA to fashion the terms of arbitration agreements on various elements: "including the way arbitrators are chosen, what their qualifications should be, which issues are arbitrable, along with procedure and choice of substantive law." It does not follow, however, that the parties can agree to override that specific language of the FAA.

Souter concludes that the text of the FAA compels the conclusion that the grounds for review stated in the Act are exclusive. After all, the Act states the court "must grant unless" one of the prescribed defects is found. This is not language giving latitude to the parties for supplementation. Moreover, this strict reading of the text conforms to sound public policy:

> Instead of fighting the test, it makes more sense to see the three provisions, Sections 9–11, as substantiating a national policy favoring arbitration with just the limited review needed to maintain arbitration's essential virtue of resolving disputes straightaway.
>
> Any other reading opens the door to the full-bore legal and evidentiary appeals that can "render informal arbitration merely a prelude to a more cumbersome and time-consuming judicial review process," and bring arbitration theory to grief in post-arbitration process.

While limiting freedom of action under the FAA, Souter points out that not all doors are closed to parties such as Hall Street who seek expanded review. One option suggested in the decision is for a party to proceed with arbitration under state or common law to which the FAA limits would not apply. Another option is to turn to the District Court's inherent authority to manage cases under the Federal Rules. Why would it not be possible for the parties and the court to agree on arbitration with judicial review under Rule 16 of the Federal Rules of Civil Procedures?

Competing camps still clash on the issue of judicial review of arbitral awards. Two strong federal principles apply: (1) contractual arbitration agreements should be enforced as written; and (2) private parties should be encouraged to arbitrate disputes.[13] Does *Hall Street* undermine these policies?

---

13. Marica Coyle, *Justices Take Critical Look at Arbitration*, 30 Nat'l L. J. (Oct. 29, 2007).

Should these policies be controlling? Eric P. Tuckman, general counsel for the American Arbitration Association, indicates that party autonomy is to be honored within the arbitration process itself, but should end when the matter gets to court. Two additional principles are also important: finality and predictability. According to Tuckman, the path advocated by Hall Street on appeal was "an incompatible hybrid between arbitration and litigation."[14]

For some, the result of *Hall Street* is sound policy. Litigators naturally push for arbitration to become more like litigation, believing that it is their duty to bring all of the tools of litigation to bear on arbitration, including discovery, motion practice, and judicial review. Arbitrators seem to have little incentive to go against the desires of the parties, seeking instead to honor party autonomy and encourage additional appointments. They may be intrigued by the greater complexity of the case when it becomes a surrogate for more difficult and interesting litigation. If paid by the hour rather than by the appointment, some may have financial incentives to expand arbitration in these ways. In short, we can find overall pressures for counsel and arbitrators to embrace the expansion of arbitration. Clients in the heat of battle will often agree, although on reflection they may lament the greater cost and delay accompanying that expansion. Courts, too, have a natural inclination to evaluate arbitrations for legal error, for that is what courts do. Thus ultimately, the path urged by Hall Street seemed destined to reduce the benefits of arbitration as a cost-effective, time-efficient tool for resolving disputes. The *Hall Street* decision seems to be a positive in that it limits the role of the court in the arbitration process and holds back the pressure to expand arbitration into litigation.

[2] *Edstrom Indus. v. Companion Life Ins. Co.*

While the Hall Street question was pending before the Supreme Court, the Seventh Circuit Court of Appeals faced a related issue in *Edstrom Indus. v. Companion Life Ins. Co.*, decided little more than a month before *Hall Street.*[15] The Edstrom court explained: "The question in our case is different. It is whether the arbitrator can be directed to apply specific substantive norms and held to the application."

The underlying dispute involved the application of a "stop loss" insurance policy provision controlled by Wisconsin law. When entering into the policy, the insured falsely stated that it had no beneficiaries whose policy payments would exceed $32,500, when in fact a baby covered as a dependent of an employee had severe medical problems that reached a cost care of $890,000. When Companion learned about the dependent baby, it increased the

14. *Id.* at 9.
15. Edstrom Indus. v. Companion Life Ins. Co., 2008 WL 351450 (7th Cir. 2008).

deductible under the policy retroactively from $65,000 to $450,000, and arbitration followed.

The arbitration agreement under the policy stated that the arbitrator must "strictly apply" the law. Wisconsin law provided that insurance companies could not avoid policy obligations based on inaccurate representations unless the insured "knew or should have known that the representation was false."

The arbitrator ignored the statute and ruled in Companion's favor, stating that Companion had a "complete and unfettered right" to revise its policy. Edstrom attacked the award in court, arguing the arbitrator failed to strictly apply Wisconsin law by ignoring the relevant statute.

On appeal, Companion argued that the arbitration decision should be upheld. It should not matter if the arbitrator correctly or incorrectly applied the Wisconsin statute as according to Companion, all that was required was that the court be able to imagine an interpretive path connecting the statute to the arbitrator's decision.

Judge Richard A. Posner wrote the decision for the court, stating:

> And it is true that errors of law committed by arbitrators are not grounds for setting aside an arbitral award. That would transform the judicial role in arbitration into appellate review of the award. The parties' effort to shift the resolution of their dispute from the court system, by agreeing to arbitration, would be thwarted.
>
> But precisely because arbitration is a creature of contract, the arbitrator cannot disregard the lawful directions the parties have given them. If they tell him to apply Wisconsin law, he cannot apply New York law.
>
> When parties agree to arbitrate their disputes they opt out of the court system, and when one of them challenges the resulting arbitration award he perforce does so not on the ground that the arbitrators made a mistake but that they violated the agreement to arbitrate, as by corruption, evident partiality, exceeding their powers, etc.—conduct to which the parties did not consent when they included an arbitration clause in their contract. (quoting *Wise v. Wachovia Securities LLC*, 450 F.3d 265, 269 (7th Cir. 2006)).
>
> The arbitration clause in this case told the arbitrator to apply Wisconsin law "strictly."
>
> This unusual stipulation, like other exact directive language in arbitration clauses, limited the extent to which the arbitrator could indulge his fancy, here in interpreting Wisconsin insurance law.

For these reasons, the court remanded the case to the arbitrator to determine if Edstrom knew or should have known about the sick baby when it applied for coverage.

[3] How Are the Cases Reconciled?

How are *Edstrom* and *Hall Street* reconciled? One way is via the distinction between directions to the court and directions to the arbitrator. In *Hall Street*, the directions given by the agreement directed the court to do something that was beyond the scope of the FAA. That does not occur in *Edstrom*, where instead the direction is given regarding the conduct of the arbitrator. The court review is the limited to the determination whether the arbitrator followed its direction, not whether there is an error of law.

However, is that a level of review within the scope of the FAA? What does *Edstrom* say to that question? Is that interpretation sound? When *Edstrom* is reviewed, the court appears to be reviewing the case for an error of law. But on closer reading, the error it notes was made by the district court, not the arbitrator. Rather, it appears that the arbitrator is told to follow his instructions, to apply Wisconsin law strictly, and to not ignore the Wisconsin statute. Could Hall Street's goal of judicial review be achieved in a similar manner? Could the parties get around *Hall Street* by simply stating in the arbitration agreement that the arbitrator must "strictly" apply the law, then appeal to the court when they conclude the arbitrator has not, asking the district court to interpret the law to determine if it was strictly applied, and if finding it was not, vacating the arbitration decision? Would that not achieve the same purpose sought by Hall Street? And would it run afoul of the *Hall Street* decision?

If we conclude that *Hall Street* and *Edstrom* are in conflict regarding the allowed scope of appeal, are the cases reconcilable on the grounds that *Hall Street* applies the FAA and *Edstrom* applies the Wisconsin arbitration statute? Does anything turn on this difference? Can parties trying to avoid *Hall Street* rely on the Supreme Court's suggestion—"The FAA is not the only way into court for parties wanting review of arbitration awards: they may contemplate enforcement under the state statutory or common law, for example, where judicial review of different scope is arguable"—and take the *Edstrom* path to expanded judicial review?

These questions show that much room and uncertainty remains for litigation over the scope of judicial review available for arbitral decisions.

[D] Who May Invoke Arbitration?

Who may invoke arbitration? Clearly, the actual parties to an arbitration agreement may invoke the clause if there has been no waiver. Questions exist, however, regarding the standing of other affected parties to invoke an arbitration agreement, as shown in a 2008 decision of first impression by the Illinois Appellate Court, *Equistar Chemicals LP v. Hartford Steam Boiler Inspection and Ins. Company of Connecticut.*[16]

16. Equistar Chemicals LP v. Hartford Steam Boiler Inspection and Ins. Co. of Conn., 2008 WL 613132 (Ill. App. 4th Dist. 2008).

Equistar Chemicals and Trigen Cinergy Solutions were parties to an agreement containing an arbitration clause. After Trigen incurred damage to a turbine generator at an ethanol plant, Hartford, Trigen's insurance company, paid Trigen $950,000. Hartford then sought arbitration to seek recovery from Equistar for the damage relying on an arbitration clause in the agreement between Trigen and Equistar. Equistar's request for a stay of arbitration was denied by the court and an appeal followed.

Equistar argued a party cannot be compelled to arbitrate until it has agreed to submit to arbitration. In this instance, the only parties that had agreed to arbitrate were Trigen and Equistar. This was fitting, as the parties had a long-standing contractual relationship, interacted on a daily basis, and were familiar with each other's resources. Equistar argued that it had not agreed to arbitrate with Hartford and should not be compelled to do so.

The Court recognized that "the right to compel arbitration typically stems from contract and generally may not be invoked by a nonsignatory to the contract." Nevertheless, the law recognizes a number of circumstances where nonsignatories may be bound by a contract, including incorporation by reference, assumption, agency, veil-piercing or alter ego, estoppel, and third-party beneficiary status. Given that nonsignatories may be bound by contract, it seems to follow that nonsignatories may also claim the benefit of an arbitration clause under appropriate circumstances.

This presented a question of first impression for the Illinois court. A California court had previously concluded that insurer-subrogee status was not an exception to the general rule preventing nonsignatories from invoking an arbitration agreement. In contrast, a New York court had ruled that a nonsignatory insurer-subrogee was bound to an arbitration clause that bound its insured. Thus, if the insured was bound to arbitration, its insurer could similarly be bound to arbitration.

The Illinois court was sympathetic to the New York decision. A party who asserts the right of subrogation must step into the shoes of the one whose claim it has paid and can only enforce the rights that party could enforce. The court applied this to Hartford, stating: "If Trigen would have been required to arbitrate the negligence action against Equistar, then Hartford should be similarly bound. Distinguishing between whether Hartford has a 'right' or an 'obligation' to arbitrate is merely a matter of semantics where Hartford is required to arbitrate."[17]

Given that Hartford's subrogee status gave it standing to invoke the arbitration clause, the trial court did not err in denying Equistar's motion to stay arbitration.

---

17. *Id.*

Public Policy and Patent Validity

Parties' freedom to arbitrate has sometimes been denied by the courts. Prior to 1982, mediation was not available for patent disputes because it was held that the courts had exclusive jurisdiction over them. The courts also recognized a strong public policy in determining the validity of patents. Thus, private agreements regarding the validity of a patent were deemed to be unenforceable. Moreover, even private arbitration was deemed to violate public policy and was unenforceable. This changed in 1982 when the Patent Act was amended to recognize the right of parties to final and private resolution of patent disputes. As a result, questions of patent validity can be referred to arbitration for full and binding disposition with awards that are enforceable under the FAA.[1]

1. *See* Charles Lickson, *The Use of Alternative Dispute Resolution in Intellectual Property, Technology-Related or Innovation-Based Disputes,* 55 AM. JUR. TRIALS 483 (2007)

7.02 Litigation Involving Mediation

Litigation involving mediation is infrequent because the process is usually nonbinding. If mediation succeeds, the parties enter into a private agreement; if it fails, the parties go on with the battle. Sometimes, however, mediation succeeds, and yet the parties continue with the battle. Such was the case in the high-profile dispute among board members over relocation of the Terra Museum of American Art in Chicago, home of a significant art collection amassed by Daniel J. Terra, including Samuel F. B. Morse's *Gallery of the Louvre.* A report in *Art in America* summarized the dispute.

[A] Terra Museum Dispute

In September [2001], board members Ronald Gidwitz, chairman of the foundation's strategic planning committee, and Dean Buntrock, another committee member, filed a suit against the . . . the Terra Foundation for the Arts—which also oversees the American Museum in Giverny, France—to prevent it from moving the museum out of Chicago. Although no such decision was ever made at a committee level, [foundation chairman Paul Hayes] Tucker told A.i.A. that the board unanimously agreed that the current facility is inadequate. The defendants claim that the suit is attempting to interfere with the foundation's ability to govern itself. The plaintiffs allege financial waste and mismanagement in a conscious effort to cause the museum to fail, thereby justifying a move. They also assert that Judith Terra wants to take the museum to Washington D.C.,

> where she lives, to improve her social status, an allegation that Tucker calls preposterous. The Illinois attorney general's office has sided with Gidwitz and Buntrock, which Tucker says, could have serious implications for all foundations. The parties have agreed to non-binding mediation.[18]

The dispute attracted attention due to in part to its prominent participants—including a former senator, the former French ambassador to the United States, the former U.S. ambassador to France, the wife of the mayor of Chicago and two former corporate CEOs—and to its international scope reaching from Chicago through Washington DC to Paris and Giverney, France.

The case was filed in the Circuit Court of Cook County, Illinois, on September 22, 2000. The attorney general of Illinois moved to intervene on September 25, 2000. James Terra, heir and executor of Terra's estate, was also permitted to intervene as a plaintiff. On February 5, 2001, Judge Dorothy Kirie Kinnaird appointed my law partner, David Hilliard, as mediator. Mediation sessions occurred from February through June, 2001. In May 2001, the media reported that a tentative settlement had been reached. However, litigation over the mediated settlement began soon after.[19]

On June 8, 2001, Judge Kinnaird enjoined the individual defendants from holding a meeting of the Terra Board outside the mediation process. Then on June 29, 2001, the individual defendants filed suit in federal court to prevent a vote by the Board on the mediated settlement, but the motion was denied that night at 10:00 pm.[20] The Seventh Circuit dismissed the appeal on August 29, 2001.

The final mediated settlement agreement was approved on June 29, 2001 by the Board by a vote of six to two, with three members absent. Judge Kinnaird issued an order implementing the agreement on July 26, 2001.

Three of the defendants—Judith Terra, second wife of Daniel Terra; Paul Tucker, Chairman of the Foundation; and Senator Alan Simpson—filed suit against the Terra Foundation seeking to overthrow the July 26, 2001 order on the grounds that it was a "naked seizure." On May 28, 2004, the Appellate Court of Illinois affirmed the July 26, 2001 order.[21] On October 6, 2004, the Illinois Supreme Court denied the defendants' Petition for Leave to Appeal.

The Terra case illustrates circumstances in which a mediated settlement can result in continued litigation. It was a multiparty dispute in which the mediated settlement was approved by a board over the objection of several board members.

---

18. Stephanie Cash, *Battle in Chicago over Terra's Plan to Move*, Art in Amer. (Apr. 2001).
19. David C. Hilliard, *The Art of Mediation: The Terra Museum War*, presentation to the Chicago Bar Association Creative Arts Committee.
20. 151 F.Supp.2d 931.
21. Buntrock v. Terra, 348 Ill.App.3d 875 (2004).

The Appellate Court's decision is instructive on dealing with a challenge to a mediated settlement. Excerpts follow (with omissions not noted in the quoted text):

> On appeal, the defendant Directors contend that the trial court improperly approved the settlement without an independent inquiry into whether or not the settlement was fair, adequate, reasonable and in the best interests of The Foundation, whether or not plaintiffs were likely to succeed on the merits, and whether there were conflicts of interests as a result of the intervention of the Attorney General.
>
> On February 5, 2001, at the suggestion of the three defendant Directors, the trial court ordered the parties to pursue mediation, appointed a mediator from among the candidates proposed by the defendant Directors, and stayed the proceedings.
>
> After more than four months of mediation, the foundation and the Attorney General reached a tentative agreement to settle the case.
>
> On June 29, 2001, eight of the board's 11 members, including two of the three defendant directors, attended a board meeting, either in person or by telephone. The conversation was recorded and transcribed. Following a lengthy discussion of the terms of the settlement, the board voted six-to-two in favor of the resolution that the foundation enter into the settlement. Defendant directors Judith Terra and Dr. Tucker voted against the resolution. Defendant Simpson did not participate in the meeting, either in person or by telephone.
>
> On July 24, 2001, a hearing commenced on the Foundation's motion for approval of the settlement. The trial court approved the settlement with one minor change regarding what the parties agreed to say about the settlement. The court specifically found that the settlement was a "just and appropriate conclusion" to the litigation; that it did not place significant restrictions on the Foundation's ability "to conduct its mission of providing education and art throughout the world"; and that the "very, very contested and * * * tortuous history" of the litigation, in which "there has been a contest [on] virtually every issue that has been raised," the Board, which the court described [as] not having been "functional * * * for almost a year now * * * will be able to make decisions * * * [a]nd the business of art will be able to go ahead, as opposed to the business of litigation."
>
> The defendant Directors contend that the trial court improperly approved the settlement of a derivative action without an independent inquiry into whether or not the settlement was fair, adequate, reasonable and in the best interests of the corporation, whether or not plaintiff's were likely to succeed on the merits, and whether there were conflicts of interests as a result of the intervention of the Attorney General.
>
> An appellate court will not review a consent order because an order entered by consent is no more than a court's recording of an agreement reached by the parties in settlement of a dispute and is not a judicial determination of their rights. An order cannot be reviewed on appeal unless the trial court was required to make a judicial determination.

> The defendant Directors complained to the trial court that they believed the two directors changed their votes on the settlement due to coercion on the part of the Attorney General. The record shows that the trial court listened to audio tapes of the Board meeting wherein the settlement was voted on, reviewed the transcript of the tape of the meeting, and found that the decision of two Board members in favor of the settlement was not the product of coercion. The trial court concluded that there was no disqualifying conflict because there was no proof that the two Directors had actually changed their declared positions as a result of the acknowledged personal pressures.
>
> There is strong policy in favor of settlement in order to avoid costly and time-consuming litigation.
>
> In order to show a conflict of interest in the settlement and entry of the consent order, the defendant Directors must make a *prima facie* case showing of interest by the directors that conflicts with the interests of the Foundation. The defendant Directors did not establish that Directors Stebbins and Marshall were "interested" in the settlement, or were directly or indirectly a party to the settlement as required in order to establish a conflict of interest.
>
> The defendant Directors further contend that the trial court's approval of the settlement was an abuse of discretion because the plaintiffs were "highly unlikely" to prevail on their claims concerning the permissible use of the Foundation's assets.
>
> Here, the materials submitted to the trial court demonstrated the existence of a *bona fide* claim that the Foundation's key charitable purpose was the operation of a museum of American art in the Chicago metropolitan area. As such, the defendant Directors have not shown that they would have prevailed on their claims disputing the intent of the donor of the Foundation.
>
> Because plaintiffs' claims are not derivative lawsuits, no judicial determination was required or made in this case relating to the "adequacy" or "fairness" of the settlement. The settlement reflected the Board's exercise of its inherent rights to amend the by-laws of the Foundation and to govern the Foundations' affairs. The trial court did not abuse its discretion in approving the settlement of litigation without an independent inquiry.[22]

The lesson of this case is that even a mediated settlement can result in further litigation if there are dissatisfied parties. However, litigation is not likely to change the result, as a consent order resulting from a mediation or settlement is not normally subject to review. Other efforts based on fraud or coercion may be possible, but will be difficult to establish in a well-managed mediation.

In Terra, the dispute arose surrounding the enforcement of a detailed settlement agreement. Disputes over enforcement of a mediated settlement can arise from confusion or misunderstanding about the terms of settlement.

---

22. *Id.*

[B] NTP and RIM Dispute

The patent litigation between NTP, Inc. and Research in Motion (RIM) over Blackberry technology yielded a reported settlement in early 2005.[23] Press releases stated that the parties had signed a "binding term sheet" that settled all litigation between them that was to be followed by definitive licensing and settlement agreements. For reasons kept under seal, the parties reached an impasse on the agreements and the Court ruled in favor of NTP that the term sheet had not created a valid and enforceable settlement agreement. The litigation continued. Ultimately, the parties announced a settlement in which RIM paid $612.5 million.

The dispute between RIM and NTP over the initial "binding term sheet" illustrates an area of particular concern for counsel in mediations: enforcement of the settlement terms in the face of subsequent disagreement. Another example of a dispute involving settlement is *Olam v. Congress Mortgage Co.*[24] The parties signed a memorandum of understanding following a day-long mediation. Later, the plaintiff failed to sign a more detailed, formal settlement agreement, and the defendants filed a motion to enforce the settlement. The court compelled testimony of the mediator regarding the terms of settlement.

[C] Term Sheet Tips

To avoid disputes of this type, seasoned mediators will call upon the advocates to prepare a statement of settlement terms before concluding the final mediation session. Roderick M. Thompson, an experienced litigator, arbitrator, and mediator from San Francisco, provides these tips for a term sheet used to conclude a mediation:[25]

- Ensure that the term sheet is an enforceable agreement. The term sheet should specifically state that the parties intend that it be binding and enforceable and reflect their mutual agreement to enter a final settlement. Have the parties sign the term sheet as well as counsel.
- Provide for expedited resolution of disputes involving the final terms. If there are disputes over the draft of a "definitive agreement," it is useful to have the dispute decided by the mediator rather than engaging in litigation with the court over enforcement. The term sheet could also provide for expedited arbitration with respect to disputes over the terms.

---

23. *See* Roderick M. Thompson, *Some Magic Words to Use in a Term Sheet Signed During Mediation*, IP Litigator 43 (May–June 2006).
24. Olam v. Congress Mortgage Co., 68 F. Supp. 2d 1110 (N.D.Cal. 1999).
25. Thompson, *supra* note 22.

- Make sure that the term sheet is admissible. The results of mediation may be inadmissible in subsequent court proceedings. An exception usually exists for the settlement agreement, but it is important to ensure that the term sheet qualifies. Therefore, a term sheet should include an express statement that the parties agree that it will be admissible in any proceedings for the purpose of enforcing or interpreting a settlement.

[D] Confidentiality

One of the hallmarks of ADR is confidentiality. This is often cited as a benefit, although as we have noted, it is not always a feature in practice. Some have called "complete confidentiality" an illusion.[26] The issue of confidentiality has resulted in a number of court decisions showing a trend to preserving confidentiality subject to some limitations:

Cincinnati Gas and Elec. Co. v. General Elec. Co.[27] The court ruled that the press and public have no constitutional right to access the records of a court-annexed summary jury trial.

Olam v. Congress Mortgage Co.[28] The court ruled that a mediator could be compelled to testify on the final terms of settlement where the parties waived their right under state law to mediation confidentiality.

Foxgate Homeowner's Ass'n v. Bramalea California, Inc.[29] The court ruled that statutory confidentiality prevented a mediator from reporting to the court on misconduct of a participant during the mediation.

In re Grand Jury Subpoena[30] The court held that mediation records were not immune from a grand jury subpoena when the information was relevant to a criminal proceeding.

Understanding ADR as a core competency for lawyers includes an understanding of the litigated disputes arising from ADR. The goal of inexpensive, efficient dispute resolution can be undermined by court litigation arising from the ADR. Such litigation is particularly frustrating as it is largely a sideshow that doesn't involve the merits of the dispute, but instead invokes the very procedures the parties intended to spare themselves by foregoing courtroom adjudication. To help avoid these pitfalls, attorneys should pay attention to the legal trends relating to ADR litigation when drafting agreements and or prosecuting ADR proceedings.

---

26. Roderick M. Thompson, *The Illusion of Complete Confidentiality in Mediation*, IP LITIGATOR (Nov.–Dec. 2001).
27. Cincinnati Gas and Elec. Co. v. General Elec. Co., 854 F.2d 900 (6th Cir. 1988).
28. Olam v. Congress Mortgage Co., 68 F. Supp. 2d 1110 (N.D.Cal. 1999).
29. Foxgate Homeowner's Ass'n v. Bramalea California, Inc., 26 Cal. 4th 1 (2001).
30. In re Grand Jury Subpoena, 148 F.3d 47 (5th Cir. 1998).

CHAPTER

8

Strategy and Advocacy

Much that can be and has been said about effective trial advocacy also applies to ADR and need not be repeated here. Arbitration and mediation, however, present special opportunities and challenges for strategy and advocacy that differ from traditional litigation.

8.01 Contractual Provisions

In arbitration, unique considerations arise from the contractual clauses that bring a matter to arbitration in the first instance. This is the first opportunity for arbitration strategy and advocacy, yet it is often ignored.

Many drafters of contracts are unfamiliar with the arbitration options and strategies and merely repeat boilerplate provisions giving little thought to the client's goals. However, careful consideration of these drafting issues can have a significant effect on the client's position in a future dispute over the contract.

Some of the key strategic concerns when drafting an arbitration clause include:

- *Language.* Are the words carefully selected to avoid confusion at bullthe time of dispute? Do you want ambiguities or loopholes that may allow you to avoid arbitration in certain circumstances? Has the language addressed all of the strategic considerations in a manner best suited to your client? A poorly drafted arbitration clause can result in litigation over its enforceability. In the *CooperNeff* case discussed in Chapter 7, the language of the clause was challenged as being "substantively unconscionable" because it reserved for the employer an exclusive right of access to the courts. Although not ultimately a basis for rejecting the arbitration clause, it contributed to a lengthy delay while litigation proceeded on a motion to compel arbitration.
- *Location.* One of the options to consider at the drafting stage is the location of any future arbitration. This may be more of a factor in international disputes than domestic ones, yet the choice of location can have important implications on the cost of the arbitration, compliance with discovery demands, final enforcement of the judgment, etc.
- *Choice of law.* This can also affect the outcome of a conflict if the law relating to the merits of the dispute or to the enforcement of the award vary by legal jurisdiction.
- *Selection of the neutral(s).* You have the ability to identify the desired background of the neutral. Should the neutrals be selected by the parties or by the arbitration institution? Do you want particular industry or legal expertise? Do you want one neutral or a panel of three? What type of ADR experience do you seek? Should you look for a neutral with judicial experience or with ADR experience? What are the differences and implications of that choice?
- *Rules.* You should give careful consideration to the rules that will govern the arbitration. Many institutions such as American Arbitration Association, International Chamber of Commerce, and World Intellectual Property Organization have existing rules that can be reviewed beforehand. Rules selection can affect your client's interests.
- *Process.* It is possible to stage the use of ADR for the dispute. Do you wish to require the parties to first attempt to negotiate a private settlement, followed by use of mediation and ultimately arbitration?

8.02 Case Management

Effective case management can also be critical for obtaining desired outcomes in arbitration. Carmen Casado, a case manager at the International Centre for Dispute Resolution, provides some useful tips applicable to practitioners in all forms of arbitration.[1]

1. Know arbitration terminology
2. Avoid dilatory tactics
3. Maintain good rapport with the case manager
4. Learn about the arbitral institution's rules and services
5. Ensure that the neutral's qualifications fit the case
6. Use stipulations to fast-forward your case
7. Act in a timely manner

8.03 Initiating Mediation

Mediation can come about in four basic ways: (1) by contract, (2) ad hoc, (3) as part of a larger ADR process, or (4) via court-annexed mediation. Each presents strategic considerations.

[A] Mediation by Contract

It is increasingly common for parties to include mediation clauses as part of licensing agreements and other business contracts. Mediation may be a first or second step in a broader dispute resolution clause ending with arbitration. Alternatively, some businesses are limiting the dispute resolution clause to mediation without addressing other options in recognition of the effectiveness of the mediation process.

For example, Phillip Armstrong at Georgia-Pacific says his company's practice has changed with increased experience. In the early period of Georgia-Pacific's ADR program, the company used dispute resolution clauses that all included arbitration. With time, Georgia-Pacific shifted to a clause that ends with mediation. "With some exceptions, the company's current view is that if it cannot reach a settlement with an adversary using the steps provided in the ADR clause, it prefers to keep its options open."[2] Thus, Georgia-Pacific has crafted a practice that retains the option of going to court or to arbitration if agreed to by the parties.

---

1. Carmen Casado, *10 Tips for Beginning Practitioners from an ICDR Case Manager*, DISPUTE RESOLUTION J., (Feb.–Apr. 2007).
2. Phillip M. Armstrong, *Georgia-Pacific's ADR Program: A Critical Review after 10 Years*, DISPUTE RESOLUTION J. (May–July 2005).

Other companies prefer to omit mediation from the dispute resolution clauses of its agreements. Rio Tinto Alcan, for example, is reluctant to include mediation as a mandatory first step. According to Rio Tinto's in-house counsel, Michael Stanek, mediation could require the company to disclose strategy, thus providing an advantage to the opposing party's litigation counsel if mediation does not resolve the dispute. It is not about hiding information, he says, which will come out eventually in any event, but it is a concern about revealing strategy. Echoing Georgia-Pacific, Rio Tinto prefers to keep its options open as well, but in a different way. Rather than mandating mediation by contract, Rio Tinto favors a clause requiring senior management to negotiate as such negotiations are typically independent of evidence or litigation strategy. Mediation remains an ad hoc option if appropriate.[3]

[B] Ad Hoc Mediation

Ad hoc mediation, or mediation by party agreement, is an option in most disputes. The challenge is how to trigger the agreement without appearing weak. Parties and counsel frequently express concern that raising settlement will signal weakness about the client's willingness to invest in trial or the client's concerns about the merits of its position.

Generally, experienced counsel can introduce the possibility of settlement or mediation in a way that does not reflect weakness. One might say to the opposing counsel, "My client has suggested this, but I wonder if this might not be a case that would benefit from mediation. What do you think?" Another approach is to blame the discussion on the court: "We're confident about our case and ready to proceed, but the judge will ask if we've considered settlement. What do you think about mediation?"

Another way to trigger ad hoc mediation is through reliance on a company policy. Several organizations have encouraged companies and counsel to make a pledge to use ADR. The International Trademark Association has encouraged brand owners to sign the following pledge:

> We recognize that for many trademark disputes there is a less expensive, more effective method of resolution than the traditional lawsuit or Trademark Office proceedings. Alternative Dispute Resolution (ADR) procedures involve collaborative techniques, which can often spare businesses the high costs of litigation.
>
> In recognition of this, we subscribe to the following statements of principle on behalf of this company and its subsidiaries worldwide:
>
> In the event of a non-urgent, non-counterfeiting trademark dispute between our company and another company which has made or will then make a similar statement, we are prepared to explore with that other party resolution of the

3. Panel Discussion, ICDR North American Dispute Resolution Series, Chicago, Illinois, April 25, 2008.

> dispute through negotiation or ADR techniques. If either party believes that the dispute is not suitable for ADR techniques, or if such techniques do not produce results satisfactory to the disputants, either party may proceed with litigation or other proceedings as the case may be.We agree that our name and address will be published on the INTA website to enable third parties to identify us as a signor of this pledge.[4]

The companies who have signed this pledge include the owners of many famous brands, including Intel, IKEA, Harley-Davidson, Kodak, and Home Depot. Other organizations both public and private have made similar pledges for their members (e.g., CPR and the United Kingdom).[5] When they are signatories to a pledge of this type, parties can rely on it as a basis for suggesting ADR to the opposing party in a dispute.

[C] Mediation Annexed to Other Forms of ADR

Mediation can also be triggered in the context of arbitration or other type of mediation. When arbitration is mandated by a contractual agreement, the case manager of the arbitration institution may suggest mediation as an option, or the parties my raise it independently. The AAA Commercial Arbitration Rules, for example, suggest mediation as a possible step in the process. Rule 8 of those rules states:

> At any stage of the proceedings, the parties may agree to conduct a mediation conference under the Commercial Mediation Procedures in order to facilitate settlement. The mediator shall not be an arbitrator appointed to the case. Where the parties to a pending arbitration agree to mediate under the AAA's rules, no additional administrative fee is required to initiate the mediation.[6]

[D] Court-Annexed Mediation

Finally, mediation may be triggered by the court. Both state and federal courts offer mediation programs. The Northern District of Illinois advises all parties in Lanham Act cases of the option to mediate and requires those parties to inform the court of their decision. That court has magistrates available to conduct mediations; it also maintains a list of attorneys certified as Lanham Act mediators.

---

4. http://www.inta.org/index.php?option=com_content&task=view&id=1384&Itemid=227&getcontent=4.
5. *See* http://www.cpradr.org/CMS_disp.asp?page=CPR_PledgeIntro&M=11.1; *see also* http://www.dca.gov.uk/civil/adr/adrrep_0102.htm.
6. *Commercial Arbitration Rules and Mediation Procedures*, American Arbitration Association, effective September 1, 2007.

Mediation Mistakes

Francis Carling, an experienced mediator in New York, has offered seven bad habits that mediation advocates should avoid.[1] Carling recommends that advocates strive to avoid these mistakes:

1. Expecting to win.

   "The goal of mediation is settlement—which means both sides must give up idle dreams of victory and come to mediation ready to compromise."

2. Failing to prepare.

   "Waiting to see what the mediator comes up with, and only then starting to think carefully about settlement options, can scuttle the mediation or produce a bad result."

3. Treating the mediator like a judge.

   Don't try to persuade the mediator that you are likely to win at trial. It is not his or her job to decide the merits of the dispute. The mediator is looking for practical suggestions for compromise

4. Lying excessively.

   Mediators expect some bluffing and lack of complete candor in the mediation process, but "making wildly unrealistic, and untrue, claims about your client's ability to compromise just wastes time and may cause a mediation to fail needlessly."

5. Killing the messenger.

   When a mediator articulates the position of the other side or presses for results and compromise, he or she is probably doing the same with the other side. Don't take it personally or let yourself or your client get angry.

6. Looking to the mediator for the right number.

   "The mediator is there to facilitate the process, not to tell you what the settlement should be."

7. Disrespecting confidentiality.

   Don't try to use mediation to seek discovery, provoke concessions, prompt revelations, or commit the parties to fixed positions. The purpose of mediation is settlement, not to gain an advantage at trial. To paraphrase a popular advertising campaign, "what happens in mediation, stays in mediation."

---

1. Carling, Francis, "Seven Habits of Ineffective Advocates in Mediation," Litigation Update, American Bar Association Section of Litigation.

8.04 Four Areas of Mediation Advocacy Focus

Effective advocacy in mediation involves four areas of focus, each identified by a word beginning with the letter *p*: *Process*, *Position*, *Preparation*, and *Presentation*.

[A] Process

Process involves an understanding of the overall mediation process. While there is no set procedure, most mediations follow a set pattern. Variations can exist depending on the practices of the mediator, so it is useful to understand the process the selected mediator will follow. It is also important to ensure that the client understands the process.

[B] Position

Position involves understanding what your client seeks to achieve in settlement. It is generally a mistake to enter a mediation, negotiation, or settlement conference simply hoping to get the best result you can. With this attitude. you are unlikely to achieve your goal, you will inevitably have to compromise, and you will be unhappy with the result. It is far better to establish a desired position as the minimal acceptable outcome and work against that. You may be able to achieve a better result and leave the proceeding as a victor rather than victim. If the minimal acceptable outcome is not achieved, you can also leave the proceeding and continue with litigation.

[C] Preparation

The difference between success and failure in most areas of legal practice is preparation, and it is critical for excellent advocacy in mediation. Several years ago I served as a mediator in a trademark infringement dispute between two major corporations in the food industry. At the initial mediation session, the plaintiff's counsel was clearly well prepared. He made a comprehensive and convincing presentation about the scope of the plaintiff's rights and the ways in which the defendant's conduct was likely to cause confusion. The presentation was directed at the decision makers for the defendant as much as at me, the mediator.

The defendant's counsel took a different approach. He merely asserted that the defendant had a different view of the merits and that the defendant was open minded about the possibility of settlement. In our private caucuses, defendant's counsel took a backseat to the principals of the company in the discussion of the relevant facts and settlement possibilities.

The dispute was not resolved at that initial mediation session. We continued negotiations by phone for several more weeks. However, not long after the initial mediation session, I heard from the defendant's counsel, who said he was being replaced on the case by a new attorney. As we discussed the matter further, it became apparent that his weak preparation and lack of involvement at the mediation session was a key factor in the client's decision. I have often wondered if things would have been different for him if he'd been better prepared and more engaged at the mediation. The lesson is that preparation can not only be the key to achieving successful results but to retaining a client.

[D] Presentation

The final *p* in mediation advocacy is presentation. The style of presentation during mediation can dramatically affect the results in your favor. An effective mediation presentation style is not the same as the dramatic presentation style likely to be effective before a jury, or even the firmly aggressive style likely to be successful at a bench trial. Instead, the most effective presentation style for mediation seems to be that of a confident, credible problem solver.

It is important to be confident in your knowledge of the facts and law. Doing so conveys a strong message to the opponent and the mediator—you understand your situation, and you are confident that you can ultimately prevail. But for confidence to be credible, it must be backed by knowledge and preparation. Strive to be the most knowledgeable person in the room regarding the facts and law. Knowledge of this type gives your opinions credibility. Finally, approach the session with a problem-solving mentality. We are gathered with a common purpose—to settle this lawsuit—so let's do our best to achieve that purpose. By making a presentation that conveys a confident, credible problem-solving attitude, you have a stronger chance of gaining the mediator as your ally in the settlement negotiations. In short, the key to confidence and credibility is superior knowledge. The way to obtaining superior knowledge is through preparation. Ultimately, preparation will be your key to success.

8.05 A New Mind-Set

Advocacy in ADR is best served by adopting a new mind-set. Vince Lombardi famously said "winning isn't every thing, it's the only thing," which is an apt summary of the traditional mind-set in most negotiation and litigation.

Seven Mediation Tips

Veteran attorney J. William Frank, III, has experienced ADR as a participant and as a neutral. He offers these ideas for effective strategy and advocacy in mediation.

1. Think about the problem and relationship in a lateral sense—give or get, need or want—not necessarily who will stop and who will pay money. In other words, focus on interests not legal position.
2. Know what you rationally can expect out of the case if it goes to trial, and let the mediator know. Also give the mediator ideas on how to settle and on barriers to settlement.
3. Educate your own client about the process. The client needs to understand that the mediator is not the decision maker, but instead is a facilitator. The client should understand that role.
4. Prepare the decision maker to talk at the mediation. The company spokesperson can be a very effective advocate. The lawyer should not be the sole mouthpiece.
5. Bring a company representative that is good at both listening and communicating.
6. Have patience. Keep emotions in check. Set out your case without name calling. Be prepared to spend time to allow the process to take its course. Bring a real decision maker.
7. Think creatively.

The advocate presses the view that her client is right and the other side is wrong, that her client must win and the opponent lose. All resources are directed at establishing and maintaining a hard position and at trying to compel the opponent to concede to that position in negotiation or the judge or jury to adopt that position in adjudication. It is a warrior mind-set. In some instances, it may be an effective one in the sense that it achieves the client's desired goal and provides a solution to the client's problem. More often than not, however, it is a mind-set that fails to reach the best solution for the client.

The new mind-set needed in today's world is one that is not limited to that of the warrior, but rather considers other options for achieving the client's goals. Winning isn't everything, and it may not even be the best thing.

A variety of models aid in creating the mind-set for advocacy in ADR. These models are useful in adjudication and arbitration with respect to process and persuasion, but are especially so for mediation and negotiation in which there is a premium on reaching agreement with the adversary.

One of the models to consider is the one explained in the classic, *Getting to Yes: Negotiating Agreement Without Giving In*, by Roger Fisher and William Ury of the Harvard Negotiation Project.[7] *Getting to Yes* advocates a method of principled negotiation that focuses on interests rather than positions. The Principled Negotiation model involves four principles or propositions:

- Separate the people from the problem
- Focus on interests, not positions
- Invent options for mutual gain
- Insist on objective criteria

Another useful model for creating an effective ADR mind-set is found in Steven Covey's best seller *The Seven Habits of Highly Effective People*. The fourth habit identified by Covey is "seek first to understand, then to be understood." This habit leads the advocate to consider the opponent's point of view.[8]

Finally, it always is wise to consider the advice of the first Illinois lawyer elected president. "Discourage litigation," Abraham Lincoln wrote, in his Notes for a Law Lecture:

> Persuade your neighbors to compromise whenever you can. Point out to them how the nominal winner is often the real loser—in fees, expenses and waste of time. As a peacemaker, the lawyer has a superior opportunity of being a good man. There will still be business enough.

---

7. Roger Fisher & William Ury, Getting to Yes: Negotiating Agreement Without Giving In (1981).
8. Which echoes a line from the Peace Prayer attributed to Saint Francis: "Grant that I should not so much seek . . . to be understood, as to understand."

Conclusion

Why then has ADR become an essential competency for lawyers? One answer is this: little has changed in the century since Ambrose Bierce's *The Devil's Dictionary* (1911) defined a litigant as "a person about to give up his skin for the hope of retaining his bones." If anything, a principal change in litigation since that time has been a greater loss of skin.

The legal world around us is reacting to this loss of skin by creating alternative models for resolving disputes. Whether or not we embrace ADR, our court systems and policy makers keep building new systems as alternatives to traditional litigation. The early models of arbitration and mediation have borne many offspring: hybrids annexed to the courts, variations operating parallel to the courts, and new systems dealing with the special problems created by a flat world without boundaries populated by travelers on the Internet moving at the speed of thought. Thus, we see—in addition to traditional litigation and the first responders such as arbitration and mediation—alternatives such as the Illinois Mandatory Arbitration program, the United States Trademark Office's Trademark Trial and Appeal Board, the National Advertising Division's process for resolving advertising disputes, the ICANN UDRP (the Uniform Dispute Resolution Policy of the Internet Corporation for Assigned Names and Numbers), and many others. More are yet to come. As lawyers, if we remain stuck in our litigation competency, we stand still as the world passes us by.

In-house counsel have the opportunity to embrace these alternatives as best practices for solving the problems of their companies. As they look around, they see their colleagues saving money, protecting confidences, preserving relationships, achieving better results in individual disputes, and creating internal processes and systems that reduce the loss of time and money to the litigation process. As in-house counsel recognize these potential benefits, they seek outside counsel who embrace these alternatives as well. Arbitration and mediation, if handled badly, may fail to produce promised benefits, and may yield less effective results than litigation handled well. Therefore, in-house counsel will look for those who can handle ADR well.

Outside counsel who embrace ADR will find greater opportunities for serving clients and will have an advantage when in-house counsel seek help.

Those of us who are outside counsel are destined to encounter arbitration, mediation, and the various hybrids arising in the legal world. We can't avoid it. Indeed, as we look to the future, we can see the domain of traditional litigation shrinking while the domains of the alternatives increase, multiply, and become more varied. Get on the bus, or get left behind.

These trends also provide a need and an opportunity for legal education. Once the basics are taught, law school offerings focus heavily on litigation skills, a reaction from the desire in the seventies and eighties for courses to become more relevant to real practice. However, leading law schools have expanded their offerings in alternative forms of dispute resolution. In addition to moot court competitions, we see negotiation competitions, courses in mediation, and clinical programs using hybrid proceedings based on arbitration. More can and should be done going forward.

Litigation has been my vocation for more than half my life. I have seen it produce results both good and bad. I have seen it help clients—and cause greater pain.

Litigation arises from a problem, from our client's pain. When I was young, I was taught a worthy goal was to always leave the place you visit better than it was before—cleaner, safer, happier. As lawyers, perhaps we should adopt that perspective. When faced with a client's problem, we should strive to leave the situation better for our involvement than it was before.

Litigation is often a necessary tool. Sometimes, though, it is not the best tool. It can be crude and damaging, and it can exacerbate the problem, leaving behind a new problem or a bigger problem. It some cases, it also leaves behind the old problem as well.

Litigation need not be abandoned as it can be useful. But what we advocate is adding a new set of tools to the lawyer's toolkit. We advocate acquiring a new competency. ADR provides an opportunity for lawyers to be better. Dare we aspire to even more? Perhaps even to become peacemakers? At least we can be a key factor in the solution instead of an aggravation of the problem. ADR might be the right tool for *that* in your next dispute. Nothing is lost by exploring the possibility, and you might help your client save some skin.

APPENDIX

A

The Federal Arbitration Act (FAA)

The Federal Arbitration Act provides the legal frame work for arbitrations involving disputes arising in interstate commerce.

Arbitration

Chapter 1. General Provisions

Section 1. "Maritime transactions" and "commerce" defined; exceptions to operation of title

"Maritime transaction," as herein defined, means charter parties, bills of lading of water carriers, agreements relating to wharfage, supplies furnished vessels or repairs to vessels, collisions, or any other matters in foreign commerce which, if the subject of controversy, would be embraced within admiralty jurisdiction; "commerce," as herein defined, means commerce among the several States or with foreign nations, or in any Territory of the United States or in the District of Columbia, or between any such Territory and another, or between any such Territory and any State or foreign nation, or between the District of Columbia and any State or Territory or foreign nation, but nothing herein contained shall apply to contracts of employment of seamen, railroad employees, or any other class of workers engaged in foreign or interstate commerce.

Section 2. Validity, irrevocability, and enforcement of agreements to arbitrate

A written provision in any maritime transaction or a contract evidencing a transaction involving commerce to settle by arbitration a controversy thereafter arising out of such contract or transaction, or the refusal to perform the whole or any part thereof, or an agreement in writing to submit to arbitration an existing controversy arising out of such a contract, transaction, or refusal, shall be valid, irrevocable, and enforceable, save upon such grounds as exist at law or in equity for the revocation of any contract.

Section 3. Stay of proceedings where issue therein referable to arbitration

If any suit or proceeding be brought in any of the courts of the United States upon any issue referable to arbitration under an agreement in writing for such arbitration, the court in which such suit is pending, upon being satisfied that the issue involved in such suit or proceeding is referable to arbitration under such an agreement, shall on application of one of the parties stay the trial of the action until such arbitration has been had in accordance with the terms of the agreement, providing the applicant for the stay is not in default in proceeding with such arbitration.

Section 4. Failure to arbitrate under agreement; petition to United States court having jurisdiction for order to compel arbitration; notice and service thereof; hearing and determination

A party aggrieved by the alleged failure, neglect, or refusal of another to arbitrate under a written agreement for arbitration may petition any United States district court which, save for such agreement, would have jurisdiction under Title 28, in a civil action or in admiralty of the subject matter of a suit arising out of the controversy between the parties, for an order directing that such arbitration proceed in the manner provided for in such agreement. Five days' notice in writing of such application shall be served upon the party in default. Service thereof shall be made in the manner provided by the Federal Rules of Civil Procedure. The court shall hear the parties, and upon being satisfied that the making of the agreement for arbitration or the failure to comply therewith is not in issue, the court shall make an order directing the parties to proceed to arbitration in accordance with the terms of the agreement. The hearing and proceedings, under such agreement, shall be within the district in which the petition for an order directing such arbitration is filed. If the making of the arbitration agreement or the failure, neglect, or refusal to perform the same be in issue, the court shall proceed summarily to the trial thereof. If no jury trial be demanded by the party alleged to be in default, or if the matter in dispute is within admiralty jurisdiction, the court shall hear and determine such issue. Where such an issue is raised, the party alleged to be in default may, except in cases of admiralty, on or before the return day of the notice of application, demand a jury trial of such issue, and upon such demand the court shall make an order referring the issue or issues to a jury in the manner provided by the Federal Rules of Civil Procedure, or may specially call a jury for that purpose. If the jury find that no agreement in writing for arbitration was made or that there is no default in proceeding thereunder, the proceeding shall be dismissed. If the jury find that an agreement for arbitration was made in writing and that there is a default in proceeding thereunder, the court shall make an order summarily directing the parties to proceed with the arbitration in accordance with the terms thereof.

Section 5. Appointment of arbitrators or umpire

If in the agreement provision be made for a method of naming or appointing an arbitrator or arbitrators or an umpire, such method shall be followed; but if no method be provided therein, or if a method be provided and any party thereto shall fail to avail himself of such method, or if for any other reason there shall be a lapse in the naming of an arbitrator or arbitrators or umpire, or in filling a vacancy, then upon the application of either party to the controversy the court shall designate and appoint an arbitrator or arbitrators or umpire, as the case may require, who shall act under the said agreement with the same force and effect as if he or they had been specifically named therein; and unless otherwise provided in the agreement the arbitration shall be by a single arbitrator.

Section 6. Application heard as motion

Any application to the court hereunder shall be made and heard in the manner provided by law for the making and hearing of motions, except as otherwise herein expressly provided.

Section 7. Witnesses before arbitrators; fees; compelling attendance

The arbitrators selected either as prescribed in this title or otherwise, or a majority of them, may summon in writing any person to attend before them or any of them as a witness and in a proper case to bring with him or them any book, record, document, or paper which may be deemed material as evidence in the case. The fees for such attendance shall be the same as the fees of witnesses before masters of the United States courts. Said summons shall issue in the name of the arbitrator or arbitrators, or a majority of them, and shall be signed by the arbitrators, or a majority of them, and shall be directed to the said person and shall be served in the same manner as subpoenas to appear and testify before the court; if any person or persons so summoned to testify shall refuse or neglect to obey said summons, upon petition the United States district court for the district in which such arbitrators, or a majority of them, are sitting may compel the attendance of such person or persons before said arbitrator or arbitrators, or punish said person or persons for contempt in the same manner provided by law for securing the attendance of witnesses or their punishment for neglect or refusal to attend in the courts of the United States.

Section 8. Proceedings begun by libel in admiralty and seizure of vessel or property

If the basis of jurisdiction be a cause of action otherwise justiciable in admiralty, then, notwithstanding anything herein to the contrary, the party claiming to be aggrieved may begin his proceeding hereunder by seizure of the vessel or other property of the other party according to the usual course of admiralty proceedings, and the court shall then have jurisdiction to direct the parties to proceed with the arbitration and shall retain jurisdiction to enter its decree upon the award.

Section 9. Award of arbitrators; confirmation; jurisdiction; procedure

If the parties in their agreement have agreed that a judgment of the court shall be entered upon the award made pursuant to the arbitration, and shall specify the court, then at any time within one year after the award is made any party to the arbitration may apply to the court so specified for an order confirming the award, and thereupon the court must grant such an order unless the award is vacated, modified, or corrected as prescribed in sections 10 and 11 of this title. If no court is specified in the agreement of the parties, then such application may be made to the United States court in and for the district within which such award was made. Notice of the application shall be served upon the adverse party, and thereupon the court shall have jurisdiction of such party as though he had appeared generally in the proceeding. If the adverse party is a resident of the district within which the award was made, such service shall be made upon the adverse party or his attorney as prescribed by law for service of notice of motion in an action in the same court. If the adverse party shall be a nonresident, then the notice of the application shall be served by the marshal of any district within which the adverse party may be found in like manner as other process of the court.

Section 10. Same; vacation; grounds; rehearing

1. In any of the following cases the United States court in and for the district wherein the award was made may make an order vacating the award upon the application of any party to the arbitration:

   1. Where the award was procured by corruption, fraud, or undue means.
   2. Where there was evident partiality or corruption in the arbitrators, or either of them.
   3. Where the arbitrators were guilty of misconduct in refusing to postpone the hearing, upon sufficient cause shown, or in refusing to hear evidence pertinent and material to the controversy; or of any other misbehavior by which the rights of any party have been prejudiced.
   4. Where the arbitrators exceeded their powers, or so imperfectly executed them that a mutual, final, and definite award upon the subject matter submitted was not made.
   5. Where an award is vacated and the time within which the agreement required the award to be made has not expired the court may, in its discretion, direct a rehearing by the arbitrators.

2. The United States district court for the district wherein an award was made that was issued pursuant to section 590 of title 5 may make an order vacating the award upon the application of a person, other than a party to the arbitration, who is adversely affected or aggrieved by the award, if the use of arbitration or the award is clearly inconsistent with the factors set forth in section 582 of title 5.

Section 11. Same; modification or correction; grounds; order

In either of the following cases the United States court in and for the district wherein the award was made may make an order modifying or correcting the award upon the application of any party to the arbitration—

a. Where there was an evident material miscalculation of figures or an evident material mistake in the description of any person, thing, or property referred to in the award.

b. Where the arbitrators have awarded upon a matter not submitted to them, unless it is a matter not affecting the merits of the decision upon the matter submitted.

c. Where the award is imperfect in matter of form not affecting the merits of the controversy.

The order may modify and correct the award, so as to effect the intent thereof and promote justice between the parties.

Section 12. Notice of motions to vacate or modify; service; stay of proceedings

Notice of a motion to vacate, modify, or correct an award must be served upon the adverse party or his attorney within three months after the award is filed or delivered. If the adverse party is a resident of the district within which the award was made, such service shall be made upon the adverse party or his attorney as prescribed by law for service of notice of motion in an action in the same court. If the adverse party shall be a nonresident then the notice of the application shall be served by the marshal of any district within which the adverse party may be found in like manner as other process of the court. For the purposes of the motion any judge who might make an order to stay the proceedings in an action brought in the same court may make an order, to be served with the notice of motion, staying the proceedings of the adverse party to enforce the award.

Section 13. Papers filed with order on motions; judgment; docketing; force and effect; enforcement

The party moving for an order confirming, modifying, or correcting an award shall, at the time such order is filed with the clerk for the entry of judgment thereon, also file the following papers with the clerk:

a. The agreement; the selection or appointment, if any, of an additional arbitrator or umpire; and each written extension of the time, if any, within which to make the award.

b. The award.

c. Each notice, affidavit, or other paper used upon an application to confirm, modify, or correct the award, and a copy of each order of the court upon such an application.

The judgment shall be docketed as if it was rendered in an action.

The judgment so entered shall have the same force and effect, in all respects, as, and be subject to all the provisions of law relating to, a judgment in an action; and it may be enforced as if it had been rendered in an action in the court in which it is entered.

Section 14. Contracts not affected

This title shall not apply to contracts made prior to January 1, 1926.

Section 15. Inapplicability of the Act of State doctrine

Enforcement of arbitral agreements, confirmation of arbitral awards, and execution upon judgments based on orders confirming such awards shall not be refused on the basis of the Act of State doctrine.

Section 16. Appeals

a. An appeal may be taken from

1. an order—
    A. refusing a stay of any action under section 3 of this title,
    B. denying a petition under section 4 of this title to order arbitration to proceed,
    C. denying an application under section 206 of this title to compel arbitration,
    D. confirming or denying confirmation of an award or partial award, or
    E. modifying, correcting, or vacating an award;
2. an interlocutory order granting, continuing, or modifying an injunction against an arbitration that is subject to this title; or
3. a final decision with respect to an arbitration that is subject to this title.

b. Except as otherwise provided in section 1292(b) of title 28, an appeal may not be taken from an interlocutory order—

1. granting a stay of any action under section 3 of this title;
2. directing arbitration to proceed under section 4 of this title;
3. compelling arbitration under section 206 of this title; or
4. refusing to enjoin an arbitration that is subject to this title.

Chapter 2. Convention on the Recognition and Enforcement of Foreign Arbitral Awards

Section 201. Enforcement of Convention

The Convention on the Recognition and Enforcement of Foreign Arbitral Awards of June 10, 1958, shall be enforced in United States courts in accordance with this chapter.

Section 202. Agreement or award falling under the Convention

An arbitration agreement or arbitral award arising out of a legal relationship, whether contractual or not, which is considered as commercial, including a transaction, contract, or agreement described in section 2 of this title, falls under the Convention. An agreement or award arising out of such a relationship which is entirely between citizens of the United States shall be deemed not to fall under the Convention unless that relationship involves property located abroad, envisages performance or enforcement abroad, or has some other reasonable relation with one or more foreign states. For the purpose of this section a corporation is a citizen of the United States if it is incorporated or has its principal place of business in the United States.

Section 203. Jurisdiction; amount in controversy

An action or proceeding falling under the Convention shall be deemed to arise under the laws and treaties of the United States. The district courts of the United States (including the courts enumerated in section 460 of title 28) shall have original jurisdiction over such an action or proceeding, regardless of the amount in controversy.

Section 204. Venue

An action or proceeding over which the district courts have jurisdiction pursuant to section 203 of this title may be brought in any such court in which save for the arbitration agreement an action or proceeding with respect to the controversy between the parties could be brought, or in such court for the district and division which embraces the place designated in the agreement as the place of arbitration if such place is within the United States.

Section 205. Removal of cases from State courts

Where the subject matter of an action or proceeding pending in a State court relates to an arbitration agreement or award falling under the Convention, the defendant or the defendants may, at any time before the trial thereof, remove such action or proceeding to the district court of the United States for the district and division embracing the place where the action or proceeding is pending. The procedure for removal of causes otherwise provided by law shall apply, except that the ground for removal provided in this section need not appear on the face of the complaint but may be shown in the petition for removal. For the purposes of Chapter 1 of this title any action or proceeding removed under this section shall be deemed to have been brought in the district court to which it is removed.

Section 206. Order to compel arbitration; appointment of arbitrators

A court having jurisdiction under this chapter may direct that arbitration be held in accordance with the agreement at any place therein provided for, whether that place is within or without the United States. Such court may also appoint arbitrators in accordance with the provisions of the agreement.

Section 207. Award of arbitrators; confirmation; jurisdiction; proceeding

Within three years after an arbitral award falling under the Convention is made, any party to the arbitration may apply to any court having jurisdiction under this chapter for an order confirming the award as against any other party to the arbitration. The court shall confirm the award unless it finds one of the grounds for refusal or deferral of recognition or enforcement of the award specified in the said Convention.

Section 208. Chapter 1; residual application

Chapter 1 applies to actions and proceedings brought under this chapter to the extent that chapter is not in conflict with this chapter or the Convention as ratified by the United States.

Chapter 3. Inter-American Convention on International Commercial Arbitration

Section 301. Enforcement of Convention

The Inter-American Convention on International Commercial Arbitration of January 30, 1975, shall be enforced in United States courts in accordance with this chapter.

Section 302. Incorporation by reference

Sections 202, 203, 204, 205, and 207 of this title shall apply to this chapter as if specifically set forth herein, except that for the purposes of this chapter "the Convention" shall mean the Inter-American Convention.

Section 303. Order to compel arbitration; appointment of arbitrators; locale

a. A court having jurisdiction under this chapter may direct that arbitration be held in accordance with the agreement at any place therein provided for, whether that place is within or without the United States. The court may also appoint arbitrators in accordance with the provisions of the agreement.

b. In the event the agreement does not make provision for the place of arbitration or the appointment of arbitrators, the court shall direct that the arbitration shall be held and the arbitrators be appointed in accordance with Article 3 of the Inter-American Convention.

Section 304. Recognition and enforcement of foreign arbitral decisions and awards; reciprocity

Arbitral decisions or awards made in the territory of a foreign State shall, on the basis of reciprocity, be recognized and enforced under this chapter only if that State has ratified or acceded to the Inter-American Convention.

Section 305. Relationship between the Inter-American Convention and the Convention on the Recognition and Enforcement of Foreign Arbitral Awards of June 10, 1958

When the requirements for application of both the Inter-American Convention and the Convention on the Recognition and Enforcement of Foreign Arbitral Awards of June 10, 1958, are met, determination as to which Convention applies shall, unless otherwise expressly agreed, be made as follows:

1. If a majority of the parties to the arbitration agreement are citizens of a State or States that have ratified or acceded to the Inter-American Convention and are member States of the Organization of American States, the Inter-American Convention shall apply.
2. In all other cases the Convention on the Recognition and Enforcement of Foreign Arbitral Awards of June 10, 1958, shall apply.

Section 306. Applicable rules of Inter-American Commercial Arbitration Commission

a. For the purposes of this chapter the rules of procedure of the Inter-American Commercial Arbitration Commission referred to in Article 3 of the Inter-American Convention shall, subject to subsection (b) of this section, be those rules as promulgated by the Commission on July 1, 1988.

b. In the event the rules of procedure of the Inter-American Commercial Arbitration Commission are modified or amended in accordance with the procedures for amendment of the rules of that Commission, the Secretary of State, by regulation in accordance with section 553 of title 5, consistent with the aims and purposes of this Convention, may prescribe that such modifications or amendments shall be effective for purposes of this chapter.

Section 307. Chapter 1; residual application

Chapter 1 applies to actions and proceedings brought under this chapter to the extent chapter 1 is not in conflict with this chapter or the Inter-American Convention as ratified by the United States.

APPENDIX

B

AAA Arbitration Rules[1]

The American Arbitration Association provides the following rules for commercial arbitration. These serve as a good model for understanding the process and procedure of typical arbitrations. The rules of other organizations are similar in many respects but may have material differences that should be reviewed in the appropriate circumstances.

Commercial Arbitration Rules

R-1. Agreement of Parties

(a) The parties shall be deemed to have made these rules a part of their arbitration agreement whenever they have provided for arbitration by the American Arbitration Association (hereinafter AAA) under its Commercial Arbitration Rules or for arbitration by the AAA of a domestic commercial dispute without specifying particular rules. These rules and any amendment of them shall apply in the form in effect at the time the administrative requirements are met for a demand for arbitration or submission agreement received by the AAA. The parties, by written agreement, may vary the procedures set forth in these rules. After appointment of the arbitrator, such modifications may be made only with the consent of the arbitrator.

(b) Unless the parties or the AAA determines otherwise, the Expedited Procedures shall apply in any case in which no disclosed claim or counterclaim exceeds $75,000, exclusive of interest and arbitration fees and costs. Parties may also agree to use these procedures in larger cases. Unless the parties agree otherwise, these procedures will not apply in cases involving more than two parties. The Expedited Procedures shall be applied as described in Sections E-1 through E-10 of these rules, in addition to any other portion of these rules that is not in conflict with the Expedited Procedures.

(c) Unless the parties agree otherwise, the Procedures for Large, Complex Commercial Disputes shall apply to all cases in which the disclosed claim or counterclaim of any party is at least $500,000, exclusive of claimed interest,

1. Copyright by American Arbitration Association.

arbitration fees and costs. Parties may also agree to use the Procedures in cases involving claims or counterclaims under $500,000, or in nonmonetary cases. The Procedures for Large, Complex Commercial Disputes shall be applied as described in Sections L-1 through L-4 of these rules, in addition to any other portion of these rules that is not in conflict with the Procedures for Large, Complex Commercial Disputes.

(d) All other cases shall be administered in accordance with Sections R-1 through R-54 of these rules.

R-2. AAA and Delegation of Duties

When parties agree to arbitrate under these rules, or when they provide for arbitration by the AAA and an arbitration is initiated under these rules, they thereby authorize the AAA to administer the arbitration. The authority and duties of the AAA are prescribed in the agreement of the parties and in these rules, and may be carried out through such of the AAA's representatives as it may direct. The AAA may, in its discretion, assign the administration of an arbitration to any of its offices.

R-3. National Roster of Arbitrators

The AAA shall establish and maintain a National Roster of Commercial Arbitrators ("National Roster") and shall appoint arbitrators as provided in these rules. The term "arbitrator" in these rules refers to the arbitration panel, constituted for a particular case, whether composed of one or more arbitrators, or to an individual arbitrator, as the context requires.

R-4. Initiation under an Arbitration Provision in a Contract

(a) Arbitration under an arbitration provision in a contract shall be initiated in the following manner:

(i) The initiating party (the "claimant") shall, within the time period, if any, specified in the contract(s), give to the other party (the "respondent") written notice of its intention to arbitrate (the "demand"), which demand shall contain a statement setting forth the nature of the dispute, the names and addresses of all other parties, the amount involved, if any, the remedy sought, and the hearing locale requested.

(ii) The claimant shall file at any office of the AAA two copies of the demand and two copies of the arbitration provisions of the contract, together with the appropriate filing fee as provided in the schedule included with these rules.

(iii) The AAA shall confirm notice of such filing to the parties.

(b) A respondent may file an answering statement in duplicate with the AAA within 15 days after confirmation of notice of filing of the demand is sent by the AAA. The respondent shall, at the time of any such filing, send a copy of the answering statement to the claimant. If a counterclaim is asserted, it shall contain a statement setting forth the nature of the counterclaim, the amount involved, if any, and the remedy sought. If a counterclaim is made, the party making the counterclaim shall forward to the AAA with the answering statement the appropriate fee provided in the schedule included with these rules.

(c) If no answering statement is filed within the stated time, respondent will be deemed to deny the claim. Failure to file an answering statement shall not operate to delay the arbitration.

(d) When filing any statement pursuant to this section, the parties are encouraged to provide descriptions of their claims in sufficient detail to make the circumstances of the dispute clear to the arbitrator.

R-5. Initiation under a Submission

Parties to any existing dispute may commence an arbitration under these rules by filing at any office of the AAA two copies of a written submission to arbitrate under these rules, signed by the parties. It shall contain a statement of the nature of the dispute, the names and addresses of all parties, any claims and counterclaims, the amount involved, if any, the remedy sought, and the hearing locale requested, together with the appropriate filing fee as provided in the schedule included with these rules. Unless the parties state otherwise in the submission, all claims and counterclaims will be deemed to be denied by the other party.

R-6. Changes of Claim

After filing of a claim, if either party desires to make any new or different claim or counterclaim, it shall be made in writing and filed with the AAA. The party asserting such a claim or counterclaim shall provide a copy to the other party, who shall have 15 days from the date of such transmission within which to file an answering statement with the AAA. After the arbitrator is appointed, however, no new or different claim may be submitted except with the arbitrator's consent.

R-7. Jurisdiction

(a) The arbitrator shall have the power to rule on his or her own jurisdiction, including any objections with respect to the existence, scope or validity of the arbitration agreement.

(b) The arbitrator shall have the power to determine the existence or validity of a contract of which an arbitration clause forms a part. Such an arbitration clause shall be treated as an agreement independent of the other terms of the contract. A decision by the arbitrator that the contract is null and void shall not for that reason alone render invalid the arbitration clause.

(c) A party must object to the jurisdiction of the arbitrator or to the arbitrability of a claim or counterclaim no later than the filing of the answering statement to the claim or counterclaim that gives rise to the objection. The arbitrator may rule on such objections as a preliminary matter or as part of the final award.

R-8. Mediation

At any stage of the proceedings, the parties may agree to conduct a mediation conference under the Commercial Mediation Procedures in order to facilitate settlement. The mediator shall not be an arbitrator appointed to the case.

Where the parties to a pending arbitration agree to mediate under the AAA's rules, no additional administrative fee is required to initiate the mediation.

R-9. Administrative Conference

At the request of any party or upon the AAA's own initiative, the AAA may conduct an administrative conference, in person or by telephone, with the parties and/or their representatives. The conference may address such issues as arbitrator selection, potential mediation of the dispute, potential exchange of information, a timetable for hearings and any other administrative matters.

R-10. Fixing of Locale

The parties may mutually agree on the locale where the arbitration is to be held. If any party requests that the hearing be held in a specific locale and the other party files no objection thereto within 15 days after notice of the request has been sent to it by the AAA, the locale shall be the one requested. If a party objects to the locale requested by the other party, the AAA shall have the power to determine the locale, and its decision shall be final and binding.

R-11. Appointment from National Roster

If the parties have not appointed an arbitrator and have not provided any other method of appointment, the arbitrator shall be appointed in the following manner:

(a) Immediately after the filing of the submission or the answering statement or the expiration of the time within which the answering statement is to be filed, the AAA shall send simultaneously to each party to the dispute an identical list of 10 (unless the AAA decides that a different number is appropriate) names of persons chosen from the National Roster. The parties are encouraged to agree to an arbitrator from the submitted list and to advise the AAA of their agreement.

(b) If the parties are unable to agree upon an arbitrator, each party to the dispute shall have 15 days from the transmittal date in which to strike names objected to, number the remaining names in order of preference, and return the list to the AAA. If a party does not return the list within the time specified, all persons named therein shall be deemed acceptable. From among the persons who have been approved on both lists, and in accordance with the designated order of mutual preference, the AAA shall invite the acceptance of an arbitrator to serve. If the parties fail to agree on any of the persons named, or if acceptable arbitrators are unable to act, or if for any other reason the appointment cannot be made from the submitted lists, the AAA shall have the power to make the appointment from among other members of the National Roster without the submission of additional lists.

(c) Unless the parties agree otherwise when there are two or more claimants or two or more respondents, the AAA may appoint all the arbitrators.

R-12. Direct Appointment by a Party

(a) If the agreement of the parties names an arbitrator or specifies a method of appointing an arbitrator, that designation or method shall be followed. The notice of appointment, with the name and address of the arbitrator, shall be filed with the AAA by the appointing party. Upon the request of any appointing party, the AAA shall submit a list of members of the National Roster from which the party may, if it so desires, make the appointment.

(b) Where the parties have agreed that each party is to name one arbitrator, the arbitrators so named must meet the standards of Section R-17 with respect to impartiality and independence unless the parties have specifically agreed pursuant to Section R-17(a) that the party-appointed arbitrators are to be non-neutral and need not meet those standards.

(c) If the agreement specifies a period of time within which an arbitrator shall be appointed and any party fails to make the appointment within that period, the AAA shall make the appointment.

(d) If no period of time is specified in the agreement, the AAA shall notify the party to make the appointment. If within 15 days after such notice has been sent, an arbitrator has not been appointed by a party, the AAA shall make the appointment.

R-13. Appointment of Chairperson by Party-Appointed Arbitrators or Parties

(a) If, pursuant to Section R-12, either the parties have directly appointed arbitrators, or the arbitrators have been appointed by the AAA, and the parties have authorized them to appoint a chairperson within a specified time and no appointment is made within that time or any agreed extension, the AAA may appoint the chairperson.

(b) If no period of time is specified for appointment of the chairperson and the party-appointed arbitrators or the parties do not make the appointment within 15 days from the date of the appointment of the last party-appointed arbitrator, the AAA may appoint the chairperson.

(c) If the parties have agreed that their party-appointed arbitrators shall appoint the chairperson from the National Roster, the AAA shall furnish to the party-appointed arbitrators, in the manner provided in Section R-11, a list selected from the National Roster, and the appointment of the chairperson shall be made as provided in that Section.

R-14. Nationality of Arbitrator

Where the parties are nationals of different countries, the AAA, at the request of any party or on its own initiative, may appoint as arbitrator a national of a country other than that of any of the parties. The request must be made before the time set for the appointment of the arbitrator as agreed by the parties or set by these rules.

R-15. Number of Arbitrators

If the arbitration agreement does not specify the number of arbitrators, the dispute shall be heard and determined by one arbitrator, unless the AAA, in its discretion, directs that three arbitrators be appointed. A party may request three arbitrators in the demand or answer, which request the AAA will consider in exercising its discretion regarding the number of arbitrators appointed to the dispute.

R-16. Disclosure

(a) Any person appointed or to be appointed as an arbitrator shall disclose to the AAA any circumstance likely to give rise to justifiable doubt as to the arbitrator's impartiality or independence, including any bias or any financial or personal interest in the result of the arbitration or any past or present relationship with the parties or their representatives. Such obligation shall remain in effect throughout the arbitration.

(b) Upon receipt of such information from the arbitrator or another source, the AAA shall communicate the information to the parties and, if it deems it appropriate to do so, to the arbitrator and others.

(c) In order to encourage disclosure by arbitrators, disclosure of information pursuant to this Section R-16 is not to be construed as an indication that the arbitrator considers that the disclosed circumstance is likely to affect impartiality or independence.

R-17. Disqualification of Arbitrator

(a) Any arbitrator shall be impartial and independent and shall perform his or her duties with diligence and in good faith, and shall be subject to disqualification for

(i) partiality or lack of independence,
(ii) inability or refusal to perform his or her duties with diligence and in good faith, and
(iii) any grounds for disqualification provided by applicable law. The parties may agree in writing, however, that arbitrators directly appointed by a party pursuant to Section R-12 shall be nonneutral, in which case such arbitrators need not be impartial or independent and shall not be subject to disqualification for partiality or lack of independence.

(b) Upon objection of a party to the continued service of an arbitrator, or on its own initiative, the AAA shall determine whether the arbitrator should be disqualified under the grounds set out above, and shall inform the parties of its decision, which decision shall be conclusive.

R-18. Communication with Arbitrator

(a) No party and no one acting on behalf of any party shall communicate ex parte with an arbitrator or a candidate for arbitrator concerning the arbitration, except that a party, or someone acting on behalf of a party, may communicate ex parte with a candidate for direct appointment pursuant to Section R-12 in order to advise the candidate of the general nature of the controversy and of the anticipated proceedings and to discuss the candidate's qualifications, availability, or independence in relation to the parties or to discuss the suitability of candidates for selection as a third arbitrator where the parties or party-designated arbitrators are to participate in that selection.

(b) Section R-18(a) does not apply to arbitrators directly appointed by the parties who, pursuant to Section R-17(a), the parties have agreed in writing are non-neutral. Where the parties have so agreed under Section R-17(a), the AAA shall as an administrative practice suggest to the parties that they agree further that Section R-18(a) should nonetheless apply prospectively.

R-19. Vacancies

(a) If for any reason an arbitrator is unable to perform the duties of the office, the AAA may, on proof satisfactory to it, declare the office vacant. Vacancies shall be filled in accordance with the applicable provisions of these rules.

(b) In the event of a vacancy in a panel of neutral arbitrators after the hearings have commenced, the remaining arbitrator or arbitrators may continue with the hearing and determination of the controversy, unless the parties agree otherwise.

(c) In the event of the appointment of a substitute arbitrator, the panel of arbitrators shall determine in its sole discretion whether it is necessary to repeat all or part of any prior hearings.

R-20. Preliminary Hearing

(a) At the request of any party or at the discretion of the arbitrator or the AAA, the arbitrator may schedule as soon as practicable a preliminary hearing with the parties and/or their representatives. The preliminary hearing may be conducted by telephone at the arbitrator's discretion.

(b) During the preliminary hearing, the parties and the arbitrator should discuss the future conduct of the case, including clarification of the issues and claims, a schedule for the hearings and any other preliminary matters.

R-21. Exchange of Information

(a) At the request of any party or at the discretion of the arbitrator, consistent with the expedited nature of arbitration, the arbitrator may direct

i) the production of documents and other information, and
ii) the identification of any witnesses to be called.

(b) At least five business days prior to the hearing, the parties shall exchange copies of all exhibits they intend to submit at the hearing.

(c) The arbitrator is authorized to resolve any disputes concerning the exchange of information.

R-22. Date, Time, and Place of Hearing

The arbitrator shall set the date, time, and place for each hearing. The parties shall respond to requests for hearing dates in a timely manner, be cooperative in scheduling the earliest practicable date, and adhere to the established hearing schedule. The AAA shall send a notice of hearing to the parties at least 10 days in advance of the hearing date, unless otherwise agreed by the parties.

R-23. Attendance at Hearings

The arbitrator and the AAA shall maintain the privacy of the hearings unless the law provides to the contrary. Any person having a direct interest in the arbitration is entitled to attend hearings. The arbitrator shall otherwise have the power to require the exclusion of any witness, other than a party or other essential person, during the testimony of any other witness. It shall be discretionary with the arbitrator to determine the propriety of the attendance of any other person other than a party and its representatives.

R-24. Representation

Any party may be represented by counsel or other authorized representative. A party intending to be so represented shall notify the other party and the AAA of the name and address of the representative at least three days prior to the date set for the hearing at which that person is first to appear. When such a representative initiates an arbitration or responds for a party, notice is deemed to have been given.

R-25. Oaths

Before proceeding with the first hearing, each arbitrator may take an oath of office and, if required by law, shall do so. The arbitrator may require witnesses to testify under oath administered by any duly qualified person and, if it is required by law or requested by any party, shall do so.

R-26. Stenographic Record

Any party desiring a stenographic record shall make arrangements directly with a stenographer and shall notify the other parties of these arrangements at least three days in advance of the hearing. The requesting party or parties shall pay the cost of the record. If the transcript is agreed by the parties, or determined by the arbitrator to be the official record of the proceeding, it must be provided to the arbitrator and made available to the other parties for inspection, at a date, time, and place determined by the arbitrator.

R-27. Interpreters

Any party wishing an interpreter shall make all arrangements directly with the interpreter and shall assume the costs of the service.

R-28. Postponements

The arbitrator may postpone any hearing upon agreement of the parties, upon request of a party for good cause shown, or upon the arbitrator's own initiative.

R-29. Arbitration in the Absence of a Party or Representative

Unless the law provides to the contrary, the arbitration may proceed in the absence of any party or representative who, after due notice, fails to be present or fails to obtain a postponement. An award shall not be made solely on the default of a party. The arbitrator shall require the party who is present to submit such evidence as the arbitrator may require for the making of an award.

R-30. Conduct of Proceedings

(a) The claimant shall present evidence to support its claim. The respondent shall then present evidence to support its defense. Witnesses for each party shall also submit to questions from the arbitrator and the adverse party. The arbitrator has the discretion to vary this procedure, provided that the parties are treated with equality and that each party has the right to be heard and is given a fair opportunity to present its case.

(b) The arbitrator, exercising his or her discretion, shall conduct the proceedings with a view to expediting the resolution of the dispute and may direct the order of proof, bifurcate proceedings and direct the parties to focus their presentations on issues the decision of which could dispose of all or part of the case.

(c) The parties may agree to waive oral hearings in any case.

R-31. Evidence

(a) The parties may offer such evidence as is relevant and material to the dispute and shall produce such evidence as the arbitrator may deem necessary to an understanding and determination of the dispute. Conformity to legal rules of evidence shall not be necessary. All evidence shall be taken in the presence of all of the arbitrators and all of the parties, except where any of the parties is absent, in default or has waived the right to be present.

(b) The arbitrator shall determine the admissibility, relevance, and materiality of the evidence offered and may exclude evidence deemed by the arbitrator to be cumulative or irrelevant.

(c) The arbitrator shall take into account applicable principles of legal privilege, such as those involving the confidentiality of communications between a lawyer and client.

(d) An arbitrator or other person authorized by law to subpoena witnesses or documents may do so upon the request of any party or independently.

R-32. Evidence by Affidavit and Post-hearing Filing of Documents or Other Evidence

(a) The arbitrator may receive and consider the evidence of witnesses by declaration or affidavit, but shall give it only such weight as the arbitrator deems it entitled to after consideration of any objection made to its admission.

(b) If the parties agree or the arbitrator directs that documents or other evidence be submitted to the arbitrator after the hearing, the documents or other evidence shall be filed with the AAA for transmission to the arbitrator. All parties shall be afforded an opportunity to examine and respond to such documents or other evidence.

R-33. Inspection or Investigation

An arbitrator finding it necessary to make an inspection or investigation in connection with the arbitration shall direct the AAA to so advise the parties. The arbitrator shall set the date and time and the AAA shall notify the parties. Any party who so desires may be present at such an inspection or investigation. In the event that one or all parties are not present at the inspection or investigation, the arbitrator shall make an oral or written report to the parties and afford them an opportunity to comment.

R-34. Interim Measures**

(a) The arbitrator may take whatever interim measures he or she deems necessary, including injunctive relief and measures for the protection or conservation of property and disposition of perishable goods.

(b) Such interim measures may take the form of an interim award, and the arbitrator may require security for the costs of such measures.

(c) A request for interim measures addressed by a party to a judicial authority shall not be deemed incompatible with the agreement to arbitrate or a waiver of the right to arbitrate.

** The Optional Rules may be found below.

R-35. Closing of Hearing

The arbitrator shall specifically inquire of all parties whether they have any further proofs to offer or witnesses to be heard. Upon receiving negative replies or if satisfied that the record is complete, the arbitrator shall declare the hearing closed. If briefs are to be filed, the hearing shall be declared closed as of the final date set by the arbitrator for the receipt of briefs. If documents are to be filed as provided in Section R-32 and the date set for their receipt is later than that set for the receipt of briefs, the later date shall be the closing date of the hearing. The time limit within which the arbitrator is required to make the award shall commence, in the absence of other agreements by the parties, upon the closing of the hearing.

R-36. Reopening of Hearing

The hearing may be reopened on the arbitrator's initiative, or upon application of a party, at any time before the award is made. If reopening the hearing would prevent the making of the award within the specific time agreed on by the parties in the contract(s) out of which the controversy has arisen, the matter may not be reopened unless the parties agree on an extension of time. When no specific date is fixed in the contract, the arbitrator may reopen the hearing and shall have 30 days from the closing of the reopened hearing within which to make an award.

R-37. Waiver of Rules

Any party who proceeds with the arbitration after knowledge that any provision or requirement of these rules has not been complied with and who fails to state an objection in writing shall be deemed to have waived the right to object.

R-38. Extensions of Time

The parties may modify any period of time by mutual agreement. The AAA or the arbitrator may for good cause extend any period of time established by these rules, except the time for making the award. The AAA shall notify the parties of any extension.

R-39. Serving of Notice

(a) Any papers, notices, or process necessary or proper for the initiation or continuation of an arbitration under these rules, for any court action in connection therewith, or for the entry of judgment on any award made under these rules may be served on a party by mail addressed to the party, or its representative at the last known address or by personal service, in or outside the state where the arbitration is to be held, provided that reasonable opportunity to be heard with regard to the dispute is or has been granted to the party.

(b) The AAA, the arbitrator and the parties may also use overnight delivery or electronic facsimile transmission (fax), to give the notices required by these rules. Where all parties and the arbitrator agree, notices may be transmitted by electronic mail (E-mail), or other methods of communication.

(c) Unless otherwise instructed by the AAA or by the arbitrator, any documents submitted by any party to the AAA or to the arbitrator shall simultaneously be provided to the other party or parties to the arbitration.

R-40. Majority Decision

When the panel consists of more than one arbitrator, unless required by law or by the arbitration agreement, a majority of the arbitrators must make all decisions.

R-41. Time of Award

The award shall be made promptly by the arbitrator and, unless otherwise agreed by the parties or specified by law, no later than 30 days from the date of closing the hearing, or, if oral hearings have been waived, from the date of the AAA's transmittal of the final statements and proofs to the arbitrator.

R-42. Form of Award

(a) Any award shall be in writing and signed by a majority of the arbitrators. It shall be executed in the manner required by law.

(b) The arbitrator need not render a reasoned award unless the parties request such an award in writing prior to appointment of the arbitrator or unless the arbitrator determines that a reasoned award is appropriate.

R-43. Scope of Award

(a) The arbitrator may grant any remedy or relief that the arbitrator deems just and equitable and within the scope of the agreement of the parties, including, but not limited to, specific performance of a contract.

(b) In addition to a final award, the arbitrator may make other decisions, including interim, interlocutory, or partial rulings, orders, and awards. In any interim, interlocutory, or partial award, the arbitrator may assess and apportion the fees, expenses, and compensation related to such award as the arbitrator determines is appropriate.

(c) In the final award, the arbitrator shall assess the fees, expenses, and compensation provided in Sections R-49, R-50, and R-51. The arbitrator may apportion such fees, expenses, and compensation among the parties in such amounts as the arbitrator determines is appropriate.

(d) The award of the arbitrator(s) may include:

(i) interest at such rate and from such date as the arbitrator(s) may deem appropriate; and

(ii) an award of attorneys' fees if all parties have requested such an award or it is authorized by law or their arbitration agreement.

R-44. Award upon Settlement

If the parties settle their dispute during the course of the arbitration and if the parties so request, the arbitrator may set forth the terms of the settlement in a "consent award." A consent award must include an allocation of arbitration costs, including administrative fees and expenses as well as arbitrator fees and expenses.

R-45. Delivery of Award to Parties

Parties shall accept as notice and delivery of the award the placing of the award or a true copy thereof in the mail addressed to the parties or their representatives at the last known addresses, personal or electronic service of the award, or the filing of the award in any other manner that is permitted by law.

R-46. Modification of Award

Within 20 days after the transmittal of an award, any party, upon notice to the other parties, may request the arbitrator, through the AAA, to correct any clerical, typographical, or computational errors in the award. The arbitrator is not empowered to redetermine the merits of any claim already decided. The other parties shall be given 10 days to respond to the request. The arbitrator shall dispose of the request within 20 days after transmittal by the AAA to the arbitrator of the request and any response thereto.

R-47. Release of Documents for Judicial Proceedings

The AAA shall, upon the written request of a party, furnish to the party, at the party's expense, certified copies of any papers in the AAA's possession that may be required in judicial proceedings relating to the arbitration.

R-48. Applications to Court and Exclusion of Liability

(a) No judicial proceeding by a party relating to the subject matter of the arbitration shall be deemed a waiver of the party's right to arbitrate.

(b) Neither the AAA nor any arbitrator in a proceeding under these rules is a necessary or proper party in judicial proceedings relating to the arbitration.

(c) Parties to an arbitration under these rules shall be deemed to have consented that judgment upon the arbitration award may be entered in any federal or state court having jurisdiction thereof.

(d) Parties to an arbitration under these rules shall be deemed to have consented that neither the AAA nor any arbitrator shall be liable to any party in any action for damages or injunctive relief for any act or omission in connection with any arbitration under these rules.

R-49. Administrative Fees

As a not-for-profit organization, the AAA shall prescribe an initial filing fee and a case service fee to compensate it for the cost of providing administrative services. The fees in effect when the fee or charge is incurred shall be applicable. The filing fee shall be advanced by the party or parties making a claim or counterclaim, subject to final apportionment by the arbitrator in the award. The AAA may, in the event of extreme hardship on the part of any party, defer or reduce the administrative fees.

R-50. Expenses

The expenses of witnesses for either side shall be paid by the party producing such witnesses. All other expenses of the arbitration, including required travel and other expenses of the arbitrator, AAA representatives, and any witness and the cost of any proof produced at the direct request of the arbitrator, shall be borne equally by the parties, unless they agree otherwise or unless the arbitrator in the award assesses such expenses or any part thereof against any specified party or parties.

R-51. Neutral Arbitrator's Compensation

(a) Arbitrators shall be compensated at a rate consistent with the arbitrator's stated rate of compensation.

(b) If there is disagreement concerning the terms of compensation, an appropriate rate shall be established with the arbitrator by the AAA and confirmed to the parties.

(c) Any arrangement for the compensation of a neutral arbitrator shall be made through the AAA and not directly between the parties and the arbitrator.

R-52. Deposits

The AAA may require the parties to deposit in advance of any hearings such sums of money as it deems necessary to cover the expense of the arbitration, including the arbitrator's fee, if any, and shall render an accounting to the parties and return any unexpended balance at the conclusion of the case.

R-53. Interpretation and Application of Rules

The arbitrator shall interpret and apply these rules insofar as they relate to the arbitrator's powers and duties. When there is more than one arbitrator and a difference arises among them concerning the meaning or application of these rules, it shall be decided by a majority vote. If that is not possible, either an arbitrator or a party may refer the question to the AAA for final decision. All other rules shall be interpreted and applied by the AAA.

R-54. Suspension for Nonpayment

If arbitrator compensation or administrative charges have not been paid in full, the AAA may so inform the parties in order that one of them may advance the required payment. If such payments are not made, the arbitrator may order the suspension or termination of the proceedings. If no arbitrator has yet been appointed, the AAA may suspend the proceedings.

APPENDIX C

Hall Street Associates LLC v. Mattel Inc.

JUSTICE SOUTER delivered the opinion of the Court.[1]

The Federal Arbitration Act (FAA or Act), 9 U. S. C. §1 et seq., provides for expedited judicial review to confirm, vacate, or modify arbitration awards. §§ 9–11 (2000 ed. and Supp. V). The question here is whether statutory grounds for prompt vacatur and modification may be supplemented by contract. We hold that the statutory grounds are exclusive.

I

This case began as a lease dispute between landlord, petitioner Hall Street Associates, L. L. C., and tenant, respondent Mattel, Inc. The property was used for many years as a manufacturing site, and the leases provided that the tenant would indemnify the landlord for any costs resulting from the failure of the tenant or its predecessor lessees to follow environmental laws while using the premises. App. 88–89.

Tests of the property's well water in 1998 showed high levels of trichloroethylene (TCE), the apparent residue of manufacturing discharges by Mattel's predecessors between 1951 and 1980. After the Oregon Department of Environmental Quality (DEQ) discovered even more pollutants, Mattel stopped drawing from the well and, along with one of its predecessors, signed a consent order with the DEQ providing for cleanup of the site.

After Mattel gave notice of intent to terminate the lease in 2001, Hall Street filed this suit, contesting Mattel's right to vacate on the date it gave, and claiming that the lease obliged Mattel to indemnify Hall Street for costs of cleaning up the TCE, among other things. Following a bench trial before the United States District Court for the District of Oregon, Mattel won on the termination issue, and after an unsuccessful try at mediating the indemnification claim, the parties proposed to submit to arbitration. The District Court was amenable, and the parties drew up an arbitration

1. JUSTICE SCALIA joins all but footnote 8 of this opinion. No. 06-989, 552 U.S. ___, 2008 WL 762537 (Mar. 25, 2008).

agreement, which the court approved and entered as an order. One paragraph of the agreement provided that

> "[t]he United States District Court for the District of Oregon may enter judgment upon any award, either by confirming the award or by vacating, modifying or correcting the award. The Court shall vacate, modify or correct any award: (i) where the arbitrator's findings of facts are not supported by substantial evidence, or (ii) where the arbitrator's conclusions of law are erroneous." App. to Pet. for Cert. 16a.

Arbitration took place, and the arbitrator decided for Mattel. In particular, he held that no indemnification was due, because the lease obligation to follow all applicable federal, state, and local environmental laws did not require compliance with the testing requirements of the Oregon Drinking Water Quality Act (Oregon Act); that Act the arbitrator characterized as dealing with human health as distinct from environmental contamination.

Hall Street then filed a District Court Motion for Order Vacating, Modifying And/Or Correcting the arbitration decision, App. 4, on the ground that failing to treat the Oregon Act as an applicable environmental law under the terms of the lease was legal error. The District Court agreed, vacated the award, and remanded for further consideration by the arbitrator. The court expressly invoked the standard of review chosen by the parties in the arbitration agreement, which included review for legal error, and cited *LaPine Technology Corp. v. Kyocera Corp.*, 130 F. 3d 884, 889 (CA9 1997), for the proposition that the FAA leaves the parties "free . . . to draft a contract that sets rules for arbitration and dictates an alternative standard of review." App. to Pet. for Cert. 46a.

On remand, the arbitrator followed the District Court's ruling that the Oregon Act was an applicable environmental law and amended the decision to favor Hall Street. This time, each party sought modification, and again the District Court applied the parties' stipulated standard of review for legal error, correcting the arbitrator's calculation of interest but otherwise upholding the award. Each party then appealed to the Court of Appeals for the Ninth Circuit, where Mattel switched horses and contended that the Ninth Circuit's recent en banc action overruling *LaPine* in *Kyocera Corp. v. Prudential-Bache Trade Servs., Inc.*, 341 F. 3d 987, 1000 (2003), left the arbitration agreement's provision for judicial review of legal error unenforceable. Hall Street countered that *Kyocera* (the later one) was distinguishable, and that the agreement's judicial review provision was not severable from the submission to arbitration.

The Ninth Circuit reversed in favor of Mattel in holding that, "[u]nder *Kyocera* the terms of the arbitration agreement controlling the mode of judicial review are unenforceable and severable." 113 Fed. Appx. 272, 272–273 (2004). The Circuit instructed the District Court on remand to

> "return to the application to confirm the original arbi tration award (not the subsequent award revised after reversal), and . . . confirm that award, unless . . . the award should be vacated on the grounds allowable under 9 U. S. C. §10, or modified or corrected under the grounds allowable under 9 U. S. C. §11." *Id.*, at 273.

After the District Court again held for Hall Street and the Ninth Circuit again reversed,[2] we granted certiorari to decide whether the grounds for vacatur and modification provided by §§10 and 11 of the FAA are exclusive. 550 U. S. __ (2007). We agree with the Ninth Circuit that they are, but vacate and remand for consideration of independent issues.

II

Congress enacted the FAA to replace judicial indisposition to arbitration with a "national policy favoring [it] and plac[ing] arbitration agreements on equal footing with all other contracts." *Buckeye Check Cashing, Inc. v. Cardegna*, 546 U. S. 440, 443 (2006). As for jurisdiction over controversies touching arbitration, the Act does nothing, being "something of an anomaly in the field of federal-court jurisdiction" in bestowing no federal jurisdiction but rather requiring an independent jurisdictional basis. *Moses H. Cone Memorial Hospital v. Mercury Constr. Corp.*, 460 U. S. 1, 25, n. 32 (1983); see, *e.g.*, 9 U. S. C. §4 (providing for action by a federal district court "which, save for such [arbitration] agreement, would have jurisdiction under title 28").[3] But in cases falling within a court's jurisdiction, the Act makes contracts to arbitrate "valid, irrevocable, and enforceable," so long as their subject involves "commerce." §2. And this is so whether an agreement has a broad reach or goes just to one dispute, and whether enforcement be sought in state court or federal. See *ibid.*; *Southland Corp. v. Keating*, 465 U. S. 1, 15–16 (1984).

The Act also supplies mechanisms for enforcing arbitration awards: a judicial decree confirming an award, an order vacating it, or an order modifying or correcting it. §§ 9–11. An application for any of these orders will get streamlined treatment as a motion, obviating the separate contract action that would usually be necessary to enforce or tinker with an arbitral

2. On remand, the District Court vacated the arbitration award, because it supposedly rested on an implausible interpretation of the lease and thus exceeded the arbitrator's powers, in violation of 9 U.S.C. §10. Mattel appealed, and the Ninth Circuit reversed, holding that implausibility is not a valid ground for vacating or correcting an award under §10 or §11. 196 Fed. Appx. 476, 477–478 (2006).
3. Because the FAA is not jurisdictional, there is no merit in the argument that enforcing the arbitration agreement's judicial review provision would create federal jurisdiction by private contract. The issue is entirely about the scope of judicial review permissible under the FAA.

award in court.[4] §6. Under the terms of § 9, a court "must" confirm an arbitration award "unless" it is vacated, modified, or corrected "as prescribed" in §§ 10 and 11. Section 10 lists grounds for vacating an award, while § 11 names those for modifying or correcting one.[5]

The Courts of Appeals have split over the exclusiveness of these statutory grounds when parties take the FAA shortcut to confirm, vacate, or modify an award, with some saying the recitations are exclusive, and others regarding them as mere threshold provisions open to expansion by agreement.[6] As mentioned already, when this litigation started, the Ninth Circuit was on the threshold side of the split, see *LaPine*, 130 F. 3d, at 889, from which it later

---

4. Unlike Justice Stevens, see *post*, at 2 (dissenting opinion), we understand this expedited review to be what each of the parties understood it was seeking from time to time; neither party's pleadings were amended to raise an independent state-law contract claim or defense specific to the arbitration agreement.
5. Title 9 U.S.C. §10(a) (2000 ed., Supp. V) provides:
   "(a) In any of the following cases the United States court in and for the district wherein the award was made may make an order vacating the award upon the application of any party to the arbitration–
   "(1) where the award was procured by corruption, fraud, or undue means;
   "(2) where there was evident partiality or corruption in the arbitration or either of them;
   "(3) where the arbitrators were guilty of misconduct in refusing to postpone the hearing; upon sufficient causes shown, or in refusing to hear evidence pertinent and material to the controversy; or any other misbehavior by which the rights of any party have been prejudiced; or
   "(4) where the arbitration exceeded their powers, or so imperfectly executed them that a mutual, final, and definite award upon the subject matter submitted was not made."
   Title 9 U.S.C. §11 (2000 ed.) provides
   "In either of the following cases the United States court in and for the district wherein the award was made may make an order modifying or correcting the award upon the application of any party to the arbitration–
   "(a) Where there was an evident material miscalculation of figures or an evident material mistake in the description of any person, thing, or property referred to in the award.
   "(b) Where the arbitrators have awarded upon a matter not submitted to them, unless it is a matter not affecting the merits of the decision upon the matter submitted.
   "(c) Where the award is imperfect in matter of form not affecting the merits of the controversy.
   "The order may modify and correct the award, so as to effect the intent thereof and promote justice between the parties."
6. The Ninth and Tenth Circuits have held that parties may not contract for expanded judicial review. See *Kyocera Corp. v. Prudential-Bache Trade Servs., Inc.*, 341 F. 3d 987, 1000 (CA9 2003); *Bowen v. Amoco Pipeline Co.*, 254 F. 3d 925, 936 (CA10 2001). The First, Third, Fifth, and Sixth Circuits, meanwhile, have held that parties may so contract. See *Puerto Rico Tel. Co. v. U. S. Phone Mfg. Corp.*, 427 F. 3d 21, 31 (CA1 2005); *Jacada (Europe), Ltd. v. International Marketing Strategies, Inc.*, 401 F. 3d 701, 710 (CA6 2005); *Roadway Package System, Inc. v. Kayser*, 257 F. 3d 287, 288 (CA3 2001); *Gateway Technologies, Inc. v. MCI Telecommunications Corp.*, 64 F. 3d 993, 997 (CA5 1995). The Fourth Circuit has taken the latter side of the split in an unpublished opinion, see *Syncor Int'l Corp. v. McLeland*, 120 F. 3d 262 (1997), while the Eighth Circuit has expressed agreement with the former side in dicta, see *UHC Management Co. v. Computer Sciences Corp.*, 148 F. 3d 997–998 (1998).

departed en banc in favor of the exclusivity view, see *Kyocera*, 341 F. 3d, at 1000, which it followed in this case, see 113 Fed. Appx., at 273. We now hold that §§10 and 11 respectively provide the FAA's exclusive grounds for expedited vacatur and modification.

III

Hall Street makes two main efforts to show that the grounds set out for vacating or modifying an award are not exclusive, taking the position, first, that expandable judicial review authority has been accepted as the law since *Wilko v. Swan*, 346 U. S. 427 (1953). This, however, was not what *Wilko* decided, which was that §14 of the Securities Act of 1933 voided any agreement to arbitrate claims of violations of that Act, see *id.*, at 437–438, a holding since overruled by *Rodriguez de Quijas v. Shear-son/American Express, Inc.*, 490 U. S. 477, 484 (1989). Although it is true that the Court's discussion includes some language arguably favoring Hall Street's position, arguable is as far as it goes.

The *Wilko* Court was explaining that arbitration would undercut the Securities Act's buyer protections when it remarked (citing FAA §10) that "[p] ower to vacate an [arbitration] award is limited," 346 U. S., at 436, and went on to say that "the interpretations of the law by the arbitrators in contrast to manifest disregard [of the law] are not subject, in the federal courts, to judicial review for error in interpretation," *id.*, at 436–437. Hall Street reads this statement as recognizing "manifest disregard of the law" as a further ground for vacatur on top of those listed in §10, and some Circuits have read it the same way. See, *e.g.*, *McCarthy v. Citigroup Global Markets, Inc.*, 463 F. 3d 87, 91 (CA1 2006); *Hoeft v. MVL Group, Inc.*, 343 F. 3d 57, 64 (CA2 2003); *Prestige Ford v. Ford Dealer Computer Servs., Inc.*, 324 F. 3d 391, 395–396 (CA5 2003); *Scott v. Prudential Securities, Inc.*, 141 F. 3d 1007, 1017 (CA11 1998). Hall Street sees this supposed addition to §10 as the camel's nose: if judges can add grounds to vacate (or modify), so can contracting parties.

But this is too much for *Wilko* to bear. Quite apart from its leap from a supposed judicial expansion by interpretation to a private expansion by contract, Hall Street overlooks the fact that the statement it relies on expressly rejects just what Hall Street asks for here, general review for an arbitrator's legal errors. Then there is the vagueness of *Wilko's* phrasing. Maybe the term "manifest disregard" was meant to name a new ground for review, but maybe it merely referred to the §10 grounds collectively, rather than adding to them. See, *e.g.*, *Mitsubishi Motors Corp. v. Soler Chrysler-Plymouth, Inc.*, 473 U. S. 614, 656 (1985) (Stevens, J., dissenting) ("Arbitration awards are only reviewable for manifest disregard of the law, 9 U. S. C. §§ 10, 207"); *I/S Stavborg v. National Metal Converters, Inc.*, 500 F. 2d 424, 431 (CA2 1974). Or, as some courts have thought, "manifest disregard" may have been shorthand for §10(a)(3) or §10(a)(4), the subsections authorizing vacatur when the arbitrators were "guilty of misconduct" or "exceeded their powers." See, *e.g., Kyocera*, supra, at 997. We, when speaking as a Court, have merely taken the *Wilko* language as we found it, without embellishment, see *First Options of Chicago, Inc. v. Kaplan*, 514 U. S. 938, 942 (1995), and now that its meaning is implicated, we see no reason to accord it the significance that Hall Street urges.

Second, Hall Street says that the agreement to review for legal error ought to prevail simply because arbitration is a creature of contract, and the FAA is "motivated, first and foremost, by a congressional desire to enforce agreements into which parties ha[ve] entered." *Dean Witter Reynolds Inc. v. Byrd*, 470 U. S. 213, 220 (1985). But, again, we think the argument comes up short. Hall Street is certainly right that the FAA lets parties tailor some, even many features of arbitration by contract, including the way arbitrators are chosen, what their qualifications should be, which issues are arbitratable, along with procedure and choice of substantive law. But to rest this case on the general policy of treating arbitration agreements as enforceable as such would be to beg the question, which is whether the FAA has textual features at odds with enforcing a contract to expand judicial review following the arbitration.

To that particular question we think the answer is yes, that the text compels a reading of the §§10 and 11 categories as exclusive. To begin with, even if we assumed §§10 and 11 could be supplemented to some extent, it would stretch basic interpretive principles to expand the stated grounds to the point of evidentiary and legal review generally. Sections 10 and 11, after all, address egregious departures from the parties' agreed-upon arbitration: "corruption," "fraud," "evident partiality," "misconduct," "misbehavior," "exceed[ing] . . . powers," "evident material miscalculation," "evident material mistake," "award[s]upon a matter not submitted;" the only ground with any softer focus is "imperfect[ions]," and a court may correct those only if they go to "[a] matter of form not affecting the merits." Given this emphasis on extreme arbitral conduct, the old rule of *ejusdem generis* has an implicit lesson to teach here. Under that rule, when a statute sets out a series of specific items ending with a general term, that general term is confined to covering subjects comparable to the specifics it follows. Since a general term included in the text is normally so limited, then surely a statute with no textual hook for expansion cannot authorize contracting parties to supplement review for specific instances of outrageous conduct with review for just any legal error.

"Fraud" and a mistake of law are not cut from the same cloth.

That aside, expanding the detailed categories would rub too much against the grain of the §9 language, where provision for judicial confirmation carries no hint of flexibility. On application for an order confirming the arbitration award, the court "must grant" the order "unless the award is vacated, modified, or corrected as prescribed in sections 10 and 11 of this title." There is nothing malleable about "must grant," which unequivocally tells courts to grant confirmation in all cases, except when one of the "prescribed" exceptions applies. This does not sound remotely like a provision meant to tell a court what to do just in case the parties say nothing else.[7]

In fact, anyone who thinks Congress might have understood § 9 as a default provision should turn back to §5 for an example of what Congress thought a default provision would look like:

> [i]f in the agreement provision be made for a method of naming or appointing an arbitrator . . . such method shall be followed; but if no method be provided therein, or if a method be provided and any party thereto shall fail to avail himself of such method, . . . then upon the application of either party to the controversy the court shall designate and appoint an arbitrator. . . .

"[I]f no method be provided" is a far cry from "must grant . . . unless" in § 9.

Instead of fighting the text, it makes more sense to see the three provisions, §§ 9–11, as substantiating a national policy favoring arbitration with just the limited review needed to maintain arbitration's essential virtue of resolving disputes straightaway. Any other reading opens the door to the full-bore legal and evidentiary appeals that can "rende[r] informal arbitration merely a prelude to a more cumbersome and time-consuming judicial review process," *Kyocera*, 341 F. 3d, at 998; cf. *Ethyl Corp. v. United Steelworkers of America*, 768 F. 2d 180, 184 (CA7 1985), and bring arbitration theory to grief in post-arbitration process.

Nor is *Dean Witter*, 470 U. S. 213, to the contrary, as Hall Street claims it to be. *Dean Witter* held that state-law claims subject to an agreement to arbitrate could not be remitted to a district court considering a related, nonarbitrable federal claim; the state-law claims were to go to arbitration immediately. *Id.*, at 217. Despite the opinion's language "reject[ing] the suggestion that the overriding goal of the [FAA] was to promote the

---

7. Hall Street claims that §9 supports its position, because it allows a court to confirm an award only "[i]f the parties in their agreement have agreed that a judgment of the court shall be entered upon the award made pursuant to the arbitration." Hall Street argues that this language "expresses Congress's intent that a court must enforce the agreement of the parties as to whether, and under what circumstances, a judgment shall be entered." Reply Brief for Petitioner 5; *see also* Brief for Petitioner 22–24. It is a peculiar argument, converting agreement as a necessary condition for judicial enforcement into a sufficient condition for a court to bar enforcement. And the text is otherwise problematical for Hall Street: §9 says that if the parties have agreed to judicial enforcement, the court "must grant" confirmation unless grounds for vacatur or modification exist under §10 or §11. The sentence nowhere predicates the court's judicial action on the parties' having agreed to specific standards; if anything, it suggests that, so long as the parties contemplated judicial enforcement, the court must undertake such enforcement under the statutory criteria. In any case, the arbitration agreement here did not specifically predicate entry of judgment on adherence to its judicial-review standard. See App. to Pet. for Cert. 15a. To the extent Hall Street argues otherwise, it contests not the meaning of the FAA but the Ninth Circuit's severability analysis, upon which it did not seek certiorari.

expeditious resolution of claims," *id.*, at 219, the holding mandated immediate enforcement of an arbitration agreement; the Court was merely trying to explain that the inefficiency and difficulty of conducting simultaneous arbitration and federal court litigation was not a good enough reason to defer the arbitration, see *id.*, at 217.

When all these arguments based on prior legal authority are done with, Hall Street and Mattel remain at odds over what happens next. Hall Street and its *amici* say parties will flee from arbitration if expanded review is not open to them. See, *e.g.*, Brief for Petitioner 39; Brief for New England Legal Foundation et al. as *Amici Curiae* 15. One of Mattel's *amici* foresees flight from the courts if it is. See Brief for U. S. Council for Int'l Business as *Amicus Curiae* 29–30. We do not know who, if anyone, is right, and so cannot say whether the exclusivity reading of the statute is more of a threat to the popularity of arbitrators or to that of courts. But whatever the consequences of our holding, the statutory text gives us no business to expand the statutory grounds.[8]

In holding that §§10 and 11 provide exclusive regimes for the review provided by the statute, we do not purport to say that they exclude more searching review based on authority outside the statute as well. The FAA is not the only way into court for parties wanting review of arbitration awards: they may contemplate enforcement understate statutory or common law, for

---

8. The history of the FAA is consistent with our conclusion. The text of the FAA was based upon that of New York's arbitration statute. See S. Rep. No. 536, 68th Cong., 1st Sess., 3 (1924) ("The bill . . . follows the lines of the New York arbitration law enacted in 1920 . . ."). The New York Arbitration Law incorporated pre-existing provisions of the New York Code of Civil Procedure. See 1920 N. Y. Laws p. 806. Section 2373 of the code said that, upon application by a party for a confirmation order, "the court must grant such an order, unless the award is vacated, modified, or corrected, as prescribed by the next two sections." 2 N. Y. Ann. Code Civ. Proc. (Stover 6th ed. 1902) (hereinafter Stover). The subsequent sections gave grounds for vacatur and modification or correction virtually identical to the 9 U. S. C. §§10 and 11 grounds. See 2 Stover §§2374, 2375.

In a brief submitted to the House and Senate Subcommittees of the Committees on the Judiciary, Julius Henry Cohen, one of the primary drafters of both the 1920 New York Act and the proposed FAA, said, "The grounds for vacating, modifying, or correcting an award are limited. If the award [meets a condition of §10], then and then only the award may be vacated. . . . If there was [an error under §11], then and then only it may be modified or corrected. . . ." Arbitration of Interstate Commercial Disputes, Joint Hearings before the Subcommittees of the Committees on the Judiciary on S. 1005 and H. R. 646, 68th Cong., 1st Sess., 34 (1924). The House Report similarly recognized that "an award may . . . be entered as a judgment, subject to attack by the other party for fraud and corruption and similar undue influence, or for palpable error in form." H. R. Rep. No. 96, 68th Cong., 1st Sess., 2 (1924).

In a contemporaneous campaign for the promulgation of a uniform state arbitration law, Cohen contrasted the New York Act with the Illinois Arbitration and Awards Act of 1917, which required an arbitrator, at the request of either party, to submit any question of law arising during arbitration to judicial determination. See Handbook of the National Conference of Commissioners on Uniform State Laws and Proceedings 97–98 (1924); 1917 Ill. Laws p. 203.

example, where judicial review of different scope is arguable. But here we speak only to the scope of the expeditious judicial review under §§9, 10, and 11, deciding nothing about other possible avenues for judicial enforcement of arbitration awards.

Although one such avenue is now claimed to be revealed in the procedural history of this case, no claim to it was presented when the case arrived on our doorstep, and no reason then appeared to us for treating this as anything but an FAA case. There was never any question about meeting the FAA §2 requirement that the leases from which the dispute arose be contracts "involving commerce." 9 U. S. C. §2; see *Allied-Bruce Terminix Cos. v. Dobson,* 513 U. S. 265, 277 (1995) (§2 "exercise[s] Congress' commerce power to the full"). Nor is there any doubt now that the parties at least had the FAA in mind at the outset; the arbitration agreement even incorporates FAA §7, empowering arbitrators to compel attendance of witnesses. App. to Pet. for Cert. 13a.

While it is true that the agreement does not expressly invoke FAA §9, §10, or §11, and none of the various motions to vacate or modify the award expressly said that the parties were relying on the FAA, the District Court apparently thought it was applying the FAA when it alluded to the Act in quoting *LaPine*, 130 F. 3d, at 889, for the then unexceptional proposition that "'[f]ederal courts can expand their review of an arbitration award beyond the FAA's grounds, when . . . the parties have so agreed.'" App. to Pet. for Cert. 46a. And the Ninth Circuit, for its part, seemed to take it as a given that the District Court's direct and prompt examination of the award depended on the FAA; it found the expanded-review provision unenforceable under Kyocera and remanded for confirmation of the original award "unless the district court determines that the award should be vacated on the grounds allow-able under 9 U. S. C. §10, or modified or corrected under the grounds allowable under 9 U. S. C. §11." 113 Fed. Appx., at 273. In the petition for certiorari and the principal briefing before us, the parties acted on the same premise. See, *e.g.*, Pet. for Cert. 27 ("This Court should accept review to resolve this important issue of statutory construction under the FAA"); Brief for Petitioner 16 ("Because arbitration provisions providing for judicial review of arbitration awards for legal error are consistent with the goals and policies of the FAA and employ a standard of review which district courts regularly apply in a variety of contexts, those provisions are entitled to enforcement under the FAA").

One unusual feature, however, prompted some of us to question whether the case should be approached another way. The arbitration agreement was entered into in the course of district-court litigation, was submitted to the District Court as a request to deviate from the standard sequence of trial procedure, and was adopted by the District Court as an order. See App. 46–47; App. to Pet. for Cert. 4a–8a. Hence a question raised by this Court at oral argument: should the agreement be treated as an exercise of the District Court's authority to manage its cases under Federal Rules of Civil Procedure 16? See, *e.g.*, Tr. of Oral Arg. 11–12. Supplemental briefing at the Court's behest joined issue on the question, and it appears that Hall Street suggested something along these lines in the Court of Appeals, which did not address the suggestion.

We are, however, in no position to address the question now, beyond noting the claim of relevant case management authority independent of the FAA. The parties' supplemental arguments on the subject in this Court implicate issues of waiver and the relation of the FAA both to Rule 16 and the Alternative Dispute Resolution Act of 1998, 28 U. S. C. §651 *et seq.*, none of which has been considered previously in this litigation, or could be well addressed for the first time here. We express no opinion on these matters beyond leaving them open for Hall Street to press on remand. If the Court of Appeals finds they are open, the court may consider whether the District Court's authority to manage litigation independently warranted that court's order on the mode of resolving the indemnification issues remaining in this case.

* * * *

Although we agree with the Ninth Circuit that the FAA confines its expedited judicial review to the grounds listed in 9 U. S. C. §§10 and 11, we vacate the judgment and remand the case for proceedings consistent with this opinion.

It is so ordered.

Justice Stevens, with whom Justice Kennedy joins, dissenting.

May parties to an ongoing lawsuit agree to submit their dispute to arbitration subject to the caveat that the trial judge should refuse to enforce an award that rests on an erroneous conclusion of law? Prior to Congress' enactment of the Federal Arbitration Act (FAA or Act) in 1925, the answer to that question would surely have been "Yes."[9] Today, however, the Court holds that the FAA does not merely authorize the vacation or enforcement of awards on specified grounds, but also forbids enforcement of perfectly reasonable judicial review provisions in arbitration agreements fairly negotiated by the parties and approved by the district court. Because this result conflicts with the primary purpose of the FAA and ignores the historical context in which the Act was passed, I respectfully dissent.

Prior to the passage of the FAA, American courts were generally hostile to arbitration. They refused, with rare exceptions, to order specific enforcement of executory agreements to arbitrate.[10] Section 2 of the FAA responded to this

---

9. See *Klein v. Catara*, 14 F. Cas. 732, 735 (C. C.D. Mass. 1814) ("If the parties wish to reserve the law for the decision of the court, they may stipulate to that effect in the submission; they may restrain or enlarge its operation as they please") (Story, J.).

10. See *Red Cross Line v. Atlantic Fruit Co.*, 264 U.S. 109, 120–122 (1924); *The Atlanten*, 252 U. S. 313, 315–316 (1920). Although agreements to arbitrate were not specifically enforceable, courts did award nominal damages for the breach of such contracts.

hostility by making written arbitration agreements "valid, irrevocable, and enforceable." 9 U. S. C. §2. This section, which is the centerpiece of the FAA, reflects Congress' main goal in passing the legislation: "to abrogate the general common-law rule against specific enforcement of arbitration agreements," *Southland Corp. v. Keating*, 465 U. S. 1, 18 (1984) (STEVENS, J., concurring in part and dissenting in part), and to "ensur[e] that private arbitration agreements are enforced according to their terms," *Volt Information Sciences, Inc. v. Board of Trustees of Leland Stanford Junior Univ.*, 489 U. S. 468, 478 (1989). Given this settled understanding of the core purpose of the FAA, the interests favoring enforceability of parties' arbitration agreements are stronger today than before the FAA was enacted. As such, there is more—and certainly not less—reason to give effect to parties' fairly negotiated decisions to provide for judicial review of arbitration awards for errors of law.

Petitioner filed this rather complex action in an Oregon state court. Based on the diverse citizenship of the parties, respondent removed the case to federal court. More than three years later, and after some issues had been resolved, the parties sought and obtained the District Court's approval of their agreement to arbitrate the remaining issues subject to *de novo* judicial review. They neither requested, nor suggested that the FAA authorized, any "expedited" disposition of their case. Because the arbitrator made a rather glaring error of law, the judge refused to affirm his award until after that error was corrected. The Ninth Circuit reversed.

This Court now agrees with the Ninth Circuit's (most recent) interpretation of the FAA as setting forth the exclusive grounds for modification or vacation of an arbitration award under the statute. As I read the Court's opinion, it identifies two possible reasons for reaching this result: (1) a supposed *quid pro quo* bargain between Congress and litigants that conditions expedited federal enforcement of arbitration awards on acceptance of a statutory limit on the scope of judicial review of such awards; and (2) an assumption that Congress intended to include the words "and no other" in the grounds specified in §§10 and 11 for the vacatur and modification of awards. Neither reason is persuasive.

While §9 of the FAA imposes a 1-year limit on the time in which any party to an arbitration may apply for confirmation of an award, the statute does not require that the application be given expedited treatment. Of course, the premise of the entire statute is an assumption that the arbitration process may be more expeditious and less costly than ordinary litigation, but that is a reason for interpreting the statute liberally to favor the parties' use of arbitration. An unnecessary refusal to enforce a perfectly reasonable category of arbitration agreements defeats the primary purpose of the statute.

That purpose also provides a sufficient response to the Court's reliance on statutory text. It is true that a wooden application of "the old rule of *ejusdem generis*," ante, at 9, might support an inference that the categories listed in §§10 and 11 are exclusive, but the literal text does not compel that reading—a reading that is flatly inconsistent with the overriding interest in effectuating the clearly expressed intent of the contracting parties. A listing of grounds that must always be available to contracting parties simply does not speak to the question whether they may agree to additional grounds for judicial review.

Moreover, in light of the historical context and the broader purpose of the FAA, §§10 and 11 are best understood as a shield meant to protect parties from hostile courts, not a sword with which to cut down parties' "valid, irrevocable and enforceable" agreements to arbitrate their disputes subject to judicial review for errors of law.[11] §2.

Even if I thought the narrow issue presented in this case were as debatable as the conflict among the courts of appeals suggests, I would rely on a presumption of overriding importance to resolve the debate and rule in favor of petitioner's position that the FAA permits the statutory grounds for vacatur and modification of an award to be supplemented by contract. A decision *"not to regulate"* the terms of an agreement that does not even arguably offend any public policy whatsoever, "is adequately justified by a presumption in favor of freedom." *FCC v. Beach Communications, Inc.*, 508 U. S. 307, 320 (1993) (Stevens, J., concurring in judgment).

Accordingly, while I agree that the judgment of the Court of Appeals must be set aside, and that there may be additional avenues available for judicial enforcement of parties' fairly negotiated review provisions, see, *ante*, at 13–15, I respectfully dissent from the Court's interpretation of the FAA, and would direct the Court of Appeals to affirm the judgment of the District Court enforcing the arbitrator's final award.

Justice Breyer, dissenting.

The question presented in this case is whether "the Federal Arbitration Act . . . precludes a federal court from enforcing" an arbitration agreement that gives the court the power to set aside an arbitration award that embodies an arbitrator's mistake about the law. Pet. for Cert. i. Like the majority and Justice Stevens, and primarily for the reasons they set forth, I believe that the Act does not preclude enforcement of such an agreement. See ante, at 13 (opinion of the Court) (The Act "is not the only way into court for parties wanting review of arbitration awards"); ante, at 3–4 (Stevens, J., dissenting) (The Act is a "shield meant to protect parties from hostile courts, not a sword with which to cut down parties' 'valid, irrevocable and enforceable' agreements to arbitrate their disputes subject to judicial review for errors of law").

---

11. In the years before the passage of the FAA, arbitration awards were subject to thorough and broad judicial review. See Cohen & Dayton, The New Federal Arbitration Law, 12 Va. L. Rev. 265, 270–271 (1926); Cullinan, Contracting for an Expanded Scope of Judicial Review in Arbitration Agreements, 51 V and. L. Rev. 395, 409 (1998). In §§10 and 11 of the FAA, Congress significantly limited the grounds for judicial vacatur or modification of such awards in order to protect arbitration awards from hostile and meddlesome courts.

At the same time, I see no need to send the case back for further judicial decision making. The agreement here was entered into with the consent of the parties and the approval of the District Court. Aside from the Federal Arbitration Act itself, 9 U. S. C. §1 et seq., respondent below pointed to no statute, rule, or other relevant public policy that the agreement might violate. The Court has now rejected its argument that the agreement violates the Act, and I would simply remand the case with instructions that the Court of Appeals affirm the District Court's judgment enforcing the arbitrator's final award.

APPENDIX

D

AAA Mediation Rules[1]

The American Arbitration Association has promulgated rules applicable for commercial mediation. These provide a good model for the conduct of mediation. The AAA Mediation Rules are set forth below:

Commercial Mediation Procedures

M-1. Agreement of Parties

Whenever, by stipulation or in their contract, the parties have provided for mediation or conciliation of existing or future disputes under the auspices of the American Arbitration Association (AAA) or under these procedures, the parties and their representatives, unless agreed otherwise in writing, shall be deemed to have made these procedural guidelines, as amended and in effect as of the date of filing of a request for mediation, a part of their agreement and designate the AAA as the administrator of their mediation.

The parties by mutual agreement may vary any part of these procedures including, but not limited to, agreeing to conduct the mediation via telephone or other electronic or technical means.

M-2. Initiation of Mediation

Any party or parties to a dispute may initiate mediation under the AAA's auspices by making a request for mediation to any of the AAA's regional offices or case management centers via telephone, email, regular mail or fax. Requests for mediation may also be filed online via WebFile at www.adr.org.

The party initiating the mediation shall simultaneously notify the other party or parties of the request. The initiating party shall provide the following information to the AAA and the other party or parties as applicable:

1. A copy of the mediation provision of the parties' contract or the parties' stipulation to mediate.
2. The names, regular mail addresses, email addresses, and telephone numbers of all parties to the dispute and representatives, if any, in the mediation.

1. Copyright by American Arbitration Association.

3. A brief statement of the nature of the dispute and the relief requested.
4. Any specific qualifications the mediator should possess.

Where there is no preexisting stipulation or contract by which the parties have provided for mediation of existing or future disputes under the auspices of the AAA, a party may request the AAA to invite another party to participate in "mediation by voluntary submission." Upon receipt of such a request, the AAA will contact the other party or parties involved in the dispute and attempt to obtain a submission to mediation.

M-3. Representation

Subject to any applicable law, any party may be represented by persons of the party's choice. The names and addresses of such persons shall be communicated in writing to all parties and to the AAA.

M-4. Appointment of the Mediator

Parties may search the online profiles of the AAA's Panel of Mediators at www.aaamediation.com in an effort to agree on a mediator. If the parties have not agreed to the appointment of a mediator and have not provided any other method of appointment, the mediator shall be appointed in the following manner:

1. Upon receipt of a request for mediation, the AAA will send to each party a list of mediators from the AAA's Panel of Mediators. The parties are encouraged to agree to a mediator from the submitted list and to advise the AAA of their agreement.
2. If the parties are unable to agree upon a mediator, each party shall strike unacceptable names from the list, number the remaining names in order of preference, and return the list to the AAA. If a party does not return the list within the time specified, all mediators on the list shall be deemed acceptable. From among the mediators who have been mutually approved by the parties, and in accordance with the designated order of mutual preference, the AAA shall invite a mediator to serve.
3. If the parties fail to agree on any of the mediators listed, or if acceptable mediators are unable to serve, or if for any other reason the appointment cannot be made from the submitted list, the AAA shall have the authority to make the appointment from among other members of the Panel of Mediators without the submission of additional lists.

M-5. Mediator's Impartiality and Duty to Disclose

AAA mediators are required to abide by the Model Standards of Conduct for Mediators in effect at the time a mediator is appointed to a case. Where there is a conflict between the Model Standards and any provision of these Mediation Procedures, these Mediation Procedures shall govern. The Standards require mediators to (i) decline a mediation if the mediator cannot conduct it in an impartial manner, and (ii) disclose, as soon as practicable, all actual and potential conflicts of interest that are reasonably known to the mediator and could reasonably be seen as raising a question about the mediator's impartiality.

Prior to accepting an appointment, AAA mediators are required to make a reasonable inquiry to determine whether there are any facts that a reasonable individual would consider likely to create a potential or actual conflict of interest for the mediator. AAA mediators are required to disclose any circumstance likely to create a presumption of bias or prevent a resolution of the parties' dispute within the time-frame desired by the parties. Upon receipt of such disclosures, the AAA shall immediately communicate the disclosures to the parties for their comments.

The parties may, upon receiving disclosure of actual or potential conflicts of interest of the mediator, waive such conflicts and proceed with the mediation. In the event that a party disagrees as to whether the mediator shall serve, or in the event that the mediator's conflict of interest might reasonably be viewed as undermining the integrity of the mediation, the mediator shall be replaced.

M-6. Vacancies

If any mediator shall become unwilling or unable to serve, the AAA will appoint another mediator, unless the parties agree otherwise, in accordance with section M-4.

M-7. Duties and Responsibilities of the Mediator

1. The mediator shall conduct the mediation based on the principle of party self-determination. Self-determination is the act of coming to a voluntary, uncoerced decision in which each party makes free and informed choices as to process and outcome.

2. The mediator is authorized to conduct separate or ex parte meetings and other communications with the parties and/or their representatives, before, during, and after any scheduled mediation conference. Such communications may be conducted via telephone, in writing, via email, online, in person or otherwise.

3. The parties are encouraged to exchange all documents pertinent to the relief requested. The mediator may request the exchange of memoranda on issues, including the underlying interests and the history of the parties' negotiations. Information that a party wishes to keep confidential may be sent to the mediator, as necessary, in a separate communication with the mediator.

4. The mediator does not have the authority to impose a settlement on the parties but will attempt to help them reach a satisfactory resolution of their dispute. Subject to the discretion of the mediator, the mediator may make oral or written recommendations for settlement to a party privately or, if the parties agree, to all parties jointly.

5. In the event a complete settlement of all or some issues in dispute is not achieved within the scheduled mediation session(s), the mediator may

continue to communicate with the parties, for a period of time, in an ongoing effort to facilitate a complete settlement.

6. The mediator is not a legal representative of any party and has no fiduciary duty to any party.

M-8. Responsibilities of the Parties

The parties shall ensure that appropriate representatives of each party, having authority to consummate a settlement, attend the mediation conference.

Prior to and during the scheduled mediation conference session(s) the parties and their representatives shall, as appropriate to each party's circumstances, exercise their best efforts to prepare for and engage in a meaningful and productive mediation.

M-9. Privacy

Mediation sessions and related mediation communications are private proceedings. The parties and their representatives may attend mediation sessions. Other persons may attend only with the permission of the parties and with the consent of the mediator.

M-10. Confidentiality

Subject to applicable law or the parties' agreement, confidential information disclosed to a mediator by the parties or by other participants (witnesses) in the course of the mediation shall not be divulged by the mediator. The mediator shall maintain the confidentiality of all information obtained in the mediation, and all records, reports, or other documents received by a mediator while serving in that capacity shall be confidential.

The mediator shall not be compelled to divulge such records or to testify in regard to the mediation in any adversary proceeding or judicial forum.

The parties shall maintain the confidentiality of the mediation and shall not rely on, or introduce as evidence in any arbitral, judicial, or other proceeding the following, unless agreed to by the parties or required by applicable law:

1. Views expressed or suggestions made by a party or other participant with respect to a possible settlement of the dispute;
2. Admissions made by a party or other participant in the course of the mediation proceedings;
3. Proposals made or views expressed by the mediator; or
4. The fact that a party had or had not indicated willingness to accept a proposal for settlement made by the mediator.

M-11. No Stenographic Record

There shall be no stenographic record of the mediation process.

M-12. Termination of Mediation

The mediation shall be terminated:

1. By the execution of a settlement agreement by the parties; or
2. By a written or verbal declaration of the mediator to the effect that further efforts at mediation would not contribute to a resolution of the parties' dispute; or
3. By a written or verbal declaration of all parties to the effect that the mediation proceedings are terminated; or
4. When there has been no communication between the mediator and any party or party's representative for 21 days following the conclusion of the mediation conference.

M-13. Exclusion of Liability

Neither the AAA nor any mediator is a necessary party in judicial proceedings relating to the mediation. Neither the AAA nor any mediator shall be liable to any party for any error, act or omission in connection with any mediation conducted under these procedures.

M-14. Interpretation and Application of Procedures

The mediator shall interpret and apply these procedures insofar as they relate to the mediator's duties and responsibilities. All other procedures shall be interpreted and applied by the AAA.

M-15. Deposits

Unless otherwise directed by the mediator, the AAA will require the parties to deposit in advance of the mediation conference such sums of money as it, in consultation with the mediator, deems necessary to cover the costs and expenses of the mediation and shall render an accounting to the parties and return any unexpended balance at the conclusion of the mediation.

M-16. Expenses

All expenses of the mediation, including required traveling and other expenses or charges of the mediator, shall be borne equally by the parties unless they agree otherwise. The expenses of participants for either side shall be paid by the party requesting the attendance of such participants.

M-17. Cost of the Mediation

There is no filing fee to initiate a mediation or a fee to request the AAA to invite parties to mediate.

The cost of mediation is based on the hourly mediation rate published on the mediator's AAA profile. This rate covers both mediator compensation and an allocated portion for the AAA's services. There is a four-hour minimum charge for a mediation conference. Expenses referenced in Section M-16 may also apply.

If a matter submitted for mediation is withdrawn or cancelled or results in a settlement after the agreement to mediate is filed but prior to the mediation conference the cost is $250 plus any mediator time and charges incurred.

The parties will be billed equally for all costs unless they agree otherwise.

If you have questions about mediation costs or services visit our website at www.adr.org or contact your local AAA office.

Conference Room Rental

The costs described above do not include the use of AAA conference rooms. Conference rooms are available on a rental basis. Please contact your local AAA office for availability and rates.

APPENDIX

E

Model Standards of Conduct for Mediators[1]

The American Bar Association, the American Arbitration Association, and the Association for Conflict Resolution have adopted Model Standards of Conduct for Mediators. These Model Standards appear below:

The Model Standards of Conduct for Mediators,September 2005

The Model Standards of Conduct for Mediators was prepared in 1994 by the American Arbitration Association, the American Bar Association's Section of Dispute Resolution, and the Association for Conflict Resolution. A joint committee consisting of representatives from the same successor organizations revised the Model Standards in 2005. Both the original 1994 version and the 2005 revision have been approved by each participating organization.

Preamble

Mediation is used to resolve a broad range of conflicts within a variety of settings. These Standards are designed to serve as fundamental ethical guidelines for persons mediating in all practice contexts. They serve three primary goals: to guide the conduct of mediators; to inform the mediating parties; and to promote public confidence in mediation as a process for resolving disputes.

Mediation is a process in which an impartial third party facilitates communication and negotiation and promotes voluntary decision making by the parties to the dispute. Mediation serves various purposes, including providing the opportunity for parties to define and clarify issues, understand different perspectives, identify interests, explore and assess possible solutions, and reach mutually satisfactory agreements, when desired.

Note on Construction

These Standards are to be read and construed in their entirety. There is no priority significance attached to the sequence in which the Standards appear.

The use of the term "shall" in a Standard indicates that the mediator must follow the practice described. The use of the term "should" indicates that the practice described in the standard is highly desirable, but not required, and is to be departed from only for very strong reasons and requires careful use of judgment and discretion.

The use of the term "mediator" is understood to be inclusive so that it applies to co-mediator models.

These Standards do not include specific temporal parameters when referencing a mediation, and therefore, do not define the exact beginning or ending of a mediation. Various aspects of a mediation, including some matters covered by these Standards, may also be affected by applicable law, court rules, regulations, other applicable professional rules, mediation rules to which the parties have agreed and other agreements of the parties. These sources may create conflicts with, and may take precedence over, these Standards. However, a mediator should make every effort to comply with the spirit and intent of these Standards in resolving such conflicts. This effort should include honoring all remaining Standards not in conflict with these other sources.

These Standards, unless and until adopted by a court or other regulatory authority do not have the force of law. Nonetheless, the fact that these Standards have been adopted by the respective sponsoring entities, should alert mediators to the fact that the Standards might be viewed as establishing a standard of care for mediators.

Standard I. Self-determination

A. A mediator shall conduct a mediation based on the principle of party self-determination.

Self-determination is the act of coming to a voluntary, uncoerced decision in which each party makes free and informed choices as to process and outcome. Parties may exercise self-determination at any stage of a mediation, including mediator selection, process design, participation in or withdrawal from the process, and outcomes.

1. Although party self-determination for process design is a fundamental principle of mediation practice, a mediator may need to balance such party self-determination with a mediator's duty to conduct a quality process in accordance with these Standards.
2. A mediator cannot personally ensure that each party has made free and informed choices to reach particular decisions, but, where appropriate, a mediator should make the parties aware of the importance of consulting other professionals to help them make informed choices.

B. A mediator shall not undermine party self-determination by any party for reasons such as higher settlement rates, egos, increased fees, or outside pressures from court personnel, program administrators, provider organizations, the media or others.

Standard II. Impartiality

A. A mediator shall decline a mediation if the mediator cannot conduct it in an impartial manner. Impartiality means freedom from favoritism, bias or prejudice.

B. A mediator shall conduct a mediation in an impartial manner and avoid conduct that gives the appearance of partiality.

1. A mediator should not act with partiality or prejudice based on any participant's personal characteristics, background, values and beliefs, or performance at a mediation, or any other reason.
2. A mediator should neither give nor accept a gift, favor, loan or other item of value that raises a question as to the mediator's actual or perceived impartiality.
3. A mediator may accept or give de minimis gifts or incidental items or services that are provided to facilitate a mediation or respect cultural norms so long as such practices do not raise questions as to a mediator's actual or perceived impartiality.

C. If at any time a mediator is unable to conduct a mediation in an impartial manner, the mediator shall withdraw.

Standard III. Conflicts of Interest

A. A mediator shall avoid a conflict of interest or the appearance of a conflict of interest during and after a mediation. A conflict of interest can arise from involvement by a mediator with the subject matter of the dispute or from any relationship between a mediator and any mediation participant, whether past or present, personal or professional, that reasonably raises a question of a mediator's impartiality.

B. A mediator shall make a reasonable inquiry to determine whether there are any facts that a reasonable individual would consider likely to create a potential or actual conflict of interest for a mediator. A mediator's actions necessary to accomplish a reasonable inquiry into potential conflicts of interest may vary based on practice context.

C. A mediator shall disclose, as soon as practicable, all actual and potential conflicts of interest that are reasonably known to the mediator and could reasonably be seen as raising a question about the mediator's impartiality. After disclosure, if all parties agree, the mediator may proceed with the mediation.

D. If a mediator learns any fact after accepting a mediation that raises a question with respect to that mediator's service creating a potential or actual conflict of interest, the mediator shall disclose it as quickly as practicable. After disclosure, if all parties agree, the mediator may proceed with the mediation.

E. If a mediator's conflict of interest might reasonably be viewed as undermining the integrity of the mediation, a mediator shall withdraw from or decline to proceed with the mediation regardless of the expressed desire or agreement of the parties to the contrary.

F. Subsequent to a mediation, a mediator shall not establish another relationship with any of the participants in any matter that would raise questions about the integrity of the mediation. When a mediator develops personal or professional relationships with parties, other individuals or organizations following a mediation in which they were involved, the mediator should consider factors such as time elapsed following the mediation, the nature of the relationships established, and services offered when determining whether the relationships might create a perceived or actual conflict of interest.

Standard IV. Competence

A. A mediator shall mediate only when the mediator has the necessary competence to satisfy the reasonable expectations of the parties.

1. Any person may be selected as a mediator, provided that the parties are satisfied with the mediator's competence and qualifications. Training, experience in mediation, skills, cultural understandings and other qualities are often necessary for mediator competence. A person who offers to serve as a mediator creates the expectation that the person is competent to mediate effectively.
2. A mediator should attend educational programs and related activities to maintain and enhance the mediator's knowledge and skills related to mediation.
3. A mediator should have available for the parties' information relevant to the mediator's training, education, experience and approach to conducting a mediation.

B. If a mediator, during the course of a mediation determines that the mediator cannot conduct the mediation competently, the mediator shall discuss that determination with the parties as soon as is practicable and take appropriate steps to address the situation, including, but not limited to, withdrawing or requesting appropriate assistance.

C. If a mediator's ability to conduct a mediation is impaired by drugs, alcohol, medication or otherwise, the mediator shall not conduct the mediation.

Standard V. Confidentiality

A. A mediator shall maintain the confidentiality of all information obtained by the mediator in mediation, unless otherwise agreed to by the parties or required by applicable law.

1. If the parties to a mediation agree that the mediator may disclose information obtained during the mediation, the mediator may do so.
2. A mediator should not communicate to any non-participant information about how the parties acted in the mediation. A mediator may report, if required, whether parties appeared at a scheduled mediation and whether or not the parties reached a resolution.
3. If a mediator participates in teaching, research or evaluation of mediation, the mediator should protect the anonymity of the parties and abide by their reasonable expectations regarding confidentiality.

B. A mediator who meets with any persons in private session during a mediation shall not convey directly or indirectly to any other person, any information that was obtained during that private session without the consent of the disclosing person.

C. A mediator shall promote understanding among the parties of the extent to which the parties will maintain confidentiality of information they obtain in a mediation.

D. Depending on the circumstance of a mediation, the parties may have varying expectations regarding confidentiality that a mediator should address. The parties may make their own rules with respect to confidentiality, or the accepted practice of an individual mediator or institution may dictate a particular set of expectations.

Standard VI. Quality of the Process

A. A mediator shall conduct a mediation in accordance with these Standards and in a manner that promotes diligence, timeliness, safety, presence of the appropriate participants, party participation, procedural fairness, party competency and mutual respect among all participants.

1. A mediator should agree to mediate only when the mediator is prepared to commit the attention essential to an effective mediation.
2. A mediator should only accept cases when the mediator can satisfy the reasonable expectation of the parties concerning the timing of a mediation.
3. The presence or absence of persons at a mediation depends on the agreement of the parties and the mediator. The parties and mediator may agree that others may be excluded from particular sessions or from all sessions.

4. A mediator should promote honesty and candor between and among all participants, and a mediator shall not knowingly misrepresent any material fact or circumstance in the course of a mediation.
5. The role of a mediator differs substantially from other professional roles. Mixing the role of a mediator and the role of another profession is problematic and thus, a mediator should distinguish between the roles. A mediator may provide information that the mediator is qualified by training or experience to provide, only if the mediator can do so consistent with these Standards.
6. A mediator shall not conduct a dispute resolution procedure other than mediation but label it mediation in an effort to gain the protection of rules, statutes, or other governing authorities pertaining to mediation.
7. A mediator may recommend, when appropriate, that parties consider resolving their dispute through arbitration, counseling, neutral evaluation or other processes.
8. A mediator shall not undertake an additional dispute resolution role in the same matter without the consent of the parties. Before providing such service, a mediator shall inform the parties of the implications of the change in process and obtain their consent to the change. A mediator who undertakes such role assumes different duties and responsibilities that may be governed by other standards.
9. If a mediation is being used to further criminal conduct, a mediator should take appropriate steps including, if necessary, postponing, withdrawing from or terminating the mediation.
10. If a party appears to have difficulty comprehending the process, issues, or settlement options, or difficulty participating in a mediation, the mediator should explore the circumstances and potential accommodations, modifications or adjustments that would make possible the party's capacity to comprehend, participate and exercise self-determination.

B. If a mediator is made aware of domestic abuse or violence among the parties, the mediator shall take appropriate steps including, if necessary, postponing, withdrawing from or terminating the mediation.

C. If a mediator believes that participant conduct, including that of the mediator, jeopardizes conducting a mediation consistent with these Standards, a mediator shall take appropriate steps including, if necessary, postponing, withdrawing from or terminating the mediation.

Standard VII. Advertising and Solicitation

A. A mediator shall be truthful and not misleading when advertising, soliciting or otherwise communicating the mediator's qualifications, experience, services and fees.

1. A mediator should not include any promises as to outcome in communications, including business cards, stationery, or computer-based communications.
2. A mediator should only claim to meet the mediator qualifications of a governmental entity or private organization if that entity or organization has a recognized procedure for qualifying mediators and it grants such status to the mediator.

B. A mediator shall not solicit in a manner that gives an appearance of partiality for or against a party or otherwise undermines the integrity of the process.

C. A mediator shall not communicate to others, in promotional materials or through other forms of communication, the names of persons served without their permission.

Standard VIII. Fees and Other Charges

A. A mediator shall provide each party or each party's representative true and complete information about mediation fees, expenses and any other actual or potential charges that may be incurred in connection with a mediation.

1. If a mediator charges fees, the mediator should develop them in light of all relevant factors, including the type and complexity of the matter, the qualifications of the mediator, the time required and the rates customary for such mediation services.
2. A mediator's fee arrangement should be in writing unless the parties request otherwise.

B. A mediator shall not charge fees in a manner that impairs a mediator's impartiality.

1. A mediator should not enter into a fee agreement which is contingent upon the result of the mediation or amount of the settlement.
2. While a mediator may accept unequal fee payments from the parties, a mediator should not use fee arrangements that adversely impact the mediator's ability to conduct a mediation in an impartial manner.

Standard IX. Advancement of Mediation Practice

A. A mediator should act in a manner that advances the practice of mediation. A mediator promotes this Standard by engaging in some or all of the following:

1. Fostering diversity within the field of mediation.
2. Striving to make mediation accessible to those who elect to use it, including providing services at a reduced rate or on a pro bono basis as appropriate.
3. Participating in research when given the opportunity, including obtaining participant feedback when appropriate.
4. Participating in outreach and education efforts to assist the public in developing an improved understanding of, and appreciation for, mediation.
5. Assisting newer mediators through training, mentoring and networking.

B. A mediator should demonstrate respect for differing points of view within the field, seek to learn from other mediators and work together with other mediators to improve the profession and better serve people in conflict.

APPENDIX F

ICANN Uniform Domain Name Dispute Resolution Policy

(As approved by ICANN on October 24, 1999)[1]

1. *Purpose*. This Uniform Domain Name Dispute Resolution Policy (the "Policy") has been adopted by the Internet Corporation for Assigned Names and Numbers ("ICANN"), is incorporated by reference into your Registration Agreement, and sets forth the terms and conditions in connection with a dispute between you and any party other than us (the registrar) over the registration and use of an Internet domain name registered by you. Proceedings under Paragraph 4 of this Policy will be conducted according to the Rules for Uniform Domain Name Dispute Resolution Policy (the "Rules of Procedure"), which are available at www.icann.org/udrp/udrp-rules-24oct99. htm, and the selected administrative-dispute-resolution service provider's supplemental rules.

2. *Your Representations*. By applying to register a domain name, or by asking us to maintain or renew a domain name registration, you hereby represent and warrant to us that (a) the statements that you made in your Registration Agreement are complete and accurate; (b) to your knowledge, the registration of the domain name will not infringe upon or otherwise violate the rights of any third party; (c) you are not registering the domain name for an unlawful purpose; and (d) you will not knowingly use the domain name in violation of any applicable laws or regulations. It is your responsibility to determine whether your domain name registration infringes or violates someone else's rights.

3. *Cancellations, Transfers, and Changes*. We will cancel, transfer or otherwise make changes to domain name registrations under the following circumstances:

a. subject to the provisions of Paragraph 8, our receipt of written or appropriate electronic instructions from you or your authorized agent to take such action;

---

1. Copyright by ICANN used with permission. Available at http://www.icann.org/en/udrp/udrp-policy-24oct99.htm

b. our receipt of an order from a court or arbitral tribunal, in each case of competent jurisdiction, requiring such action; and/or
c. our receipt of a decision of an Administrative Panel requiring such action in any administrative proceeding to which you were a party and which was conducted under this Policy or a later version of this Policy adopted by ICANN. (See Paragraph 4(i) and (k) below.)

We may also cancel, transfer or otherwise make changes to a domain name registration in accordance with the terms of your Registration Agreement or other legal requirements.

4. *Mandatory Administrative Proceeding.*

This Paragraph sets forth the type of disputes for which you are required to submit to a mandatory administrative proceeding. These proceedings will be conducted before one of the administrative-dispute-resolution service providers listed at www.icann.org/udrp/approved-providers.htm (each, a "Provider").

a. Applicable Disputes. You are required to submit to a mandatory administrative proceeding in the event that a third party (a "Complainant") asserts to the applicable Provider, in compliance with the Rules of Procedure, that

(i) your domain name is identical or confusingly similar to a trademark or service mark in which the Complainant has rights; and
(ii) you have no rights or legitimate interests in respect of the domain name; and
(iii) your domain name has been registered and is being used in bad faith.
In the administrative proceeding, the Complainant must prove that each of these three elements are present.

b. Evidence of Registration and Use in Bad Faith. For the purposes of Paragraph 4(a)(iii), the following circumstances, in particular but without limitation, if found by the Panel to be present, shall be evidence of the registration and use of a domain name in bad faith:

(i) circumstances indicating that you have registered or you have acquired the domain name primarily for the purpose of selling, renting, or otherwise transferring the domain name registration to the Complainant who is the owner of the trademark or service mark or to a competitor of that Complainant, for valuable consideration in excess of your documented out-of-pocket costs directly related to the domain name; or
(ii) you have registered the domain name in order to prevent the owner of the trademark or service mark from reflecting the mark in a corresponding domain name, provided that you have engaged in a pattern of such conduct; or

(iii) you have registered the domain name primarily for the purpose of disrupting the business of a competitor; or
(iv) by using the domain name, you have intentionally attempted to attract, for commercial gain, Internet users to your web site or other on-line location, by creating a likelihood of confusion with the complainant's mark as to the source, sponsorship, affiliation, or endorsement of your web site or location or of a product or service on your web site or location.

c. How to Demonstrate Your Rights to and Legitimate Interests in the Domain Name in Responding to a Complaint. When you receive a complaint, you should refer to Paragraph 5 of the Rules of Procedure in determining how your response should be prepared. Any of the following circumstances, in particular but without limitation, if found by the Panel to be proved based on its evaluation of all evidence presented, shall demonstrate your rights or legitimate interests to the domain name for purposes of Paragraph 4(a)(ii):

(i) before any notice to you of the dispute, your use of, or demonstrable preparations to use, the domain name or a name corresponding to the domain name in connection with a bona fide offering of goods or services; or
(ii) you (as an individual, business, or other organization) have been commonly known by the domain name, even if you have acquired no trademark or service mark rights; or
(iii) you are making a legitimate noncommercial or fair use of the domain name, without intent for commercial gain to misleadingly divert consumers or to tarnish the trademark or service mark at issue.

d. Selection of Provider. The Complainant shall select the Provider from among those approved by ICANN by submitting the complaint to that Provider. The selected Provider will administer the proceeding, except in cases of consolidation as described in Paragraph 4(f).
e. Initiation of Proceeding and Process and Appointment of Administrative Panel. The Rules of Procedure state the process for initiating and conducting a proceeding and for appointing the panel that will decide the dispute (the "Administrative Panel").
f. Consolidation. In the event of multiple disputes between you and a complainant, either you or the Complainant may petition to consolidate the disputes before a single Administrative Panel. This petition shall be made to the first Administrative Panel appointed to hear a pending dispute between the parties. This Administrative Panel may consolidate before it any or all such disputes in its sole discretion, provided that the disputes being consolidated are governed by this Policy or a later version of this Policy adopted by ICANN.

g. Fees. All fees charged by a Provider in connection with any dispute before an Administrative Panel pursuant to this Policy shall be paid by the Complainant, except in cases where you elect to expand the Administrative Panel from one to three panelists as provided in Paragraph 5(b)(iv) of the Rules of Procedure, in which case all fees will be split evenly by you and the Complainant.

h. Our Involvement in Administrative Proceedings. We do not, and will not, participate in the administration or conduct of any proceeding before an Administrative Panel. In addition, we will not be liable as a result of any decisions rendered by the Administrative Panel.

i. Remedies. The remedies available to a Complainant pursuant to any proceeding before an Administrative Panel shall be limited to requiring the cancellation of your domain name or the transfer of your domain name registration to the Complainant.

j. Notification and Publication. The Provider shall notify us of any decision made by an Administrative Panel with respect to a domain name you have registered with us. All decisions under this Policy will be published in full over the Internet, except when an Administrative Panel determines in an exceptional case to redact portions of its decision.

k. Availability of Court Proceedings. The mandatory administrative proceeding requirements set forth in Paragraph 4 shall not prevent either you or the Complainant from submitting the dispute to a court of competent jurisdiction for independent resolution before such mandatory administrative proceeding is commenced or after such proceeding is concluded. If an Administrative Panel decides that your domain name registration should be canceled or transferred, we will wait ten (10) business days (as observed in the location of our principal office) after we are informed by the applicable Provider of the Administrative Panel's decision before implementing that decision. We will then implement the decision unless we have received from you during that ten (10) business day period official documentation (such as a copy of a complaint, file-stamped by the clerk of the court) that you have commenced a lawsuit against the Complainant in a jurisdiction to which the Complainant has submitted under Paragraph 3(b)(xiii) of the Rules of Procedure. (In general, that jurisdiction is either the location of our principal office or of your address as shown in our Whois database. See Paragraphs 1 and 3(b)(xiii) of the Rules of Procedure for details.) If we receive such documentation within the ten (10) business day period, we will not implement the Administrative Panel's decision, and we will take no further action, until we receive (i) evidence satisfactory to us of a resolution between the parties; (ii) evidence satisfactory to us that your lawsuit has been dismissed or withdrawn; or (iii) a copy of an order from such court dismissing your lawsuit or ordering that you do not have the right to continue to use your domain name.

5. *All Other Disputes and Litigation.* All other disputes between you and any party other than us regarding your domain name registration that are not brought pursuant to the mandatory administrative proceeding provisions of Paragraph 4 shall be resolved between you and such other party through any court, arbitration or other proceeding that may be available.

6. *Our Involvement in Disputes.* We will not participate in any way in any dispute between you and any party other than us regarding the registration and use of your domain name. You shall not name us as a party or otherwise include us in any such proceeding. In the event that we are named as a party in any such proceeding, we reserve the right to raise any and all defenses deemed appropriate, and to take any other action necessary to defend ourselves.

7. *Maintaining the Status Quo.* We will not cancel, transfer, activate, deactivate, or otherwise change the status of any domain name registration under this Policy except as provided in Paragraph 3 above.

8. *Transfers During a Dispute.*

a. Transfers of a Domain Name to a New Holder. You may not transfer your domain name registration to another holder (i) during a pending administrative proceeding brought pursuant to Paragraph 4 or for a period of fifteen (15) business days (as observed in the location of our principal place of business) after such proceeding is concluded; or (ii) during a pending court proceeding or arbitration commenced regarding your domain name unless the party to whom the domain name registration is being transferred agrees, in writing, to be bound by the decision of the court or arbitrator. We reserve the right to cancel any transfer of a domain name registration to another holder that is made in violation of this subparagraph.

b. Changing Registrars. You may not transfer your domain name registration to another registrar during a pending administrative proceeding brought pursuant to Paragraph 4 or for a period of fifteen (15) business days (as observed in the location of our principal place of business) after such proceeding is concluded. You may transfer administration of your domain name registration to another registrar during a pending court action or arbitration, provided that the domain name you have registered with us shall continue to be subject to the proceedings commenced against you in accordance with the terms of this Policy. In the event that you transfer a domain name registration to us during the pendency of a court action or arbitration, such dispute shall remain subject to the domain name dispute policy of the registrar from which the domain name registration was transferred.

9. *Policy Modifications.* We reserve the right to modify this Policy at any time with the permission of ICANN. We will post our revised Policy at least thirty (30) calendar days before it becomes effective. Unless this Policy has already

been invoked by the submission of a complaint to a Provider, in which event the version of the Policy in effect at the time it was invoked will apply to you until the dispute is over, all such changes will be binding upon you with respect to any domain name registration dispute, whether the dispute arose before, on or after the effective date of our change. In the event that you object to a change in this Policy, your sole remedy is to cancel your domain name registration with us, provided that you will not be entitled to a refund of any fees you paid to us. The revised Policy will apply to you until you cancel your domain name registration.

APPENDIX G

ICANN Rules for Uniform Domain Name Dispute Resolution Policy

(As approved by ICANN on October 24, 1999)[1]

Administrative proceedings for the resolution of disputes under the Uniform Dispute Resolution Policy adopted by ICANN shall be governed by these Rules and also the Supplemental Rules of the Provider administering the proceedings, as posted on its web site.

1. *Definitions*

In these Rules:

Complainant means the party initiating a complaint concerning a domain-name registration.

ICANN refers to the Internet Corporation for Assigned Names and Numbers.

Mutual Jurisdiction means a court jurisdiction at the location of either (a) the principal office of the Registrar (provided the domain-name holder has submitted in its Registration Agreement to that jurisdiction for court adjudication of disputes concerning or arising from the use of the domain name) or (b) the domain-name holder's address as shown for the registration of the domain name in Registrar's Whois database at the time the complaint is submitted to the Provider.

Panel means an administrative panel appointed by a Provider to decide a complaint concerning a domain-name registration.

Panelist means an individual appointed by a Provider to be a member of a Panel.

Party means a Complainant or a Respondent.

Policy means the Uniform Domain Name Dispute Resolution Policy that is incorporated by reference and made a part of the Registration Agreement.

Provider means a dispute-resolution service provider approved by ICANN. A list of such Providers appears at www.icann.org/udrp/approved-providers.htm.

---

1. Copyright by ICANN used with permission. Available at http://www.icann.org/en/udrp/udrp-rules-24oct99.htm

Registrar means the entity with which the Respondent has registered a domain name that is the subject of a complaint.

Registration Agreement means the agreement between a Registrar and a domain-name holder.

Respondent means the holder of a domain-name registration against which a complaint is initiated.

Reverse Domain Name Hijacking means using the Policy in bad faith to attempt to deprive a registered domain-name holder of a domain name.

Supplemental Rules means the rules adopted by the Provider administering a proceeding to supplement these Rules. Supplemental Rules shall not be inconsistent with the Policy or these Rules and shall cover such topics as fees, word and page limits and guidelines, the means for communicating with the Provider and the Panel, and the form of cover sheets.

2. *Communications*

(a) When forwarding a complaint to the Respondent, it shall be the Provider's responsibility to employ reasonably available means calculated to achieve actual notice to Respondent. Achieving actual notice, or employing the following measures to do so, shall discharge this responsibility:

(i) sending the complaint to all postal-mail and facsimile addresses (A) shown in the domain name's registration data in Registrar's Whois database for the registered domain-name holder, the technical contact, and the administrative contact and (B) supplied by Registrar to the Provider for the registration's billing contact; and
(ii) sending the complaint in electronic form (including annexes to the extent available in that form) by e-mail to:

(A) the e-mail addresses for those technical, administrative, and billing contacts;
(B) postmaster@<the contested domain name>; and
(C) if the domain name (or "www." followed by the domain name) resolves to an active web page (other than a generic page the Provider concludes is maintained by a registrar or ISP for parking domain-names registered by multiple domain-name holders), any e-mail address shown or e-mail links on that web page; and

(iii) sending the complaint to any address the Respondent has notified the Provider it prefers and, to the extent practicable, to all other addresses provided to the Provider by Complainant under Paragraph 3(b)(v).

(b) Except as provided in Paragraph 2(a), any written communication to Complainant or Respondent provided for under these Rules shall be made by the preferred means stated by the Complainant or Respondent, respectively (see Paragraphs 3(b)(iii) and 5(b)(iii)), or in the absence of such specification

(i) by telecopy or facsimile transmission, with a confirmation of transmission; or

(ii) by postal or courier service, postage pre-paid and return receipt requested; or

(iii) electronically via the Internet, provided a record of its transmission is available.

(c) Any communication to the Provider or the Panel shall be made by the means and in the manner (including number of copies) stated in the Provider's Supplemental Rules.

(d) Communications shall be made in the language prescribed in Paragraph 11. E-mail communications should, if practicable, be sent in plaintext.

(e) Either Party may update its contact details by notifying the Provider and the Registrar.

(f) Except as otherwise provided in these Rules, or decided by a Panel, all communications provided for under these Rules shall be deemed to have been made:

(i) if delivered by telecopy or facsimile transmission, on the date shown on the confirmation of transmission; or

(ii) if by postal or courier service, on the date marked on the receipt; or

(iii) if via the Internet, on the date that the communication was transmitted, provided that the date of transmission is verifiable.

(g) Except as otherwise provided in these Rules, all time periods calculated under these Rules to begin when a communication is made shall begin to run on the earliest date that the communication is deemed to have been made in accordance with Paragraph 2(f).

(h) Any communication by

(i) a Panel to any Party shall be copied to the Provider and to the other Party;

(ii) the Provider to any Party shall be copied to the other Party; and

(iii) a Party shall be copied to the other Party, the Panel and the Provider, as the case may be.

(i) It shall be the responsibility of the sender to retain records of the fact and circumstances of sending, which shall be available for inspection by affected parties and for reporting purposes.

(j) In the event a Party sending a communication receives notification of non-delivery of the communication, the Party shall promptly notify the Panel (or, if no Panel is yet appointed, the Provider) of the circumstances of the notification. Further proceedings concerning the communication and any response shall be as directed by the Panel (or the Provider).

3. *The Complaint*

(a) Any person or entity may initiate an administrative proceeding by submitting a complaint in accordance with the Policy and these Rules to any Provider approved by ICANN. (Due to capacity constraints or for other reasons, a Provider's ability to accept complaints may be suspended at times. In that event, the Provider shall refuse the submission. The person or entity may submit the complaint to another Provider.)

(b) The complaint shall be submitted in hard copy and (except to the extent not available for annexes) in electronic form and shall:

(i) Request that the complaint be submitted for decision in accordance with the Policy and these Rules;
(ii) Provide the name, postal and e-mail addresses, and the telephone and telefax numbers of the Complainant and of any representative authorized to act for the Complainant in the administrative proceeding;
(iii) Specify a preferred method for communications directed to the Complainant in the administrative proceeding (including person to be contacted, medium, and address information) for each of (A) electronic-only material and (B) material including hard copy;
(iv) Designate whether Complainant elects to have the dispute decided by a single-member or a three-member Panel and, in the event Complainant elects a three-member Panel, provide the names and contact details of three candidates to serve as one of the Panelists (these candidates may be drawn from any ICANN-approved Provider's list of panelists);
(v) Provide the name of the Respondent (domain-name holder) and all information (including any postal and e-mail addresses and telephone and telefax numbers) known to Complainant regarding how to contact Respondent or any representative of Respondent, including contact information based on pre-complaint dealings, in sufficient detail to allow the Provider to send the complaint as described in Paragraph 2(a);
(vi) Specify the domain name(s) that is/are the subject of the complaint;
(vii) Identify the Registrar(s) with whom the domain name(s) is/are registered at the time the complaint is filed;
(viii) Specify the trademark(s) or service mark(s) on which the complaint is based and, for each mark, describe the goods or services, if any, with which the mark is used (Complainant may also separately describe other goods and services with which it intends, at the time the complaint is submitted, to use the mark in the future.);
(ix) Describe, in accordance with the Policy, the grounds on which the complaint is made including, in particular,

(1) the manner in which the domain name(s) is/are identical or confusingly similar to a trademark or service mark in which the Complainant has rights; and

(2) why the Respondent (domain-name holder) should be considered as having no rights or legitimate interests in respect of the domain name(s) that is/are the subject of the complaint; and

(3) why the domain name(s) should be considered as having been registered and being used in bad faith

(The description should, for elements (2) and (3), discuss any aspects of Paragraphs 4(b) and 4(c) of the Policy that are applicable. The description shall comply with any word or page limit set forth in the Provider's Supplemental Rules.);

(x) Specify, in accordance with the Policy, the remedies sought;

(xi) Identify any other legal proceedings that have been commenced or terminated in connection with or relating to any of the domain name(s) that are the subject of the complaint;

(xii) State that a copy of the complaint, together with the cover sheet as prescribed by the Provider's Supplemental Rules, has been sent or transmitted to the Respondent (domain-name holder), in accordance with Paragraph 2(b);

(xiii) State that Complainant will submit, with respect to any challenges to a decision in the administrative proceeding canceling or transferring the domain name, to the jurisdiction of the courts in at least one specified Mutual Jurisdiction;

(xiv) Conclude with the following statement followed by the signature of the Complainant or its authorized representative:

> "Complainant agrees that its claims and remedies concerning the registration of the domain name, the dispute, or the dispute's resolution shall be solely against the domain-name holder and waives all such claims and remedies against (a) the dispute-resolution provider and panelists, except in the case of deliberate wrongdoing, (b) the registrar, (c) the registry administrator, and (d) the Internet Corporation for Assigned Names and Numbers, as well as their directors, officers, employees, and agents."
>
> "Complainant certifies that the information contained in this Complaint is to the best of Complainant's knowledge complete and accurate, that this Complaint is not being presented for any improper purpose, such as to harass, and that the assertions in this Complaint are warranted under these Rules and under applicable law, as it now exists or as it may be extended by a good-faith and reasonable argument."; and

(xv) Annex any documentary or other evidence, including a copy of the Policy applicable to the domain name(s) in dispute and any trademark or service mark registration upon which the complaint relies, together with a schedule indexing such evidence.

(c) The complaint may relate to more than one domain name, provided that the domain names are registered by the same domain-name holder.

4. *Notification of Complaint*

(a) The Provider shall review the complaint for administrative compliance with the Policy and these Rules and, if in compliance, shall forward the complaint (together with the explanatory cover sheet prescribed by the Provider's Supplemental Rules) to the Respondent, in the manner prescribed by Paragraph 2(a), within three (3) calendar days following receipt of the fees to be paid by the Complainant in accordance with Paragraph 19.

(b) If the Provider finds the complaint to be administratively deficient, it shall promptly notify the Complainant and the Respondent of the nature of the deficiencies identified. The Complainant shall have five (5) calendar days within which to correct any such deficiencies, after which the administrative proceeding will be deemed withdrawn without prejudice to submission of a different complaint by Complainant.

(c) The date of commencement of the administrative proceeding shall be the date on which the Provider completes its responsibilities under Paragraph 2(a) in connection with forwarding the Complaint to the Respondent.

(d) The Provider shall immediately notify the Complainant, the Respondent, the concerned Registrar(s), and ICANN of the date of commencement of the administrative proceeding.

5. *The Response*

(a) Within twenty (20) days of the date of commencement of the administrative proceeding the Respondent shall submit a response to the Provider.

(b) The response shall be submitted in hard copy and (except to the extent not available for annexes) in electronic form and shall:

(i) Respond specifically to the statements and allegations contained in the complaint and include any and all bases for the Respondent (domain-name holder) to retain registration and use of the disputed domain name (This portion of the response shall comply with any word or page limit set forth in the Provider's Supplemental Rules.);

(ii) Provide the name, postal and e-mail addresses, and the telephone and telefax numbers of the Respondent (domain-name holder) and of any representative authorized to act for the Respondent in the administrative proceeding;

(iii) Specify a preferred method for communications directed to the Respondent in the administrative proceeding (including person to be contacted, medium, and address information) for each of (A) electronic-only material and (B) material including hard copy;

(iv) If Complainant has elected a single-member panel in the Complaint (see Paragraph 3(b)(iv)), state whether Respondent elects instead to have the dispute decided by a three-member panel;
(v) If either Complainant or Respondent elects a three-member Panel, provide the names and contact details of three candidates to serve as one of the Panelists (these candidates may be drawn from any ICANN-approved Provider's list of panelists);
(vi) Identify any other legal proceedings that have been commenced or terminated in connection with or relating to any of the domain name(s) that are the subject of the complaint;
(vii) State that a copy of the response has been sent or transmitted to the Complainant, in accordance with Paragraph 2(b); and
(viii) Conclude with the following statement followed by the signature of the Respondent or its authorized representative:

> "Respondent certifies that the information contained in this Response is to the best of Respondent's knowledge complete and accurate, that this Response is not being presented for any improper purpose, such as to harass, and that the assertions in this Response are warranted under these Rules and under applicable law, as it now exists or as it may be extended by a good-faith and reasonable argument."; and

(ix) Annex any documentary or other evidence upon which the Respondent relies, together with a schedule indexing such documents.

(c) If Complainant has elected to have the dispute decided by a single-member Panel and Respondent elects a three-member Panel, Respondent shall be required to pay one-half of the applicable fee for a three-member Panel as set forth in the Provider's Supplemental Rules. This payment shall be made together with the submission of the response to the Provider. In the event that the required payment is not made, the dispute shall be decided by a single-member Panel.

(d) At the request of the Respondent, the Provider may, in exceptional cases, extend the period of time for the filing of the response. The period may also be extended by written stipulation between the Parties, provided the stipulation is approved by the Provider.

(e) If a Respondent does not submit a response, in the absence of exceptional circumstances, the Panel shall decide the dispute based upon the complaint.

6. *Appointment of the Panel and Timing of Decision*

(a) Each Provider shall maintain and publish a publicly available list of panelists and their qualifications.

(b) If neither the Complainant nor the Respondent has elected a three-member Panel (Paragraphs 3(b)(iv) and 5(b)(iv)), the Provider shall appoint, within five (5) calendar days following receipt of the response by the Provider, or the lapse of the time period for the submission thereof, a single Panelist from its list of panelists. The fees for a single-member Panel shall be paid entirely by the Complainant.

(c) If either the Complainant or the Respondent elects to have the dispute decided by a three-member Panel, the Provider shall appoint three Panelists in accordance with the procedures identified in Paragraph 6(e). The fees for a three-member Panel shall be paid in their entirety by the Complainant, except where the election for a three-member Panel was made by the Respondent, in which case the applicable fees shall be shared equally between the Parties.

(d) Unless it has already elected a three-member Panel, the Complainant shall submit to the Provider, within five (5) calendar days of communication of a response in which the Respondent elects a three-member Panel, the names and contact details of three candidates to serve as one of the Panelists. These candidates may be drawn from any ICANN-approved Provider's list of panelists.

(e) In the event that either the Complainant or the Respondent elects a three-member Panel, the Provider shall endeavor to appoint one Panelist from the list of candidates provided by each of the Complainant and the Respondent. In the event the Provider is unable within five (5) calendar days to secure the appointment of a Panelist on its customary terms from either Party's list of candidates, the Provider shall make that appointment from its list of panelists. The third Panelist shall be appointed by the Provider from a list of five candidates submitted by the Provider to the Parties, the Provider's selection from among the five being made in a manner that reasonably balances the preferences of both Parties, as they may specify to the Provider within five (5) calendar days of the Provider's submission of the five-candidate list to the Parties.

(f) Once the entire Panel is appointed, the Provider shall notify the Parties of the Panelists appointed and the date by which, absent exceptional circumstances, the Panel shall forward its decision on the complaint to the Provider.

7. *Impartiality and Independence*

A Panelist shall be impartial and independent and shall have, before accepting appointment, disclosed to the Provider any circumstances giving rise to justifiable doubt as to the Panelist's impartiality or independence. If, at any stage during the administrative proceeding, new circumstances arise that could give rise to justifiable doubt as to the impartiality or independence of the Panelist, that Panelist shall promptly disclose such circumstances to the Provider. In such event, the Provider shall have the discretion to appoint a substitute Panelist.

8. *Communication between Parties and the Panel*

No Party or anyone acting on its behalf may have any unilateral communication with the Panel. All communications between a Party and the

Panel or the Provider shall be made to a case administrator appointed by the Provider in the manner prescribed in the Provider's Supplemental Rules.

9. *Transmission of the File to the Panel*
The Provider shall forward the file to the Panel as soon as the Panelist is appointed in the case of a Panel consisting of a single member, or as soon as the last Panelist is appointed in the case of a three-member Panel.

10. *General Powers of the Panel*
(a) The Panel shall conduct the administrative proceeding in such manner as it considers appropriate in accordance with the Policy and these Rules.

(b) In all cases, the Panel shall ensure that the Parties are treated with equality and that each Party is given a fair opportunity to present its case.

(c) The Panel shall ensure that the administrative proceeding takes place with due expedition. It may, at the request of a Party or on its own motion, extend, in exceptional cases, a period of time fixed by these Rules or by the Panel.

(d) The Panel shall determine the admissibility, relevance, materiality and weight of the evidence.

(e) A Panel shall decide a request by a Party to consolidate multiple domain name disputes in accordance with the Policy and these Rules.

11. *Language of Proceedings*
(a) Unless otherwise agreed by the Parties, or specified otherwise in the Registration Agreement, the language of the administrative proceeding shall be the language of the Registration Agreement, subject to the authority of the Panel to determine otherwise, having regard to the circumstances of the administrative proceeding.

(b) The Panel may order that any documents submitted in languages other than the language of the administrative proceeding be accompanied by a translation in whole or in part into the language of the administrative proceeding.

12. *Further Statements*
In addition to the complaint and the response, the Panel may request, in its sole discretion, further statements or documents from either of the Parties.

13. *In-Person Hearings*
There shall be no in-person hearings (including hearings by teleconference, videoconference, and web conference), unless the Panel determines, in its sole discretion and as an exceptional matter, that such a hearing is necessary for deciding the complaint.

14. *Default*
(a) In the event that a Party, in the absence of exceptional circumstances, does not comply with any of the time periods established by these Rules or the Panel, the Panel shall proceed to a decision on the complaint.

(b) If a Party, in the absence of exceptional circumstances, does not comply with any provision of, or requirement under, these Rules or any request from the Panel, the Panel shall draw such inferences therefrom as it considers appropriate.

15. *Panel Decisions*
(a) A Panel shall decide a complaint on the basis of the statements and documents submitted and in accordance with the Policy, these Rules and any rules and principles of law that it deems applicable.

(b) In the absence of exceptional circumstances, the Panel shall forward its decision on the complaint to the Provider within fourteen (14) days of its appointment pursuant to Paragraph 6.

(c) In the case of a three-member Panel, the Panel's decision shall be made by a majority.

(d) The Panel's decision shall be in writing, provide the reasons on which it is based, indicate the date on which it was rendered and identify the name(s) of the Panelist(s).

(e) Panel decisions and dissenting opinions shall normally comply with the guidelines as to length set forth in the Provider's Supplemental Rules. Any dissenting opinion shall accompany the majority decision. If the Panel concludes that the dispute is not within the scope of Paragraph 4(a) of the Policy, it shall so state. If after considering the submissions the Panel finds that the complaint was brought in bad faith, for example in an attempt at Reverse Domain Name Hijacking or was brought primarily to harass the domain-name holder, the Panel shall declare in its decision that the complaint was brought in bad faith and constitutes an abuse of the administrative proceeding.

16. *Communication of Decision to Parties*
(a) Within three (3) calendar days after receiving the decision from the Panel, the Provider shall communicate the full text of the decision to each Party, the concerned Registrar(s), and ICANN. The concerned Registrar(s) shall immediately communicate to each Party, the Provider, and ICANN the date for the implementation of the decision in accordance with the Policy.

(b) Except if the Panel determines otherwise (see Paragraph 4(j) of the Policy), the Provider shall publish the full decision and the date of its implementation on a publicly accessible web site. In any event, the portion of any decision determining a complaint to have been brought in bad faith (see Paragraph 15(e) of these Rules) shall be published.

17. *Settlement or Other Grounds for Termination*
(a) If, before the Panel's decision, the Parties agree on a settlement, the Panel shall terminate the administrative proceeding.

(b) If, before the Panel's decision is made, it becomes unnecessary or impossible to continue the administrative proceeding for any reason, the Panel shall terminate the administrative proceeding, unless a Party raises justifiable grounds for objection within a period of time to be determined by the Panel.

18. *Effect of Court Proceedings*
(a) In the event of any legal proceedings initiated prior to or during an administrative proceeding in respect of a domain-name dispute that is the subject of the complaint, the Panel shall have the discretion to decide whether to suspend or terminate the administrative proceeding, or to proceed to a decision.

(b) In the event that a Party initiates any legal proceedings during the pendency of an administrative proceeding in respect of a domain-name dispute that is the subject of the complaint, it shall promptly notify the Panel and the Provider. See Paragraph 8 above.

19. Fees
(a) The Complainant shall pay to the Provider an initial fixed fee, in accordance with the Provider's Supplemental Rules, within the time and in the amount required. A Respondent electing under Paragraph 5(b)(iv) to have the dispute decided by a three-member Panel, rather than the single-member Panel elected by the Complainant, shall pay the Provider one-half the fixed fee for a three-member Panel. See Paragraph 5(c). In all other cases, the Complainant shall bear all of the Provider's fees, except as prescribed under Paragraph 19(d). Upon appointment of the Panel, the Provider shall refund the appropriate portion, if any, of the initial fee to the Complainant, as specified in the Provider's Supplemental Rules.

(b) No action shall be taken by the Provider on a complaint until it has received from Complainant the initial fee in accordance with Paragraph 19(a).

(c) If the Provider has not received the fee within ten (10) calendar days of receiving the complaint, the complaint shall be deemed withdrawn and the administrative proceeding terminated.

(d) In exceptional circumstances, for example in the event an in-person hearing is held, the Provider shall request the Parties for the payment of additional fees, which shall be established in agreement with the Parties and the Panel.

20. *Exclusion of Liability*
Except in the case of deliberate wrongdoing, neither the Provider nor a Panelist shall be liable to a Party for any act or omission in connection with any administrative proceeding under these Rules.

21. *Amendments*
The version of these Rules in effect at the time of the submission of the complaint to the Provider shall apply to the administrative proceeding commenced thereby. These Rules may not be amended without the express written approval of ICANN.

APPENDIX

H

Standing Order Setting Settlement Conference

This case has been referred for a settlement conference before Magistrate Judge Morton Denlow. All parties and their lead counsel are ORDERED TO APPEAR at the Dirksen Federal Building, 219 South Dearborn Street, Courtroom #1350, Chicago, IL on the date and time the parties agree to set the settlement conference through Judge Denlow's courtroom deputy.

Settlement Conference Preparation

Over 95 percent of all civil suits settle prior to trial. Therefore, settlement preparation should be treated as seriously as trial preparation. Planning is essential because the party who is best prepared obtains the best result. The Court has found that the following steps are essential to a successful settlement conference.

A. Format

1. PRESETTLEMENT CONFERENCE DEMAND AND OFFER. A settlement conference is more likely to be productive if, before the conference, the parties have had a written exchange of their settlement proposals. Accordingly, at least fourteen (14) days prior to the settlement conference, plaintiff's counsel shall submit a written itemization of damages and settlement demand to defendant's counsel with a brief explanation of why such a settlement is appropriate. No later than seven (7) days prior to the settlement conference, defendant's counsel shall submit a written offer to plaintiff's counsel with a brief explanation of why such a settlement is appropriate. On occasion, this process will lead directly to a settlement. If settlement is not achieved, plaintiff's counsel shall deliver or fax copies of these letters to Judge Denlow's chambers no later than five (5) business days before the conference. Do not file copies of these letters in the Clerk's Office.

2. ATTENDANCE OF PARTIES REQUIRED. Parties with ultimate settlement authority must be personally present. An insured party shall appear by a

representative of the insurer who is authorized to negotiate, and who has authority to settle the matter up to the limits of the opposing parties' existing settlement demand. An uninsured corporate party shall appear by a representative authorized to negotiate, and who has authority to settle the matter up to the amount of the opposing parties' existing settlement demand or offer. Having a client with authority available by telephone is not an acceptable alternative, except under the most extenuating circumstances.* Because the Court generally sets aside at least two hours for each conference, it is impossible for a party who is not present to appreciate the process and the reasons which may justify a change in one's perspective towards settlement.

3. MEDIATION FORMAT. The Court will generally use a mediation format: opening presentations by each side followed by a joint discussion and private caucusing by the Court with each side. The Court expects both the lawyers and the party representatives to be fully prepared to participate. The Court encourages all parties to keep an open mind in order to reassess their previous positions and to find creative means for resolving the dispute.

4. STATEMENTS INADMISSIBLE. Statements made by any party during the settlement conference are not to be used in discovery and will not be admissible at trial. Parties are encouraged to be frank and open in their discussions. The Court expects the parties to address each other with courtesy and respect.

B. Issues to Be Discussed at Settlement Conference

Parties should be prepared to discuss the following at the settlement conference:

1. What are your objectives in the litigation?
2. What issues (in and outside of this lawsuit) need to be resolved? What are the strengths and weaknesses of your case?
3. Do you understand the opposing side's view of the case? What is wrong with their perception? What is right with their perception?
4. What are the points of agreement and disagreement between the parties? Factual? Legal?
5. What are the impediments to settlement?
6. What remedies are available through litigation or otherwise?
7. Are there possibilities for a creative resolution of the dispute?
8. Do you have adequate information to discuss settlement? If not, how will you obtain sufficient information to make a meaningful settlement discussion possible?

9. Are there outstanding liens? Do we need to include a representative of the lienholder?

C. Involvement of Clients

For many clients, this will be the first time they have participated in a court-supervised settlement conference. Therefore, counsel shall provide a copy of this Standing Order to the client and shall discuss the points contained herein with the client prior to the settlement conference.

D. Visit the Court's Website

For additional information concerning Judge Denlow's practices and procedures, visit the Court's homepage on the Internet at: http://www.ilnd.uscourts.gov. There you will find published articles by Judge Denlow concerning Steps to an Effective Settlement Conference. Reading these articles will assist you in preparing for the settlement conference.

APPENDIX

I

Instructions for Settlement Conference, U.S. District Judge Matthew F. Kennelly

Over 95 percent of all civil suits are settled prior to trial. For those cases that can be resolved through settlement, early consideration of settlement can allow the parties to avoid unnecessary litigation as well as the substantial cost, expenditure of time, and distraction and anxiety that are typically part of the litigation process. Even for those cases that cannot be resolved through settlement, early consideration of settlement can allow the parties to better understand the factual and legal nature of their dispute and thus focus the issues to be litigated.

Given the importance of settlement, and the fact that it is by settlement that the vast majority of cases are resolved, settlement preparation should be treated as seriously as trial preparation. Set forth below are the procedures that the Court will require the parties to follow in preparing for the settlement conference and the procedures that the Court typically will employ in conducting the conference.

For many clients, this will be the first time they have participated in a court-supervised settlement conference. Counsel are directed to provide a copy of this Standing Order to their clients and to discuss the procedures with them in advance of the conference. Any party who wishes to vary any of the procedures described in this Standing Order should make an appropriate request to the Court prior to the exchange of settlement letters described below.

1. Pre-conference demand and offer. Settlement conferences are more likely to be productive if the parties have previously exchanged demands and offers and have made a good faith effort to settle the case on their own. Accordingly, at least fourteen (14) days before the settlement conference, the plaintiff shall submit a written itemization of damages and a settlement demand to the defendant. No later than seven (7) days before the settlement conference, the defendant shall submit a written offer to the plaintiff. On occasion, this process will lead directly to a settlement. If settlement is not reached, the parties shall deliver or fax copies of the letters to Judge Kennelly's chambers no later than two (2) days before the settlement conference. The letters are not to be filed with the Clerk.

2. Attendance of parties required. Parties with ultimate settlement authority must be personally present at the settlement conference, unless otherwise ordered by the Court. This means that if a party is an individual, that individual must personally attend; if a party is a corporation or governmental entity, a representative of the corporation or governmental entity who is authorized to negotiate and who has full settlement authority must personally attend; if a party requires approval by an insurer to settle, then a representative of the insurer who is authorized to negotiate and who has full settlement authority must attend. Having a client with authority available by telephone is not an acceptable alternative, except under the most extenuating circumstances (the purchase of an airplane ticket is not an extenuating circumstance). The Court sets aside a significant amount of time for each settlement conference and believes that it is impossible for a party who is not present to appreciate fully the process and the reasons that may justify a change in one's perspective towards settlement.

3. Conference format. The Court generally will follow a "mediation" format: opening presentations by each side to the other side, followed by a joint discussion with the Court and private meetings by the Court with each side. The Court expects both the lawyers and the party representatives to be fully prepared to participate in the discussions and meetings. In these discussions, the Court encourages all parties to be willing to reassess their previous positions and to be wiling to explore creative means for resolving the dispute.

4. Statements inadmissible. Any statements made by any party or attorney during the settlement conference will be inadmissible at trial. The Court expects the parties to address each other with courtesy and respect but at the same time strongly encourages the parties to be frank and open in their discussions.

5. Issues to be discussed at settlement conference. Parties should be prepared to discuss the following issues at the settlement conference:

a. What are your objectives in the litigation?
b. What issues (in and outside of this lawsuit) need to be resolved?
c. What are the strengths and weaknesses of your case?
d. Do you understand the opposing side's view of the case? What is wrong with their perception? What is right with their perception?
e. What are the points of agreement and disagreement between the parties (both factual and legal)?
f. What are the impediments to settlement?
g. What remedies are available through litigation or otherwise?
h. Are their [sic] possibilities for a creative resolution of the dispute?
i. Do you have adequate information to discuss settlement? If no, how will you obtain sufficient information to make a meaningful settlement discussion possible?
j. Are their [sic] outstanding liens? Do we need to include a representative of the lienholder?

Table of Cases

Index

M

N